Adventures in the Play-Ritual Continuum

RITUAL, FESTIVAL, AND CELEBRATION

A series edited by Jack Santino

VOLUME 1
Winter Carnival in a Western Town: Identity, Change, and the Good of the Community
LISA GABBERT

VOLUME 2
Playing Dead: Mock Trauma and Folk Drama in Staged High School Drunk Driving Tragedies
MONTANA MILLER

VOLUME 3
Pole Raising and Speech Making: Modalities of Swedish American Summer Celebration
JENNIFER EASTMAN ATTEBERY

VOLUME 4
Public Performances: Studies in the Carnivalesque and Ritualesque
JACK SANTINO, EDITOR

VOLUME 5
Claiming Space: Performing the Personal through Decorated Mortarboards
MONTANA MILLER

VOLUME 6
Adventures in the Play-Ritual Continuum
AUDUN KJUS, JAKOB LÖFGREN, CLÍONA O'CARROLL, SIMON POOLE, AND IDA TOLGENSBAKK, EDITORS

Adventures in the Play-Ritual Continuum

EDITED BY
*Audun Kjus, Jakob Löfgren, Clíona O'Carroll,
Simon Poole, and Ida Tolgensbakk*

UTAH STATE UNIVERSITY PRESS
Logan

© 2025 by University Press of Colorado

Published by Utah State University Press
An imprint of University Press of Colorado
1580 North Logan Street, Suite 660
PMB 39883
Denver, Colorado 80203-1942

All rights reserved

 The University Press of Colorado is a proud member of Association of University Presses.

The University Press of Colorado is a cooperative publishing enterprise supported, in part, by Adams State University, Colorado State University, Fort Lewis College, Metropolitan State University of Denver, University of Alaska Fairbanks, University of Colorado, University of Denver, University of Northern Colorado, University of Wyoming, Utah State University, and Western Colorado University.

ISBN: 978-1-64642-673-7 (hardcover)
ISBN: 978-1-64642-674-4 (paperback)
ISBN: 978-1-64642-675-1 (ebook)
https://doi.org/10.7330/9781646426751

Library of Congress Cataloging-in-Publication Data

Names: Kjus, Audun, editor. | O'Carroll, Clíona, editor. | Poole, Simon E., editor. | Löfgren, Jakob, editor. | Tolgensbakk, Ida, editor.
Title: Adventures in the play-ritual continuum / edited by Audun Kjus, Clíona O'Carroll, Simon Poole, Jakob Löfgren, and Ida Tolgensbakk.
Other titles: Ritual, festival, and celebration.
Description: Logan : Utah State University Press, [2024] | Series: Ritual, festival, celebration series | Includes bibliographical references and index.
Identifiers: LCCN 2024017655 (print) | LCCN 2024017656 (ebook) | ISBN 9781646426737 (hardcover) | ISBN 9781646426744 (paperback) | ISBN 9781646426751 (ebook)
Subjects: LCSH: Play—Social aspects. | Manners and customs.
Classification: LCC GV1201.38 .A38 2024 (print) | LCC GV1201.38 (ebook) | DDC 306.4/81—dc23/eng/20240814
LC record available at https://lccn.loc.gov/2024017655
LC ebook record available at https://lccn.loc.gov/2024017656

Cover photograph: A race on the beach. Photographer: Tomás Ó Muircheartaigh. Owned by the National Folklore Collection, University College Dublin. Archive number: N161.33.00001

Contents

List of Figures *vii*

1. Imagining the Play-Ritual Continuum
   Audun Kjus 3

2. Naughty Games: The Profanation of the Sacred at Scottish Hen Parties
   Sheila M. Young 33

3. The Big Question: Unwrapping the Modern Performative Marriage Proposal
   Audun Kjus 52

4. Inventive Ash Scatterings in the Swedish Archipelago
   Hanna Jansson 72

5. The Play and Ritual of Extreme Sports Races: Exploring the Cultural Logic of Endurance Events
   Karin S. Lindelöf and Annie Woube 88

6. Rules of Play, Playing with the Rules: Challenge and Cooperation between Security Forces and Football Fans in Sweden
   Katarzyna Herd 107

7. Playing in the In-Between: Practices of Play, Ritual,
and Beyond at Computer Game Festivals
Ruth Dorothea Eggel   125

8. To Leave a Receipt and Bang the Gavel: Play and
Ceremony in Celebrations of Fandom
Jakob Löfgren   143

9. Lutfisk—Nothing to Sniff At: Migration Heritages
and Ritualized Play in Scandinavian America
Lizette Gradén   163

10. Playing for Keeps: Tradition, Transformation, and
Anti-Racist Protest in an American Capital
Sallie Anna Pisera   184

11. A Frame within a Frame within a Frame within . . . : Concluding Essay
*Audun Kjus, Simon Poole, Ida Tolgensbakk, Jakob Löfgren,
and Clíona O'Carroll*   205

Index   223

List of Contributors   235

Figures

2.1. Children's games and their hen party equivalents 41
3.1. Textile box from Telemark, painted in 1805 57
3.2. Illustration is from the Codex Manesse (1305–40 Zürich): der Schenke von Limburg kneeling for his lady 58
5.1. Participants at the start of the Spartan Ultra World Championship, Åre, Sweden 89
5.2. Sign with instructions for the correct burpee 90
5.3. One of twenty-five obstacles at the Spartan Ultra World Championship, Åre, Sweden 92
5.4. Warrior "mascot" at the Spartan Ultra World Championship, Åre, Sweden 93
5.5. Instruction sign at barbed-wire obstacle, Spartan Ultra World Championship, Åre, Sweden 104
8.1. Guild of thieves' membership card, front, with the authorization of Guild president Josiah (Mr.) Boggis 146
8.2. Guild of thieves' membership card, back: the guild oath 147
8.3. Winners, presenters, and other participants in the Hugo Awards ceremony 157

9.1. Coffee mug "McOlson's Lutfisk Burgers—1 sold" 167
9.2. Cardboard fins for the lutfisk float at the Svensk Hyllningsfest parade 170
9.3. The lutfisk dinner is packed in boxes in the ASI kitchen 176
10.1. Map of downtown Madison 190
10.2. A collage of photos from the May 30, 2020, march 193

Adventures in the Play-Ritual Continuum

1

Imagining the Play-Ritual Continuum

AUDUN KJUS

Sometimes, doing research is almost like playing a game. The researcher becomes absorbed by the challenge: twisting and turning elements to find the best combination, perfecting technique, and reviewing and reiterating with great patience. At its most intense, one enters a bubble, where only the task seems relevant and the world outside appears to have little consequence. Getting close to the end, tension increases, because the outcome is still uncertain. The result could be a thing of beauty, but until it is completed there is always a risk that the project may fall apart, ending with a whimper instead of a bang. At other times, doing research is more like conducting a ritual, moving through the stipulated and institutionally sanctioned procedures, aiming to create potent models for certain phenomena in the world. And the results may, if they are effective and gain favor, acquire an elevated status, as even more real than the experiences they were built upon.

Academic discussion of the relation between play and ritual has resurfaced at irregular intervals. At the 1978 conference of the Association for the Anthropological Study of Play, anthropologist Steven J. Fox (1980, 57) stated that play and ritual appear to be closely related and interrelated activities that should be studied in tandem. However, relatively few appear to have done this. More recently, archaeologist Colin Renfrew (2017, 14) has pointed out that while physical evidence of both play and ritual may be found in archaeological source material, determining which is which is not an easy task. When working with this puzzle, Renfrew was frustrated by the blurred conceptual distinction, which added to the confusion (10). To clarify, he decided to compare a definition of play with two definitions of ritual (Bell 1997, 138–69; Burghardt 2005, 70–82; Rappaport 1999, 24). This helped him identify a number of similarities, but he was unable to find significant differences. He had to conclude that archaeologists should be open to the possibility that the remnants they uncover may have been used in the context of play, of ritual, or of both.

The idea for this book was born when two of us, who shared a project on children's games, began exploring the interesting but theoretically difficult middle ground between play and ritual. What started as a reading circle gained momentum through national and international conference panels, where we met other researchers who were grappling with similar problems, predominantly in studies of adult experience. The core content of the book consists of nine empirical studies, drawn from different strands of everyday life. This empirical bias is not accidental. Our perspective is that while, on the one hand, play appears to be a basic animal activity that evades definition and, on the other hand, ritual appears to be a concept that refers to a nearly endless variety of social arrangements, it is not likely that the relationship between the two can ever be caught within a finite theoretical understanding. Still, this should not stop us from developing analytical language to explore and interpret acts and settings that have affinity with both social registers. What the empirical phenomena studied in this book have in common is that they provide gateways to intersections and transitions between the playful and the ritual, showing the complex intermingling of play, playfulness, game, ritual, ceremony, rite, and ritualizing. In the final chapter, connections are made between the different cases, and some of the theoretical ideas suggested in this first chapter are revisited.

The remaining part of this chapter is aimed at improving the analytical relationship between the terms *play* and *ritual*. By mapping both the distance and the closeness between the two terms, the goal is to create a situation where they, without too much quarrel and discontent, can be put to work in tandem in front of the same proverbial carriage. The text moves through four approaches. Two existing well-shaped sets of criteria for identifying *play* and *ritual* are discussed, to examine how the criteria for one term relate to the other term. A similar exercise is done on a selection of empirical studies of play and ritual, respectively. This leads to a discussion of how phenomena at the extreme ends of the play-ritual continuum function differently with regard to Gregory Bateson's (2000 [1972]) play-paradox: the fact that the characters, actions, and situations that are played, both are and are not the characters, actors, and situations they depict. However, since empirical studies of play and ritual are often complicated by the layered and uneven contents of the two main concepts, I begin by offering a brief introduction of the two words and their histories.

THE TWO WORDS

Play and *ritual* are quite different words, used to describe and explain actions with many similar features. The word *play* is rooted in everyday language. According to etymologists, the original meaning was something like "a quick and lively movement." The use of phrases such as "the play of light on water" may then be considered to honor the denotation of the word, its original meaning, even if the expression today seems more like a metaphorical expansion.

Across languages, the basic words for play have generally been used to cover wide areas. They have, for instance, been used with reference to music, dance, sports, and children's games. Medieval historian Johan Huizinga (1950 [1938], 28–55) observed how the broader field of play is divided in different ways in different languages. In English, the somewhat special situation is the distinction between *play* and *game*. *Play* (from the Anglo-Saxon) refers to a special form of movement. *Game*, in contrast, originally did not refer to the appearance or physical act of playing but to the state of mind of the player. Game is a Norse word for *fun*, which makes the English expression *fun and games* a pleonasm. In German, the situation is simpler because *Spiel* is used for the entire field of play. In Norwegian (my native language), an approximate division of labor has been made between the native word *lek* and the imported word *spill* (from German). While both words originally designated a movement or an exchange, *spill* is used for sports, music, and theater and has become the dominant word for activities strictly based on rules, such as board games and card games, leaving *lek* as referring to freer forms of play.

If the aim (as with theorists such as Caillois 2001 [1961]; Fagen 1981; Huizinga 1950 [1938]; Sutton-Smith 1997) is to use the word *play* to designate a basic form of human and animal behavior, some aspects of this word quickly become apparent: it is strongly associated with children and childhood and is often used as the counterpart of earnestness or seriousness. For many, classifying something as play means defining it as *not serious*. New Zealand educator and folklorist Brian Sutton-Smith (1997, 35–47) noted that the strong link between play and childhood, as the opposite of seriousness and responsibility, does not seem to do justice to either children or play.

In vernacular use, concepts of play have a long and complex history. In comparison, the concept of *ritual* has a more specific origin and a more accountable history (Bell 1997, 3–89). The word has Latin roots and has long had its home in theology. Entries in mid-nineteenth-century dictionaries explain the word as *precepts for ceremonies during divine service*. Toward the end of the nineteenth century, the word came into use as a specialist term in the history of religion, and from then on it was also used with reference to regularities in non-Christian religious ceremonies. William Robertson Smith (1846–94) held that rituals materialized people's sense of community, and he saw in them the seeds of both religion and society. His contemporary, anthropologist Edward Burnett Tylor (1832–1917), held that the study of rituals could reveal a transition between cultural stages in the history of humankind.

The first academic ritual studies were based on a retrospective premise, where the aim was to look back through the ages to the origins of humankind. This tradition included researchers who came to consider the cultural patterns they found not as first and foremost pre-historical but rather as basic and common to humankind. Émile Durkheim (1858–1917) chose to study the natives of Australia because he assumed they had one of the most primitive cultures, but he ended up drawing general conclusions about how people construct and comprehend their collective selves through acts that allow them to sense their community (Durkheim 1912). Arnold van Gennep (1873–1957) used ethnographic data from presumptively primitive cultures as a point of departure but used these data to develop a general theory of how social positions are created by different forms of exclusion and inclusion through ritual processes (van Gennep 1960 [1909]). They were followed by shelves of anthropological studies about how ritual practices contribute to preserving and re-creating social institutions.

The anthology *Secular Ritual* (1977), edited by anthropologists Sally Falk Moore (1924–2021) and Barbara G. Myerhoff (1935–85) represented a development in this research tradition. Myerhoff and Moore argued that cultural researchers should study the production of meaning in nonreligious ceremonies, such as birthday parties, political rallies, and the opening of new buildings, using the same analytical tools as those applied to the study of religious ceremonies. They also invited researchers not only to study alien and exotic rituals but to do research in their domestic fields, in their own contemporary industrialized societies. A significant departure from previous ritual research was their foregrounding of individual agency (5).

Myerhoff and Moore did not perceive ritual as a predominantly historical legacy but as a vessel that could be utilized for various purposes. This understanding, found in a widespread manner in cultural research today, is relatively new. It only came into use toward the end of the 1970s, and it still took time before it gained acceptance. In the Nordic countries, it had its clear breakthrough in 1995 with the Swedish anthology *Gatan är vår* [The street is ours], which the editor Barbro Klein (1995, 11) placed in the lineage of Myerhoff and Moore.

At that time, however, the word *ritual* had long been a part of everyday speech, with meanings that often differ from the present-day cultural theory concept. On the one hand, people may perceive rituals as irrational and primitive (more or less as Tylor [1873] saw them). On the other hand, people may associate rituals with empty formalism. If you label ceremonial acts as *only ritual*, you use a figure of speech that has a long pedigree. Theological controversy over the efficacy and role of ritual in religious practice was a central aspect of the Reformation, when Catholics saw the many rituals of the church as revelations of divine presence while Protestants considered the same acts at best as empty gestures and at worst as scam and deception (Muir 2005, 163–201). A somewhat similar approach, but not necessarily with a negative understanding, is to use the word *ritual* simply to denote a set of regular procedures. While folklorists and anthropologists usually reserve the concept of ritual for pronounced and explicitly performed sets of acts that produce values, identities, and meaning (Ronström 2017, 240–41), social science researchers, in a tradition linked to the symbolic interactionism and micro-sociology of Erving Goffman, are inclined to use the term to refer to all forms of habitual and repetitive action—for example, studies of how we get ready for the day in the bathroom in the morning or of how we act in the company cafeteria (232–33).

What can be learned from this initial consideration of the two words? It is obvious that they have many and complex uses, and it cannot be expected that stable basic meanings can be established. But when the intention is to enter the field of tension, fluctuation, and cultural energy that lies between play and ritual, this may not be necessary. If the goal is to examine actions that are *both/and* or *neither/nor* and to study transitions from the one to the other, whether with clear fractures or elusive ambivalence, then the potential meanings of the basic concepts are part of what must be explored. Here, a crucial point and difficult question is whether the distinction between play and ritual marks two related but basically different forms of behavior, or if the distinction is based on the categories and pre-understandings that are used to interpret the behavior, and that *play* and *ritual* rather should be perceived as two different discursive and analytical approaches.

EVOLUTIONIST BACKDROP

Compared to the many volumes of ethnographic literature on ritual, the corresponding literature on play is limited. In early ethnographic studies, the category of play was also subordinated to the study of rituals. Subjects such as the history of religion, anthropology, and folkloristics aimed to discern the source and origin of cultural forms. Leading figures argued that the origin of art, religion, and legislation could be found in archaic and pre-historical religious rituals (Robertson Smith 1894, 55). In the quest to find the nascent onset of cultural expressions, some researchers also thought the study of play might provide good clues.

Edward Burnett Tylor used children's games as a key example when he introduced the term *survival* into his cultural theory. He was considering both developments in which children's playful imitations of adult serious rituals outlived their original cultural stage and thus could give clues about earlier social customs (Tylor 1873, 72) and situations where serious adult rituals ceased to be functional but were still continued as games (78).

As pointed out by Alice Bertha Gomme (1898, 458), who published the first large collection of traditional games from the British Isles, Tylor did not develop these perspectives further. In the analytical essay that sums up her book, Gomme attempted to do this herself. She categorized types of games according to their formal aspects and made assumptions about the original ritual functions of the different types. For instance, she assumed that circle games had originated as ceremonies within a community, while line games originated from ceremonies between communities (480–81). She distinguished among three different types of marriage games and related them to three different steps in the evolution of marriage ceremonies. On the question of how rituals and ceremonies had developed into games, she followed both of Tylor's suggestions. Early in the essay, she describes how children's playful imitations of adult behavior had outlived the serious original practices, sometimes by centuries (459). Toward the end, she also suggests a more continuous transmission, where the original practices have gradually been altered to suit later ideas (528).

Henry Bett (1929, 8) was one of the English folklorists who followed the first suggestion of Tylor and Gomme. For Bett, the most exciting aspect was the possible relationship between children's games and bloodthirsty heathen rituals. When children were burning figures made out to be witches or traitors during bonfire parties in spring or autumn, he assumed that they had initially copied the human sacrifices of the druids (as described by Roman authors). He interpreted singing games like "London Bridge Is Falling Down" as remnants of a custom in which the corpse of a sacrificed person was placed in the foundations of bridges, city walls, and other important constructions (114; e.g., Zumwalt 1999, 26–27).

Scottish folklorist Lewis Spence (1947, 1) followed the second suggestion of Tylor and Gomme. For instance, he reasoned that the ballgames included in calendar festivals had originally been employed to help the gods in their cosmological work (90). The movements of the ball between participating players had originally represented the movements of the sun or moon across the firmament (19). On a deeper level, he interpreted the ballgame as sympathetic magic: the gods could be lazy and exhausted and needed to be awakened and spurred into action. The human energy exerted on the playing field was meant to inspire the gods to make spring flourish and autumn ripen (190).

Spence also discussed the Robin Hood festivals held in English villages. They were celebrated in the spring, and he identified remnants of fertility rituals in them. Robin Hood was a master bowman, and the shooting of arrows was meant to make rain fall. Marian, who had to be liberated and whom Robin won with his supreme archery skills, Spence identified as the goddess of spring. The way Robin Hood died in ballads and stories, by bleeding to death, Spence (1947, 36) thought was reminiscent of an ancient blood offering.

HOMO LUDENS

Historian Johan Huizinga's book (1950 [1938]) on the history of playing, initially published in Dutch in 1938, was also situated in an evolutionist paradigm—as was most of the cultural research before World War II. The theory of cultural development was an important element in the political ideology of European imperialism. This line of thinking gave those who were at the forefront of development the right and obligation to firmly lead more backward cultures toward higher developmental stages. Like so many others, Huizinga was searching for the origin and source of culture, and he found *play* a good candidate.

Compared to the British folklorists, Huizinga did an about-face on the connection between play and ritual. He rejected the view that ritual was more fundamental, with play a reflection or degeneration. He put play first and assumed that other cultural forms had developed from play. An ambivalence in Huizinga's view on the relation between play and ritual, however, needs to be pointed out.

On the one hand, he claims that in the cultures of those labeled *primitive people*, *ritual* and *play* cannot be easily separated. He states that people in primitive societies perform their rituals "in a spirit of pure play, truly understood" (Huizinga 1950 [1938], 5). He even adds that ritual shares all formal characteristics with play (18) and warns that if we consider rituals to be serious and play as not serious, we will probably misunderstand the customs of archaic and primitive peoples (20).

On the other hand, some of his formulations show that he considers play to be the more fundamental form. From play come myths and rituals. From myths and rituals come law and order, trade and profit, arts and crafts, fiction, wisdom, and science (Huizinga 1950 [1938], 5). To Huizinga, who was leaning on an evolutionary approach, it was important that play was not only a basic form of expression but that it also historically preceded other forms. The belief that so-called primitive people did not need to distinguish between play and ritual and that such a distinction became more important in higher cultures resonates with ideas about development through cultural differentiation.

The thematic chapters of Huizinga's book can be criticized for constructing cultural history in a weak and random way. The assumption toward which we are heading, which presumably will connect the dots, is the conjecture that cultural creations such as fiction, philosophy, legislation, and warfare have developed from play. If this theory is rejected or discarded as uninteresting, one is left with arguments of little substance. The book's introductory essay easily escapes such criticism. Here, Huizinga delivers sharp and unexpected insights like pearls on a string, and there are good reasons why cultural researchers keep returning to this text.

Huizinga opens by pointing out that play must be a fundamental activity, as many species of animals play in similar manners. When watching dogs play, we quickly understand that they have rules, they pretend, and they delight in it. Huizinga makes the point that play *in itself* is meaningful for the animals engaged in it, using this observation to position himself theoretically and methodologically. He maintains that many of the earlier studies of play have focused on determining how play satisfies other needs—such as relaxation, learning, socialization, or shedding superfluous energy. In contrast, Huizinga wants to study the inherent properties of play. Something as fundamental as play deserves to be studied on its own merit, not merely to determine how it is useful for other activities and purposes. Huizinga encourages researchers to ask questions such as: what does play mean for those who play? What makes play fun, exciting, or absorbing?

For Huizinga, a decisive point is that play must be something the mind does. Play is not only a consequence of the natural external conditions under which one lives. With play, the mind actively intervenes and creates a temporary order. When entering play, certain limits are established that create a zone beyond ordinary life. In this zone, some of the conditions of existence are explored—one imagines some of life's conditions (Huizinga 1950 [1938], 4). Huizinga perceives a close connection between play and the mind's capacity to imagine. He claims that both language and mythology, when they are created, must be considered to be forms of play: language because any abstract concept is built on the most daring metaphorical leaps of the mind; mythology because it is boiling and bubbling with the urge to create and the joy of creating, in a mode of simultaneous lightheartedness and seriousness (4–5).

After this initial flight of theory, Huizinga (1950 [1938], 7–13) presents a series of overarching characteristics of play, in the paragraphs most often cited by other authors. Even if Huizinga is careful to point out that the list of characteristics should not be understood as an attempt at defining play—in his opinion, play is a phenomenon that escapes definition—the list is often referred to as "Huizinga's definition of play."

ANALYTICAL PINCER MANEUVER NO. 1

While it could be useful for Huizinga to (in some contexts) see play and ritual as identical phenomena, the goal here is to manage the concepts *play* and *ritual* as two equally valuable analytical approaches that may be used in interactive ways. As the first move in this direction, I will repeat the exercise carried out by archaeologist Colin Renfrew, but with other examples. I will examine two good lists of formal characteristics of play and ritual respectively (Huizinga 1950 [1938]; Ronström 2017), and highlight criteria in which the two social formats may appear to be different.

Characteristics of Play Related to Rituals

In Huizinga's list of formal characteristics of play, there are, as he also remarked, many items that can be directly applied to rituals, but there are also things that may appear to be different in the two settings. When Huizinga summarizes the characteristics, he writes that play is a voluntary activity that is actively and deliberately established beyond ordinary life and in which participants become absorbed through the alternating buildup and release of tension (Huizinga 1950 [1938], 13). I will discuss these three points in more detail.

PLAY IS A VOLUNTARY ACTIVITY. With one of his apt formulations, Huizinga states that if you are forced to do something, it is no longer play. He continues that only when it has been formalized as a social function can play be understood as duty or responsibility. Initially, play is a surplus phenomenon in the sense that it can be stopped or postponed, and it is only necessary to the degree that people may claim they have a need to amuse themselves (Huizinga 1950 [1938], 7–8).

Brian Sutton-Smith (1997, 35) criticized this point by Huizinga as too contingent on Western modernist rhetoric, where play is associated with childhood and leisure as the counterpart of seriousness, work, and adult life. This is a historically conditioned understanding that does not take play as a universal phenomenon into consideration. The criterion that the play activity must be voluntary demands discussion. When it comes to rituals, the criterion is inherently unreasonable. While participation in rituals may indeed be voluntary and many rituals have spectacular elements that invite voluntary participation, the opposite is just as characteristic. Rituals organize time, space, and social environments in ways that are obligatory, compulsory, and even coercive. On Christmas Eve you may lock your door and draw all your curtains, but you will still know that it is Christmas everywhere around you. If a person's status is to be changed from free citizen to convicted felon, a legal process is required. Before a candidate can be awarded a PhD, they must give a disputation. Until the 1920s, Lutheran confirmation was obligatory in Norway. For instance, the ethnologist Eilert Sundt started his career in a position at a correction facility, where his job was to forcefully confirm young people from society's lower ranks.

The binding and mandatory aspects of many rituals have gradually become less obvious in modern individualist societies. A reason for this is that the pronouncement and administration of social duties and rights have increasingly become the responsibility of strong bureaucratic systems. Baptism is no longer the act that secures a newborn baby's identity. This is guaranteed when the child is entered in the population register. In many countries a marriage must be registered by City Hall to be valid, and people may correspondingly see the public ceremony and reception as optional. However, most people who marry choose to have some public ceremony, and a naming ceremony is often arranged when parents decide not to baptize their child. You can also ask parents if arranging their children's birthday parties is optional.

All things considered, it seems strange and unreasonable that Huizinga could maintain that play and ritual share all formal characteristics, given that he opens by pointing out that play is voluntary and later attaches great importance to this point.

PLAY HAS BOUNDARIES. Play is distinguished from mundane life by marking a zone for play in time and space. Children distinguish between what is done in play and what is merely done. Often, play takes place in a venue for play that is established in advance, physically and/or ideologically, with or without deliberation. Just as play is outside ordinary life, it is not expected that it should satisfy ordinary demands or expectations. Play is an interlude that follows its own intrinsic order. This is also what gives play a recognizable form as a cultural phenomenon. When the interaction has been carried out, it can be repeated, copied, and varied. It can be included in society's cultural storeroom, preserved and passed on as tradition. Play requires a certain order. If you ignore the rules, the game is ruined—you kill the essence of the game and render it worthless (Huizinga 1950 [1938], 8–10).

The fact that both play and ritual activities are marked and framed with delineated internal spaces, which are experienced in contrast to ordinary life on the outside, is an important point in the theoretical literature of both fields. Several authors have discussed how time and space must be oriented and a controlled inner zone must be created for rituals to be effective (Gustafsson 2002, 24; Handelman 1980, 67; Ronström 2017, 238). The extent to which what happens inside the zone affects what happens on the outside begs discussion. When Huizinga first writes about this (1959 [1938], 9), he describes the inner zone of play as completely separated from the regular world and states that what happens in the play event is without consequences for ordinary life. Intuitively, this seems simplistic. Later, Huizinga also elaborates how the sense of belonging created in play activities tends to last beyond the play events. This is not to say that all play activities lead to the formation of an association or a club, but the perception of having something in common, outside of ordinary and mundane settings, may retain its sheen of magic when the interaction is over and everyone has gone home (12).

This line of thinking could be taken further, as play preferences and play experiences are often bound up with the development of personal identity. Play preferences and play styles will have bearing on who people think they are, whether they are dancers, golfers, fly fishers, or gamers. The fact that one shares experiences with, and displays oneself to, other people is an important aspect of this creation of identity. At the same time, skills articulated during play, such as strength, stamina, wisdom, and cunning—or alternatively weakness, foolishness, clumsiness, and stupidity—may be retained and continued in non-play contexts. If this is seen as a form of general seeping of significance from play to social life beyond the boundaries of play, it could indicate a sliding continuity between play and ritual.

While the properties you are assigned in ritual tend toward formal social roles, those you acquire in play may be informal but no less real. What you perform on the football field you also bring into the classroom.

Perhaps one can say that the context of ritual contains expectations that the connection between what you do in the inner framed zone and what will happen in the outside ordinary world should be more than random. In the case of ritual, some form of systematic feedback is expected. If so, it would be fitting to describe ritual as play turned inside out, with the capacity to bind and orient not only its own inner zone but also with respect to the surroundings—not only while the play lasts but afterward as well.

PLAY IS EXCITING. The excitement is founded on uncertainty. No one knows how the interaction will end. In some play activities, a result is achieved when the interaction is over, and the player must demonstrate skill to reach a good result. Other play events have no such clear conclusions, and some researchers have called for a significant differentiation to be made between types of play in this respect (Caillois 2001, 9). Still, even in forms like imaginative role-play, excitement is built from uncertainty. What is to be created this time? Where does the play activity lead us? According to Huizinga (1950, 10–11), it is how play takes place within established frames that allows it to be fully immersive. The reduced horizon produces a clarity that enables the play event to bind or enchant. In a chaotic and confusing world, the play activity can create temporary perfection, and you can (preferably on a temporary basis) lose yourself in play.

Rituals can also be exciting. Consider, for example, the religious examination of Lutheran confirmands, when everyone is listening attentively and cannot fail to notice whether you answer correctly. For some, the way certain rituals put an individual in focus and invite the attention of an entire congregation is nerve-racking and unbearable, while others find it exhilarating and thrive on it. Excitement or tension can relate to whether the ritual actions are carried out correctly. The vicar should not stumble while carrying the chalice. The best man or maid of honor should not leave the wedding rings at home. However, excitement is a more basic principle for play than for rituals. Those who have lost interest in a play activity have in principle already abandoned it. Obviously, even if you find it boring, you can still shoot marbles with grandchildren or small siblings, but in such a case it may be more precise to just call this "play" an activity. If you are not good at hiding your lack of interest in the game, you may end up ruining it for your playmate, who is engaging with earnest playfulness.

There is a striking inverted mirror pattern in that while play needs a necessary degree of protected security before it can take place, rituals are often used in uncertain or tension-filled situations—during sickness and crises, when the harvest needs to be reaped, or when the team is about to enter the field. The classical references for the connection between rituals and uncertainty are Bronislaw Malinowski's (1948, 59; 1984 [1922], 413) studies of customs in the Trobriand Islands in Melanesia. He observed that rituals tended to align around insecure situations. Very few rituals were connected to safe coastal fishing, while the uncertain fishing on the open sea swarmed with rituals.

Educator Birgitta Olofsson has observed the link between personal security and the ability to play among children. She relates the need for security to two other characteristics of children's play: reciprocity and the establishment of play zones. A characteristic of children's play is that the participants take turns being the active party, the one who acts and talks. Imagine a situation where two children are throwing a ball, and one suddenly decides to sit on the ball and refuses to yield it. The other will probably quickly abandon the play situation. If children are to enter an open interaction, they must feel confident that the playmates have honest purposes, that they are genuinely interested in playing and not inclined to exploit or harass the other player (Olofsson 1993, 26–28, 30–40, 134–40). Anyone who wants to observe these mechanisms could also visit the nearest kennel. If a dog is invited to play but does not feel safe because the other dog appears to be intimidating or violent, the invited dog will give signals that urge the potential playmate to calm down. If the loud dog complies, then the play activities can start.

Olofsson also holds that children are more ready to enter into play if they manage to establish play zones that are not easily invaded by foreign powers. Some adults have no scruples about breaking into a children's playground, thereby disturbing the running game. In avoidance of this, children may prefer to play in places that are off adults' beaten track, where the frames of the play are relatively secure and they avoid having the excitement they have worked to build suddenly ruined by intruders.

Characteristics of Rituals Related to Play

Now I will turn the tables and approach the intersection between play and ritual from the other direction. Swedish ethnologist Owe Ronström (2017) has written about the history of the ritual concept, providing a good list of characteristics and properties of rituals. I find that all the characteristics he pointed out may also apply to play, but some of them will work somewhat differently. I will discuss only the three that differ most.

RITUALS ARE BUILT ON REPETITIONS. Many rituals belong to and are repeated at particular points in time, at specific times of the year, the week, or the day. Repetitions also contribute to building structure and expectation *within* the ritual event. A similar sequence can be used to open and close a session, or the content may consist of a number of similar motif sequences. The repetitions of sequential motifs are crucial for participants' recognition of the ritual as a cultural item and for their ability to get involved (Ronström 2017, 238).

Both forms of repetitions have parallels in play. Behavioral biologists have found that animal play also occurs at regular points of time in the day and the year (Fagen 1995, 32–33). Repetition of motif sequences of actions is one of the clearest criteria for recognizing play among animals. The play event is often initiated with meta-communicative signals that are invitations to play. Thereafter, the play frame is maintained with repetitions of related actions, and it may be adjusted with further meta-communication (Fagen 1981, 48–50). Robert Fagen wonders if humans could be the only species who have games with clearly defined endings (122). Among animals, the play events normally end by being abandoned. They may also end if some of the participants break the rules of the game (337).

In some rituals, the management of conclusions will be extra important when it has a bearing that events are carried through in such a way that the end is publicly recognized. The ritual can be a means of finalizing a social exchange with a clear result.

IN RITUALS, PARTICIPANTS TAKE ON ROLES that are distributed according to given patterns. When assuming a role, it may be marked by particular gestures, a change of clothes, the wearing of a mask, or more subtly by tone of voice or physical bearing. Taking on roles creates opportunities for many kinds of play (movements back and forth), for instance, between the role and the identity of the person playing it or between the current and earlier holders of the role—and the participants can understand the various roles differently, even as they join and comply with the same formal rules for the interaction (Ronström 2017, 239). Thus, the role-play allows for a working polysemy, where different interpretations do not necessarily interfere with the ritual interaction.

Role-play is correspondingly normal in play, and it can also be highly formalized. It may be difficult to distinguish between play and ritual merely by observing the role-play, but one may envision a difference as to how the roles are understood. One could reason that in the play activity, there will be limited expectations that the role will have importance and impact beyond the framework of the play event, while roles in a ritual may be identities that are expected to have more general and lasting validity. Thus, situations can be envisioned where two persons participate in the same role-play, but while one of them may consider it a noncommittal pastime, the other may consider it an eternal pact.

RITUALS HAVE THE ABILITY TO PRODUCE WHAT THEY DISPLAY. Here, Ronström (2017, 241–48) reviews two comprehensive examples showing respectively how rituals may express ethnic belonging and royalty. Similarly, American folklorist Jack Santino (2009, 9) has characterized symbolic public acts performed with an intention to transform society as *ritualesque*. In one of the cases Santino describes, a group of women had decided to perform a *padding* of the house of a prominent and outspoken anti-feminist university professor. Having purchased a large quantity of women's sanitary pads, they drank wine for courage and wrote messages on the napkins in red ink. Late at night, they attached the politically soiled napkins to the professor's house, in clear view for the morning rush on the adjacent major traffic route (20). Santino's example of ritualesque behaviour highlights how innovative play elements can be used to invoke political interpretations of current events. While the group of women in this example were protesting against the abuse of hegemonic power, the cases explored by Ronström, with protagonists communicating royalty and ethnicity, show that defending a perceived status quo—even to the extent that the social order is portrayed as natural or eternal—can just as legitimately be labeled political.

It would be safe to say that play activities also produce what they display. The reality displayed within a play activity is something that is created and exists within the framework of the play event. An objection could be that much play involves copying things that already exist in the serious world. Children play, for example, with models of animals and cars. They can play police officer, doctor, or football star. However, as psychologist Greta G. Fein (1987, 299) has elaborated, when children, in dramatic play sequences, copy phenomena and incidents in the world, the copies they produce are only marginally direct portraits of those things in the world and are more directly voicings and variations of the child's own thoughts and feelings about those things. Typically, the play copy is a greatly reduced version of the original. With a couple of quick lines, a small change of the voice, and perhaps an old hat, the child becomes another. While the copy is often stylized, the content of emotions and meaning is produced in full scale.

Both in play and in rituals, people are engaged in portraying and imagining some particular and selected aspects of life, and again it may be difficult to distinguish between the two forms of activity. Perhaps a distinction can be made if we also have access to the perceptions of the participants in the activity. If they perceive that what they produce is unreal, then it could be play that we have witnessed; if they perceive it as super-real, however, then it could be a ritual. At any rate, a divide can be seen when rituals are used to produce duties and rights that are intended to have stable and lasting existence.

ANALYTICAL PINCER MANEUVER NO. 2

These preliminary exercises are meant as an introduction to and preparation for a series of empirical studies, and now I turn to this more practical line of academic work. When conducting empirical research, the area between play and ritual can be approached from the vantage points of both the study of play and the study of ritual. To attempt to do both at the same time in a reasonably balanced manner is an analytical challenge. I have found few texts in the research literature that support such a maneuver, but I would like to mention some studies that merit attention.

IN STUDIES EXAMINING PLAY BEHAVIOR, biologists have observed how animals can transcend the limits of play and turn the activity into something different. In Robert Fagen's (1981, 394) review of this topic, he first describes how animals establish play as safe and fair. With dogs, apes, and other mammals, it has been observed that older or obviously stronger individuals hold back and restrict themselves when they play with younger or weaker individuals. They allow themselves to be pursued and pretend to be caught. If someone is injured, physically or mentally, the play session is over.

It has also been observed that individuals may exploit the play setting to serve goals that go beyond the playful interaction. According to Fagen (1981), this primarily occurs among young carnivores when they start eating meat and when apes reach the age of sexual maturity. Fagen identifies strategies that violate the rules of the play activity, and he calls them *cheating* (394). The most common form of cheating is when individuals start insisting on always winning. When someone begins to do this, the play breaks down or shifts into aggression. An individual who does not accept any form of temporarily reduced status—who keeps opponents down using all means, nurtures quarrels, and exaggerates provocations—has stopped playing. It is perhaps less common to say that animals have rituals (this may depend on which ritual concept you apply), but a kind of behavior that serves the purpose of showing off and upholding a social status that has been won could be labeled ritual.

Folklorist Sally Sugarman (2005) has summarized some of the ritual aspects of children's play. She addresses how children might exploit the ambivalence of play. An aggressive attack may be perceived as both an insult and not an insult (129). The victim of the attack will often choose to define it as not an insult because being the target of violence is an experience fraught with shame. When it is obvious to outside observers that the victim has been injured and their social status reduced, it could be appropriate to consider such attacks as ritual rather than play. Sugarman also points to scenarios where children use play to establish social structures, as when the interaction purposefully excludes adults from the children's sphere or when children use play to demonstrate some form of courage, understood as a requirement for belonging in a group or in the elite among one's peers.

The common denominator in the readings of Fagen and Sugarman is that when play is used to build relatively stable, socially recognized identities, it may be on its way to the ritual register.

IN STUDIES EXAMINING RITUAL BEHAVIOR, play activities appear as elements in many of the ceremonial complexes. For instance, in celebrating Norway's Constitution Day, children first participate in a long, physically demanding parade. Afterward, they get soda pop and ice cream, and games and play are arranged for them. Anthropologist Margaret Thompson Drewal has studied some of the larger ritual complexes of the Yoruba, an ethnic group in West Africa. She found that play was important in all the rituals she studied, and she identified play elements such as spectacular presentations, sudden transformations of familiar symbols, and ceremonial mock duels in which daring initiative and extravagant insults were flung back and forth. Further, she found play to be a key ingredient in Yoruba ritual theory. Yoruba rituals generally involve repeating and copying events from the lives of the gods and heroes. To re-create and call into earthly existence this eternal and divine history, sensational acts that evoke emotions and raise the heartbeat are required (Drewal 1992, 73). This aspect of Yoruba culture can be generalized and seen as a valuable contribution to cultural theory, as rituals played out in open public spaces often employ play elements to engage those who attend and hold their attention.

The introduction of play elements may influence the execution of rituals in various ways. Through play, participants are drawn into proceedings that might otherwise be excessively demanding or exhausting. Elements of play may be used to create a public focus, thus ensuring the social impact of the proceedings. When rituals end in play, the play activities offer relief from the dense and intense atmosphere created through the ceremonies. As post-liminal and incorporating rites (van Gennep 1960 [1909], 11), play activities can help the participants let go of the ritual and gradually return to normal interaction.

When discussing Victor Turner's theory on the socially renewing effects of ritual liminality and *communitas*, Drewal argues that play may have an even more fundamental importance for ritual practices. Turner has given detailed descriptions of the liminal phase of transition rituals, where the novices are separated from earlier social contexts and undergo rites that symbolically erase their earlier identities and rites that are characterized by what Turner (1982, 26–27) calls *anti-structure*—ambivalence and paradox. In the liminal phase, the actors play with common expressions and meanings and make them alien so they can be understood in new, more fundamental ways. They reshuffle familiar symbolic elements, creating grotesque and unnatural combinations. This allows new expressions and insight to arise from unforeseen combinations. In opposition to Turner, Drewal (1992) finds that in the rituals she observed, play elements were not limited to the liminal stages. To the contrary, they could erupt at any stage of the ritual process (8). She argues that this cultivation of playfulness and play skills maintains the flexibility of the rituals and allows the performers to adapt their traditional cultural forms to changing circumstances. Maintaining a playful attitude prepares participants for transforming both the acts played out and their own interpretations of them.

More recently, Jens Kreinath (2020, 237–39) has studied rituals of venerating the Muslim saint Hz. Hizir in southern Turkey, and he has described how playful practices and cultural conceptions of play are important aspects of local cosmologies, for displaying and exploring basic ideas about human existence. He also follows Drewal in suggesting that play elements are used for adapting rituals to the situations at hand and to allow for spontaneous and unpredicted results (232).

Don Handelman (1977, 1980), building on Gregory Bateson's theory about framed forms of communication, has offered a more formal explanation as to why calendar and life-cycle celebrations often show combinations of play and ritual. According to Bateson (2000 [1972]), considerable effort is required to manage a break from ordinary socialization to a more particular and framed form of communication, such as play or ritual. Handelman reasons that it will be less demanding to move from one framed setting to another than to manage the initial break with the normal situation. When a play setting has been established, it will be easier to move on to a ritual setting, or if one is engaged in a ritual, one could easily add a game or two. This explains what can be called *the festival effect*, where over time a celebration that is well-known and well-liked ends up as a conglomerate of presentations, competitions, and role-play. In addition to the fact that it will be easier to attach new frames to old ones, the already existing collective attention that is generated in the established play or ritual zone will be an attractive social resource to tap into. What occurs in such a zone will already have social significance, and, to variable extents, it will be feasible to intervene with additional play or ritual frames and with new layers of symbolic messages.

THE WORD CAT HAS NO FUR AND CANNOT SCRATCH

Now that the theories of Gregory Bateson have been mentioned, the proverbial cat is out of the bag and it is time to present an important trait in play-ritual studies, derived from Bateson's ideas about meta-communication and framed utterances. Two of the researchers inspired by Bateson are Brian Sutton-Smith, when he attempts to conceptualize what play is, and Don Handelman, when he tries to distinguish between play and ritual as social forms. Many will associate the idea of framed communication with the interaction studies of Erving Goffman, but it is Bateson's articulation of frame theory, from his essay on play and fantasy (2000 [1972]), that underpins Handelman's and Sutton-Smith's discussions.

The topic of Bateson's text is the human ability to communicate about communication. We can transmit meta-linguistic signals, which primarily address language and not the phenomena to which the language refers. As Bateson (2000 [1972], 178, original emphasis) puts it, "*The word cat has no fur and cannot scratch.*" We can also send meta-communicative signals that refer to and may attempt to regulate the relationship between the communicators. For Bateson, play is good place to study meta-communicative practices. For play to occur, Bateson holds that three types of signals must be understood: (1) signs that show individuals' state and purpose, (2) signs that simulate signs of the first type, and (3) signs that enable one to discriminate between signs that are meant seriously and those that are simulated (189).

The message *this is play* expresses the fact that the consequences of the actions that follow will not be identical to the consequences of the actions that are being simulated. The dog acting within the play frame, pretending to bite, knows that the pretend bite will not have the same consequences as a real bite (Bateson 2000 [1972], 180). The fact that the characters and actions within the play frame both are and are not the characters and actions they depict opens a landslide of paradoxes. The play bite is a piece of fiction, and in a certain sense it does not really exist. But it still has real consequences (182).

According to Bateson (2000 [1972], 178), the majority of meta-linguistic and meta-communicative messages are conveyed implicitly, and he assumes that the basic ability for meta-communicative behavior must be established before words and concepts for meta-communication are clarified (180). The ability to engage in play, then, appears to be a basis for developing higher semiotic skills—that is, abilities for coding and decoding different and variable relationships between map and territory. According to Bateson, in the initial use and understanding of symbols, the map is identified with the territory. Only later, map and territory are considered to exist separately. In play, there is both identification and differentiation (185).

In his book *The Ambiguity of Play* (1997), Brian Sutton-Smith discusses how both scientific and vernacular theories about play have been spun around cultural rhetoric on topics such as destiny, power, identity, imagination, and development. Toward the end of the volume, Sutton-Smith outlines a thesis on what we do when we play (225–31). His theory starts with the fact that we fantasize and form ideas while we are present and acting in the world. While we are doing what we do to survive, we connect emotions to impressions, form concepts, and objectify our surroundings. When we enter into play, some of these experiences, feelings, and concepts are detached; they relocate in a different frame—a play frame—where they can be re-experienced, reconsidered, and developed. To illustrate this point, Sutton-Smith (20–21) cites an example from Jean Piaget, about how an infant at the mother's breast first suckles itself full, then starts playing with the breast.

The person who enters into play takes a leap into a virtual world. The playful state is then maintained through various measures until the play event is over. Sutton-Smith (1997, 150) mentions (as does Fagen above) repetitions, rules, and meta-communication as such measures and suggests that the forms of play can be ordered in a continuum with those that are (almost) fully regulated with formal rules on one end of the scale and those that are (almost) fully regulated with play signals and meta-communication on the other. He suggests that play activities generally produce stylized representations of existential matters and calls attention to how play often simulates or parodies danger and uncertainty (231). A variety of existential uncertainties are easily recognizable from play settings—for instance, the experiences of winning or losing, of receiving love, of being in a conflict, and of achieving a recognized social status (becoming someone). This again shows the connection between play and ritual activities, as rituals also deal with existential topics: life and death, the passing of the years, becoming an adult, being or becoming a healthy person. Who, where, and when are we? What caused this mess?

Sutton-Smith (1997, 195) warns that we go off track if we simply draw a line between real life and unreal play. He finds that the distinction should instead be between (1) experience and imagination on an ordinary/unmarked level and (2) experience and imagination on a virtual/marked level. Within the boundaries of play, characters, acts, and emotions are played out, which are familiar from ordinary reality but are not identified with it. The play event is moving on a meta-level more than on a mimetic level, as re-voicing and interpreting the world is more crucial than copying it.

Bearing this in mind, one could attempt to use Bateson's paradox as a pair of scales to balance between play and ritual: in both forms, virtual realities are presented when something or someone both is and is not what they portray. If the scale end with *is* weighs more, then we are leaning toward the ritual register, where the virtual state is a kind of *super-reality*. If, on the other hand, the scale end with *is not* is heavier, we are leaning toward the state of play, where the virtual world is a kind of *unreality*.

This type of sliding transition is different from what Don Handelman (1977, 187; 1980) imagined when he wrote his two articles about play and ritual as complementary but mutually exclusive social forms. Handelman also starts out from Bateson's observation that the play frame is established through meta-communication. However, he suggests that the signals which establish zones for play and for ritual offer different meta-communicative messages. On entering play, it is signaled: *this is play*. On entering ritual, the message is: *let us believe* . . . (Handelman 1980, 66). While the ritual is about what should have been, play is about what could have been (Handelman 1977, 186). Those who participate in a ritual expect it to have some sort of validity and power in the mundane world beyond the frames of the proceedings (188). The ritual thus opens an explicit and acknowledged bridge of experience between the framed and the ordinary reality.

From this first distinction, Handelman derives additional distinctions, which contribute to imbuing play and ritual with separate and complementary functions: the play frame is relatively weaker, while the ritual frame is relatively stronger. The transition to play is simpler, while the transition to ritual is more complex (Handelman 1980, 67). Play is replete with opportunities for unpredictable creativity; therefore, the assumed significance of the messages produced in the play zone must be weak. Play is defined as unserious, untrue, and unreal because it is a source of disorder that the social order needs to be protected against. Play provides a malleable environment for constructing new ideas. Ritual underlines the integrity of the moral community. In play, it is possible to immediately comment on what goes on in the social world, while a ritual is geared to commenting on truths about time and space and human affairs more slowly and in an overarching manner (Handelman 1977, 189).

POLARITY AND CONTINUITY

If the relationship between play and ritual is considered from the participant, or emic, perspective, I believe Handelman makes sound generalizations. In many cultural settings a polarized separation exists, in which the two forms are considered radically divorced and opposite; in consequence, both the concepts and the activities are assigned to different tasks in different contexts. I am not as certain, however, that Handelman was right in claiming that as forms of behavior, they are mutually exclusive. Perhaps what Handelman posited as opposites can still be encountered in an unbroken continuum in our lived experiences.

Interestingly, anthropologist Matan Shapiro (2020, 212) has argued that the relation between play and ritual should *not* be viewed as a continuum, with two distinct ends, but rather as a spectrum with subtle immersions of shades and tones. I do not find this difference in preferred metaphor alarming. I also do not imagine the play-ritual continuum to be a linear stretch between two tidy extremes, like the continuum between darkness and light. To find relations that are more similar to the play-ritual continuum, one should look to other basic animal activities. Take, for instance, the continuum between work and rest. On the surface level, it may appear tidy. One could imagine it like a graded scale between no activity and maximum activity. But often it is not that simple. For instance, you may rest while you work and work while you rest. Both rest and work come in great varieties, some of which are culturally framed and institutionalized, even to the extent that they have a history.

Arguably, the polarity between work and rest is stronger than that between play and ritual. As this chapter has elaborated, play and ritual are activities with so many shared traits that one can easily wonder if they are different words for the same basic phenomenon. But the two terms polarize and create a distinction. Somewhat paradoxically, this also happens when Shapiro discusses the dynamic organization of the religious festival he has studied. He uses the conceptual binarity between the terms *play* and *ritual* to describe and explain the different stages of the event. The idea of a play-ritual continuum may be useful to foreground the interrelatedness of the activities described by the two words, as long as one keeps in mind that the relation is often messy.

SIMILAR FIELDS OF RESEARCH

I would like to mention two fields of research with close relations to the ambitions of this book: namely, festival studies and studies of children's folklore. Researchers of children's folklore have noted that the cultural performances they observe contain elements that may be characterized both as social rituals (amplifying and confirming) and as playful interventions (testing and doubting) (Mechling 1999, 276). Creating groups with shared standards, traditions, and identities appears to be a central aspect of many events and performances, but the groups thus created are not just any groups, as they are sifted through the rules of specific games, played out in specific social and historical settings (Sutton-Smith 1999, 8). Sutton-Smith calls for persistent empirical studies of events that are often thought to be trivial and deemed to have little importance, predicting these as places where one may observe culture in the making (16–17).

Oddly, none of the case studies in this volume are about children's games (a fact that opens the possibility for a sequel). Play research in pedagogy and psychology mostly deals with children's games and imaginative role-play, but to reason about play more generally, many different versions of the phenomenon should be included in the empirical scope. With the current selection, we wanted to study a range of activities and events; thus, the book describes political demonstrations, lutfisk dinners, football matches, extreme sports races, computer game festivals, fandom ceremonies, marriage proposals, hen parties, and private ash scatterings.

Seeing this colorful bouquet of cases brings an easy transmission to the next related field of research: festival studies. Similar to the study of children's folklore, this is a field where ritual and play activities have been examined in detail in their social contexts. The public displays addressed are as varied and multifaceted as the case studies in this book. In his introduction to the rich anthology *Public Performances: Studies in the Carnivalesque and Ritualesque*, Jack Santino (2017, x) states that his aim in the coordinated study of very different kinds of events is not to reduce them to a single, simplistic paradigm but rather to sketch out similarities and differences among them and show how their generic components may be used for different situations and goals. He also explains that the concepts of carnival, as an event without real consequences, and ritual, as an event with permanent and universal consequences, are idealized constructions: "Most events will have elements of the ritualesque along with the carnivalesque, and the latter does not negate the former. The two are not antithetical, and the genre frames are multivocal" (5).

I would also like to recognize how our ambition to study expressive events in which different kinds of framed interaction mix and merge into new conglomerate and creole forms is indebted to the tradition of dynamic genre analysis. This line of research gained momentum when the works of Mikhail Bakhtin were translated to English in the late 1970s. American folklorist John D. Dorst (1983, 413) was one of the forerunners, expressing a wish to embrace the way "generic instabilities and ambiguities constitute a legitimate, though largely neglected, area of research." In the play-ritual continuum, we can expect to find genre dialogues similar to those described by Bakhtin (1986 [1929/1979], 60–61, 66), including how genres are subject to mutual influence and how style and content from simple genres are incorporated in larger, more elaborate genre formats. The capacity of play-ritual events to orient and define time, space, and social environment can be seen as parallel to what Richard Bauman and Charles L. Briggs (1990, 68) have described as the speaker's active contextualization in staging the tradition of the text. Such a perception of expressive genres as historical and dynamic leads to the understanding that they are contested and that their production of social meaning is up for grabs.

THEORY AND EMPIRICISM

The capacity of rituals to organize time and space, generate groups of outsiders and insiders, and create, re-create, and anchor existentially important concepts makes them promising places of origin for rational thought and action. Because of this, ritual studies is a cherished branch of cultural research, where play is often relegated to the role of a contrast or a supplement. The question of exactly how rituals are perceived to alter reality was one of the areas of contention between Catholic and Protestant theologians during the Reformation (Muir 2005, 163–201). Catholic theologians argued that God was physically present during the rituals and transformed the earthly substances, while Protestants asserted that the rituals contributed more indirectly, by revealing spiritual truths and strengthening believers in their belief. Then again, how did the different lay participants consider the rituals to be effective? To understand people's actions, it is a great help to have access to the concepts and theories that they themselves relate to their actions. It often makes sense to simply ask people what they intend in doing what they do. But knowledge obtained through interviews also has limitations. As often as not, we cannot fully explain what we are doing, and we may easily resort to standard explanations that we hope are acceptable to the person asking. The acts in question may be played out and have their meaning in one context while the interview about them takes place in another. Interviews must therefore be combined with the researcher's own examinations and interpretations of the words and deeds that are performed.

The theoretical construct developed in this chapter is characterized by approximation. Words like *can, may*, and *perhaps* have been used repeatedly. There is, however, reason to bear in mind Sutton-Smith's warning that one should not rely too heavily on theories when studying play and games. His own studies made it clear how the different widespread and collective perceptions of what play is and how it should be carried out are permeated by power and ideology. The collective ideas about different play activities form cultural hierarchies, in which some activities attain dominant positions and others are given subordinate roles. While people tend to hold the play forms in which they themselves participate in high esteem, those to which they are outsiders are generally considered to be of low value (Sutton-Smith 1997, 204–7). The play and ritual researcher should therefore access sources with a probing attitude and without expectations that are too narrow. Good empirical legwork is the necessary underpinning for clearer, more tenable ideas. Still, there is much to gain if our efforts lead to more reliable drafts of the simmering waters of tension and imagination that lie in between the oceans of play and ritual.

REFERENCES

Bakhtin, Mikhail. 1986 [1929/1979]. "The Problem of Speech Genres." In *Speech Genres and Other Late Essays*, edited by Caryl Emerson and Michael Holquist, 60–102. Austin: University of Texas Press.

Bateson, Gregory. 2000 [1972]. *Steps to an Ecology of Mind*. Chicago: University of Chicago Press.

Bauman, Richard, and Charles L. Briggs. 1990. "Poetics and Performance as Critical Perspectives on Language and Social Life." *Annual Review of Anthropology* 19: 59–88.

Bell, Catherine. 1997. *Ritual: Perspectives and Dimensions*. Oxford: Oxford University Press.

Bett, Henry. 1929. *The Games of Children, Their Origin and History*. London: Methuen.

Burghardt, Gordon M. 2005. *The Genesis of Animal Play: Testing the Limits*. Cambridge, MA: MIT Press.

Caillois, Roger. 2001 [1961]. *Man, Play, and Games*. Chicago: University of Illinois Press.

Dorst, John D. 1983. "Neck-Riddle as a Dialogue of Genres: Applying Bakhtin's Genre Theory." *Journal of American Folklore* 96 (382): 413–33.

Drewal, Margaret Thompson. 1992. *Yoruba Ritual: Performers, Play, Agency*. Bloomington: Indiana University Press.

Durkheim, Émile. 1912. *Les formes élémentaires de la vie religieuse: Le systéme totémique en Australie*. Paris: Libraire Félix Alcan.

Fagen, Robert. 1981. *Animal Play Behaviour*. New York: Oxford University Press.

Fagen, Robert. 1995. "Animal Play, Games of Angels, Biology, and Brian." In *The Future of Play Theory: A Multidisciplinary Inquiry into the Contributions of Brian Sutton-Smith*, edited by Anthony D. Pellegrini, 23–44. New York: State University of New York Press.

Fein, Greta G. 1987. "Pretend Play, Creativity, and Consciousness." In *Curiosity, Imagination, and Play: On the Development of Spontaneous Cognitive and Motivational Processes*, edited by Dietmar Görlitz and Joachim F. Wohlwill, 282–304. London: Lawrence Erlbaum Associates.

Fox, Steven J. 1980. "Theoretical Implications for the Study of Interrelations between Ritual and Play." In *Play and Culture: The 1978 Proceedings of the Association for the Anthropological Study of Play*, edited by Helen B. Schwartzman, 51–57. New York: Leisure.

van Gennep, Arnold. 1960 [1909]. *The Rites of Passage*. Chicago: University of Chicago Press.

Gomme, Alice Bertha. 1898. *The Traditional Games of England, Scotland, and Ireland: With Tunes, Singing-Rhymes, and Methods of Playing According to the Variants Extant and Recorded in Different Parts of the Kingdom*. London: David Nutt.

Gustafsson, Lotten. 2002. *Den förtrollade zonen: Lekar med tid, rum och identitet under Medeltidsveckan på Gotland*. Nora, Sweden: Nya Doxa.

Handelman, Don. 1977. "Play and Ritual: Complementary Frames of Meta-Communication." In *It's a Funny Thing, Humour: Proceedings from the Inter-*

national Conference on Humour and Laughter, Cardiff 1976, edited by Antony J. Chapman and Hugh C. Foot, 185–92. Oxford: Pergamon.

Handelman, Don. 1980. "Re-Thinking Naven: Play and Identity." In *Play and Culture: 1978 Proceedings of the Association for the Anthropological Study of Play*, edited by Helen B. Scwartzman, 58–70. New York: Leisure.

Huizinga, Johan. 1950 [1938]. *Homo Ludens: A Study of the Play-Element in Culture*. New York: Roy Publishers.

Klein, Barbro, ed. 1995. *Gatan är vår*. Stockholm: Carlsson.

Kreinath, Jens. 2020. "Playing with Frames of Reference in Veneration Rituals: Fractal Dynamics in Encounters with a Muslim Saint." *Anthropological Theory* 20 (2): 221–50.

Malinowski, Bronislaw. 1948. *Magic Science and Religion and Other Essays*. Boston: Beacon.

Malinowski, Bronislaw. 1984 [1922]. *Argonauts of the Western Pacific*. Prospect Heigths, IL: Waveland.

Mechling, Jay. 1999. "Children's Folklore in Residential Institutions: Summer Camps, Boarding Schools, Hospitals, and Custodial Facilities." In *Children's Folklore: A Source Book*, 2nd ed., edited by Brian Sutton-Smith, Jay Mechling, Thomas W. Johnson, and Felicia R. McMahon, 273–91. Logan: Utah State University Press.

Moore, Sally Falk, and Barbara G. Myerhoff, eds. 1977. *Secular Ritual*. Assen, the Netherlands: Van Gorcum.

Muir, Edward. 2005. *Ritual in Early Modern Europe*. Cambridge: Cambridge University Press.

Olofsson, Birgitta. 1993. *I lekens verden*. Oslo: Pedagogisk forum.

Rappaport, Roy A. 1999. *Ritual and Religion in the Making of Humanity*. Cambridge: Cambridge University Press.

Renfrew, Colin. 2017. "Introduction: Play as the Precursor of Ritual in Early Human Societies." In *Ritual, Play, and Belief in Evolution and Early Human Societies*, edited by Colin Renfrew, Iain Morley, and Michael J. Boyd, 9–20. Cambridge: Cambridge University Press.

Robertson Smith, William. 1894. *Lectures on the Religion of the Semites*, first series: *The Fundamental Institutions*. London: Adam and Charles Black.

Ronström, Owe. 2017. "Ritual och ritualisering." In *Tillämpad kulturteori*, edited by Jenny Gunnarsson Payne and Magnus Öhlander, 231–50. Lund: Studentlitteratur.

Santino, Jack. 2009. "The Ritualesque: Festival, Politics, and Popular Culture." *Western Folklore* 68 (1): 9–26.

Santino, Jack, ed. 2017. *Public Performances: Studies in the Carnevalesque and Ritualesque*. Logan: Utah State University Press.

Shapiro, Matan. 2020. "Dynamics of Movement: Intensity, Ritualized Play, and the Cosmology of Kinship Relations in Northeast Brazil." *Anthropological Theory* 20 (2): 193–220.

Spence, Lewis. 1947. *Myth and Ritual in Dance, Game, and Rhyme*. London: Watts.

Sugarman, Sally. 2005. "Playing the Game: Rituals in Children's Games." In *Rituals and Patterns in Children's Lives*, edited by Kathy Merlock and Jackson Madison, 124–38. Madison, WI: Popular Press.

Sutton-Smith, Brian. 1997. *The Ambiguity of Play*. Cambridge, MA: Harvard University Press.

Sutton-Smith, Brian. 1999. "Introduction: What Is Children's Folklore?" In *Children's Folklore: A Source Book*, 2nd ed., edited by Brian Sutton-Smith, Jay Mechling, Thomas W. Johnson, and Felicia R. McMahon, 3–17. Logan: Utah State University Press.

Turner, Victor. 1982. *From Ritual to Theatre: The Human Seriousness of Play*. New York: Paj.

Tylor, Edward Burnett. 1873. *Primitive Culture: Researches into the Development of Mythology, Philosophy, Religion, Language, Art, and Custom*. London: John Murray.

Zumwalt, Rosemary Lévy. 1999. "The Complexity of Children's Folklore." In *Children's Folklore: A Source Book*, 2nd ed., edited by Brian Sutton-Smith, Jay Mechling, Thomas W. Johnson, and Felicia R. McMahon, 23–47. Logan: Utah State University Press.

2

Naughty Games

The Profanation of the Sacred at Scottish Hen Parties

SHEILA M. YOUNG

Jenna's hen party is well under way, and the group is playing that old favorite, the children's game Pin the Tail on the Donkey. It is the bride's turn next, but once she is blindfolded the game board is removed and exchanged for a new one. Gone is the cuddly donkey, and in its place is a picture of a naked man with the groom's face superimposed on it. In place of the tail is a penis. She doesn't know it, but the bride is playing Pin the Willy on the Man and the "man" is her husband-to-be. The hens stifle their giggles. Jenna is described by her bridesmaid as "a nice girl," so this will move her out of her comfort zone. They can't wait to see her reaction once the blindfold is removed. And they're not disappointed. Jenna's face is a picture. She wasn't expecting this and has been completely taken in by it. The girls are delighted and shriek with laughter. Jenna, after her initial shock, joins in. Let's face it: how else is she supposed to react?

HISTORICAL BACKGROUND

Due to its ludic nature, with its emphasis on rule breaking, the hen party is an excellent event for examining the complex relationship between play and ritual, embodying as it does the intersection between play and

https://doi.org/10.7330/9781646426751.c002

custom/rites of passage. For my doctoral research (Young 2016) I interviewed women who had taken part in hen parties in northern Scotland between 1940 and 2016. My findings showed that until the late 1980s–early 1990s, the hen party was relatively simple and inexpensive; it lasted only one evening and was generally for working-class women, and those attending were generally from the bride's peer group. It has evolved into a complex, at times costly event, with multiple, practically statutory elements and the added complexity that it frequently extends overnight. It is celebrated by women of all socioeconomic backgrounds and ages and has moved from requiring minimal organization to being micro-managed to the last detail.

The hen party is part of the marriage cycle and today takes place in the weeks leading up to the wedding. It is part of the "engagement" or "intent to marry" period. In the past, Scottish couples took part in a number of other pre-wedding rituals, such as the engagement party, the show of presents (Bennett 2004), the *réiteach* (Martin 2007), and the blackening (and its precursor, the foot washing) (Bennett 2004; Young 2019). The blackening involves kidnapping the couple, taking them to a public space, covering then from head to toe in a disgusting concoction of foodstuffs and other products, then taking them around the local community on the back of a lorry for the amusement of those watching. While the blackening still takes place in parts of Scotland, the other rituals have more or less died out, giving the hen party added significance.

Prenuptial rituals have been classified as rites of passage, enabling the transition from one life stage to another. Arnold van Gennep (1960 [1909]) recognized that there were threshold, or *liminal*, stages in the life of an individual—for example, a passage from puberty to adulthood or from single to married status. As these liminal periods were considered dangerous for both the individual and the community, rituals were enacted to assist the individual in making the transition from one to the other. The purpose of the foot-washing ritual, for example, was to bring a couple safely to the altar and then to protect them from "the mutual dangers of the marriage bed" (Allan 1954, 190).

Today, many Scots consider marriage less transformational, since a high percentage cohabit before marriage. One bride, who had been cohabiting with her partner for seven years, said: "I think there's a lot of things that are exactly the same . . . In our day-to-day lives nothing has changed"

(EI 2011.014). The days of enacting vernacular rituals for apotropaic purposes are largely gone, so the question remains: if the hen party and subsequent marriage do not transform, what do they do? Can the hen party really be termed a ritual? There is general agreement that the term *ritual* is complex. Catherine Bell (2009, vii) claims that there is no such thing as "a universal, autonomous phenomenon called ritual." She prefers instead to think of *ritualized behavior* or *a culturally strategic way of acting in the world*, while Don Handelman (1984) prefers to avoid the term *ritual* altogether and labels rituals *events*. Interestingly, not one interviewee described the hen party as a ritual. The most common response was that it was *an event*, with *fun* and *play* as the dominant features. Two respondents described it as a "rite of passage" (van Gennep 1960 [1909]), but when pressed further it was clear that this was more in the sense of "something that you had to do" in the life cycle. Rather than a ritual in the van Gennepian sense, it is more like Bell's (2009, vii) *special event* or *ritualized behavior* or J. Lowell Lewis's (2013, 43) *type of human special event*.

Over the past two decades, the hen party has emerged as an important area of mass consumption, and an industry has emerged to provide goods and services for pre-wedding parties. It can therefore be described as a "consumption orientated rite of passage" or a ritual of "status, consumption and materialism" (Otnes and Lowrey 1993, 325). In contemporary society, both calendar customs and life traditions lend themselves well to capitalist consumer culture. The commercialization of such events should not surprise us since, as Jack Santino (1996, 4–5) puts it, "we cannot live in a money-based, profit-driven society and expect our major ritual occasions not to reflect that society."

Sharon Boden (2003) suggests, in her study of British wedding consumption, that the bridal role itself becomes a consumer identity. She calls the wedding a "spectacularly, within-reach consumer fantasy," adding that to organize one, the planner needs two contradictory personalities: that of "project manager" and that of "childish fantasizer" (21). I was struck by the similarity between the task of organizing a contemporary children's party and that of a hen party and would argue that it provides both a structural model and a context for the hen party. Alison Clarke (2007, 265) examines the contemporary British children's party and the labor it involves: "As British children's parties have evolved as more elaborate affairs, they have also become increasingly commercialised. Enterprises such as

McDonald's fast-food outlets, Kid Zone play activity areas and [the] Party Pieces catalogue . . . are widely incorporated into children's party planning across Britain." McDonald's fast-food outlets could be replaced with any of the restaurants offering hen party meal deals; Kid Zone play areas could involve any number of the activities offered to groups, such as burlesque dance classes; and the Party Pieces catalog could be any of the many websites devoted to the sale of hen party merchandise. Clarke notes that outside agencies are being used increasingly to help with planning children's parties, which she attributes to "the enormous amount of labor involved in, and the social anxiety generated by, the typical infant's birthday party in recent years" (265; see also Bronner 1999, 263–64, for links between commercial culture and child lore). Hen party organizers can empathize with these comments. Returning to Boden's notion that the wedding organizer needs to be part "childish fantasizer," I would argue that this personality trait or, put another way, the child within is channeled or recalled for both planning and taking part in the event. The hen party draws heavily on elements borrowed from a children's party. For many, childhood represents a happy time and, most important, a time free from responsibility. When asked about her favorite moment from a hen weekend, one contributor replied, "drinking Bloody Mary's at 9am in our bedroom giggling like little girls" (EI 2014.093).

The hen party also fits very well with Victor Turner (1982) and Richard Schechner's (2002) concept of ritual as performance. It has stages, sets, scenes, principal actors, other actors, stage managers, and stagehands. There is a degree of informality, casualness, and amusement to it. This shows similarities to a "pop-up street theater" since when it is over, the "cast and crew" pack up and leave the pop-up theater space, which then awaits a new performance with a new set of actors (Young 2019, 15). So it is with the hen party. A number of scholars agree that there is little distinction between play and ritual: "all are temporary worlds within the ordinary world" (Huizinga 1949, 10). Ludic behavior creates social groups that separate themselves from the outside world, with the participants entering a "magic circle" for the duration of the play (Huizinga 1949).

Within the hen party, games and activities offer the possibility of ritualized play. Games are chosen for ritualistic outcomes, but taken as a whole, the hen party is a playful ritual—yes, there are serious moments, but the general feel of the ritual is one of lightheartedness and fun. For

Handelman (1984), the frames of play suggest "let us pretend" while the frames of ritual suggest "let us believe." Play at hen parties has elements of both, and to that I would add "let us regress" and "let us transgress." Margaret Thompson Drewal (1992) and Matan Shapiro (2020) illustrate how play is used to regulate the course of a complex ritual event, with Shapiro suggesting that play and ritual should not be considered binary opposites but rather a "distributed spectrum of intensities" (212).

In the same way, the hen party as a rite of passage is multilayered. It is itself part of a macro rite of passage—engagement (or intent to marry), marriage, married—but within the macro the hen party is one of several constituent micro rites of passage within the engagement stage. The hen party itself contains a nano-tripartite structure: the journey is the separation, the content the transition, and the return home aggregation (Young 2016, 263). The bride is now ready for the next stage: the marriage.

Regardless of whether hen parties are labeled rituals, the purpose of the research described in this chapter is to focus on ritual-as-communication (Geertz 1973), to examine how the various play elements are used and how they function in the larger communication pattern the hen party constitutes. In so doing, I will show that play is used to regulate the course of the complex event. I will also interpret the messages conveyed through these games to the participants, the organizers, and the onlookers.

EVOLUTION OF THE HEN PARTY

Hen and stag parties have been largely under-researched. Indeed, John R. Gillis (1985) noted that an obsession with the legal/institutional nature of marriage led to the focus of ethnographic research on the marriage itself rather than on the buildup to marriage. The earliest references to the precursor to the hen party focus on the workplace (Bennett 2004; Charsley 1991; Dyer 1979; Livingstone 1996; Monger 1996), and they are fairly recent. Until the 1950s and 1960s, some industries in Scotland had a marriage bar, which meant that a woman had to give up her job when she got married. On the bride's final day at work, her colleagues would dress her up in a homemade coat or dress, decorated with paper flowers onto which were pinned lewd messages. To complete the parody bride outfit, she might be given a net curtain for a veil and a bouquet of weeds, and she may also have had L-plates pinned to the back of her dress (denoting that she was sexually inexperienced). She would be paraded around her place of work, to the amusement of the staff, before being taken to a public space for further embarrassment. This ritual has been given a number of names, such as "taking out" or "dressing up" (Charsley 1991), "pey off day" or "bosseler" (Monger 1996), and "bosola" (Livingstone 1996). "Jumping the chanty" (Bennett 2004) was a similar ritual that required the parody bride to carry a chanty (chamber pot) on the way to the pub. At various points the bride's friends would demand that she stop in the middle of the road (thus stopping oncoming traffic) and jump over the chanty three times for luck. She would use the chanty again, once inside the pub, to demand money from the men in the pub in exchange for a kiss. While this might appear relatively tame by today's standards, at the time it was considered risqué. It was not common for women in Scotland to go to a pub until the 1960s or 1970s, as one of my contributors, who married in 1949, illustrated: "I can honestly say I never was in a pub drinking. It was just not done" (EI 2012.077).

This situation did not change significantly until the 1980s. As it became more common and socially acceptable for women to consume alcohol, pre-wedding rituals for women became rowdier and bawdier and more in line with stag parties. Women could be tied to a tree or a lamppost or taken around town on the back of a truck, horns tooting to attract attention to the bride-to-be. Stripograms also became common. However, the hen party was still considered a working-class ritual. By the 1980s the parody bride costume was eclipsed by other fancy dress. Sallie Westwood (1984) describes the "bride's ritual" for twins working at a hosiery factory in Wales. One of the twins was dressed in an oversized Babygro with two large pink breasts sewn onto it; on the seat of the suit, across the bride's bottom, were the words "It feels good." Later in the evening the twins were taken to a male strip show.

The late 1980s represented a time of great social change in the UK. The Labour government tried to re-energize Britain's city centers, in particular the nighttime economy. The government attempted to move away from the "lager lout," male-dominated, working-class pubs to a more European café culture model (Hobbs et al. 2005) that would attract women and people from all social backgrounds. There was a re-commodification of the drink industry, the introduction of clubs and themed bars, and a move from "spit and sawdust" to "chrome and cocktails" (Measham and Brain

2005). Opening hours were lengthened, and drinks became cheaper. Britain's attempt at creating a more civilized pub scene was not successful. Rather than reducing alcohol consumption, there was an increase together with a rise in related social problems; binge drinking among young women was a particular problem (Bromley and Ormston 2005; Thurnell-Read 2011; Wilson 2005; Winlow and Hall 2006). The hen party would not have taken the form it has without these changes, which enabled women to occupy spaces formerly occupied by men and resulted in a "ladette culture," defined as "a young woman who behaves in a boisterously assertive or crude manner and engages in heavy drinking sessions" (Jackson and Tinkler 2007, 254).

By the 2000s, hen parties in the UK had taken off and their equivalent in North America, the bachelorette party, was also gaining in popularity. Diane Tye and Anne Marie Powers (1998) and Beth Montemurro (2006) argue that the bachelorette party in Canada and the US was eclipsing other pre-wedding rituals, such as the bridal shower, due to the generally rather formal nature of the bridal shower in comparison with the more enjoyable bachelorette party. Both place great emphasis on the function of bachelorette party games as encouraging transgressive behavior.

Hen and stag parties became more aligned during the 2010s, in part due to the greater equality of the sexes, but the internet also played a role. Companies offered services to both hens and stags and used the same website to do so; one section for hens, one for stags. Both offered complete hen/stag party packages or parts thereof, such as activities, fancy dress clothing, and foodstuffs. There was little to distinguish between them, save perhaps in the area of activities, with men favoring more outdoor/competitive activities such as paintballing and canyoning and women preferring spa sessions and cocktail-making classes. As a result, the form became the same; through digital globalization, hen and stag parties became relatively similar throughout the English-speaking world (Young 2019, 172).

TYPES OF GAMES AND ACTIVITIES

Although there have been changes in all areas of the hen party, perhaps the greatest change has been in their content, that is, how the time is filled. One of the most important component parts is what Robert Stebbins

(1997, 18) terms *casual leisure*, defined as an "immediately, intrinsically rewarding, relatively short-lived pleasurable activity requiring little or no special training to enjoy it." Stebbins divides casual leisure into six main types: play, passive entertainment, active entertainment, sociable conversation, relaxation, and sensory stimulation. All are found at hen parties, but I will focus on two here: play and active entertainment, which I term collectively *games and activities*.

Games and activities command a disproportionate amount of space on hen party websites, which affirms the prominent place they occupy at the majority of those parties. The sheer variety is astonishing; there is literally something for everyone. Interviewees described their hen parties using terms such as *tame* and *wild*, and it was clear from my research that rather than being on a continuum, hen parties sat at one end or the other; there was little in between. Games and activities are similarly aligned. The Go Bananas website, for example, describes two types of hen party packages: "Show us action and as many men's bottoms as possible" and "Girls relaxing weekend with no men perving over you." The most popular activities at the tame end of the scale are Spa Treatments, Afternoon Tea, and various outdoor activities. At the wild end of the scale are Male Strip Show, Foreplay Lessons, and Burlesque Dance Classes. Popular "tame" games are homemade quizzes and treasure hunts. The most popular "wild" games were the quiz Mr and Mrs, Pin the Willy on the Man, and Cock-a-Hoop. Most hen parties also include drinking games.

The sharp rise in games and activities during the past decade is commensurate with the increase in the duration of hen parties. Of the thirty-eight hen parties studied, a total of 108 games/activities were engaged in. Seventeen weekend hen parties included 4 or more games/activities, and they all took place post-2010. Prior to 2010, most hen parties lasted only a single evening and involved just one game or activity. The greatest number of games/activities at a single hen party was 10 at a weekend event in a self-catered accommodation.

The hen party has produced a group of games that are unique, since they will only be played there. They do not fit into any traditional classification system for children's games (Avedon and Sutton-Smith 1971; Gomme 1894; Opie and Opie 1969; Whittaker 2012) but rather occupy their own niche (Young 2019). Traditional childhood games such as Pin the Tail on the Donkey, Snakes and Ladders, and Hoopla are adapted, subverted, and

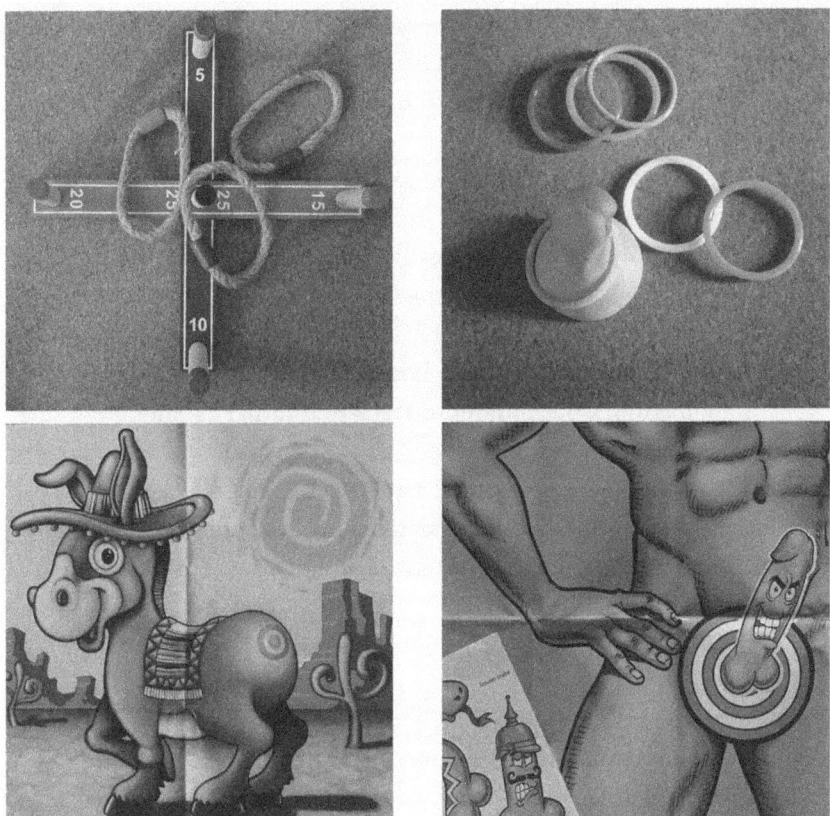

FIGURE 2.1. Children's games and their hen party equivalents. Photo by Iain Young.

parodied; and a "profanation of the sacred" (Bouissac 1990) takes place. They become Pin the Willy on the Man, Willies and Ladders, and Cock-a-Hoop (figure 2.1).

There is something unsettling and shocking about these games, stripped of their innocence and turned into something entirely different. Initially, we are transported back to our childhood and to the fun of birthday parties. In subverting this, we are tampering with the innocence and naïveté of childhood while also giving it a final nod as the responsibilities of adulthood beckon. The next time we will play these games (the original ones, that is) is probably at our own children's birthday parties.

Even adult games, such as the quiz Mr and Mrs, the most popular hen party game, are subverted. In place of benign questions such as the groom's shoe size or the groom's favorite holiday destination, the bride might be asked the groom's favorite part of her body or the most adventurous place they have had sex. One bride recalled being asked these questions in front of her mother and mother-in-law and feeling utterly mortified.

These games are not children's games, since they have been tampered with. Further, they are not, in a sense, adult games, because they are instantly recognizable as games from childhood. They occupy a liminal space in which normal behaviors are abandoned in favor of more transgressive, though licensed, behavior. This type of casual leisure has been termed "abnormal" or "wild leisure" (Rojek 2000) or "deviant leisure" (Stebbins 1997), but I prefer to think of it rather as "naughty games" (Young 2019). No harm is intended; the participants are simply being naughty. The good news is that the naughtiness is permissible; no resulting punishment or admonishment arises from these transgressions, apart from the bride's ordeal, which is intentional.

SOURCING OF GAMES AND ACTIVITIES

The task of sourcing games and activities lies with the organizers, generally bridesmaids or siblings. The amount of discussion as to the sort of casual leisure the bride wants is very dependent on the relative tameness or wildness of the hen party. The wilder the hen party, the less input the bride might have.

Once selected, the games and activities have to be sourced. They can be shop-bought or homemade. Many hen (and stag) party websites, such as the Hen Party Superstore, sell themselves as a one-stop shop, providing both ideas and services. They appeal to those with little desire to devote a good deal of time to organization, and in general their main function is to take much of the pressure off the organizers: "Sit back, chill, and let us organise accommodation, activities and entertainment . . . We handle the stressful stuff so you can be all about the fun" (www.henweekends.co.uk).

While homemade games and activities were more stressful to organize, in the interviews I conducted they were more common among those from a higher socioeconomic background. Indeed, some of my interviewees considered the shop-bought games "cheap and tacky," since "it is the appearance of natural, rather than artifice, that marks a higher cultural value" (Skeggs 2004, 101). Furthermore, opting for someone else to do the organization was deemed to constitute divesting responsibility and not showing the bride sufficient love and respect.

SOCIAL AND EMOTIONAL DYNAMICS

While the hen party, to both participants and onlookers, might seem to be simply a fun event, much is communicated below the radar. For communication to happen, there have to be transmitters and receivers (or players), as well as stages (or playgrounds) on which this takes place. At the hen party, the transmitters or players can be both inside and outside the group, and the playgrounds can be in either a public or a private space. Hen party games are always chosen with a function in mind: to deliver certain messages, some explicit, others implicit. Very little spontaneity is involved in the order in which games are played; most hen parties follow a fairly strict schedule. Weekend hen parties tend to begin on Friday evening and do not finish until around lunchtime on Sunday, which means that around thirty hours need to be filled, although not all of those hours feature games and activities. Nevertheless, this is still considerable time to fill; to keep the momentum going, there has to be a good balance of activity and passivity. Games and activities punctuate the proceedings—offering structure, regulating the course of the event (Drewal 1992; Shapiro 2020), and creating a "spectrum of intensities" (Shapiro 2020, 212).

THE PLAYERS AND THE PLAYGROUNDS

The decision of who takes part in a game is very much dependent on its function. Games and activities can be engaged in, in teams or individually. At times, the game is played only by the "central person" (Sutton-Smith 1959), that is, the bride, since in ritual "a collective passage always has solo passages embedded within it" (Glaser and Strauss 1971, 122). The focus of the ritual is on the bride, who is expected to take part and to do so with good humor, as we saw with Jenna. The games are carefully controlled by individuals or the group, who monitor the bride and referee the prizes and penalties. Getting a quiz answer wrong might result in a punishment—for example, forcing the bride to drink a shot. The bride is generally set up to fail, producing the outcome the group has desired—in this case, getting the bride drunk to loosen her inhibitions for the tasks ahead of her. At times, the role is reversed and the bride becomes the judge. For example, at one hen party each member had to gift the bride a pair of underwear, and she had to judge the giver's identity.

As a rite of passage, the hen party ritual is intended to include an element of frisson; the bride should not know what lies ahead of her, and she should expect some surprises (usually unpleasant). These come in the form of trials, and it is the games and activities that constitute the trials. It is up to the organizers to decide how much discomfort the bride will endure. Jenna's trial was relatively tame, but other brides were expected to perform simulated sex with a male stripper or play Dares with complete strangers.

The same game or activity can be designed to generate different responses from different members of the group. The bride may find it embarrassing to walk down the town's main street carrying a huge, inflatable phallus, but her hens will probably find it hilarious. Semi-forced coercion is necessary to achieve the rituals' goals. Enduring hardship is an accepted part of the ritual for both the bride and the organizers. The bride does not want to be "the enemy of ritual . . . the spoilsport" (Myerhoff 1977, 199), so she must be willing to take a hit for the amusement of her friends. This time, she is on the receiving end; the next time, she will be on the giving end.

Refusing to take part in a game is problematic, and not only for the bride. I would argue that hen party games diverge from the mainstream here in that they are not actually volitional, as various game scholars have suggested (Caillois 1961; Huizinga 1949; Whittaker 2012). They are semi-coercive, since they specify the roles certain people take. While refusal to take part in a game was unusual according to the subjects I interviewed, refusing to take part in an activity did happen. Three hens refused to take part in a burlesque dance class and went shopping instead. At another hen party, several people were not interested in a craft-making activity and refused to do it. In both cases the impact was felt within the group; there was a breach of solidarity. This rupture leads to "perceptions and feelings of mild deviance from the projected shape of the passage" (Glaser and Strauss 1971, 73). For the passage to continue successfully, the agents need to address this issue swiftly.

TAKING PLACE AND ACTING OUT

At Jenna's party, Pin the Willie on the Man was played in a private space, whereas the activity the following evening was played out in a public space. The group donned fancy dress (school-themed, since Jenna is a teacher) and Jenna, dressed as a nerdy *male* pupil, was escorted through a crowded hotel restaurant, clearly embarrassed, as the restaurant guests laughed and clapped. Jenna wore a sash with the words "Jenna's Hennie" emblazoned on it. The public group message was clear: "It's Jenna's hen party. We normally would not wear fancy dress to a restaurant but this is a one-off event, and we are licensed to do this. We are going to make her feel uncomfortable, and this will amuse us." The message received by the onlookers was: "This woman, called Jenna, is on her hen party and obviously getting married soon. We, as part of Scottish society, find the high jinks of the group amusing, but we recognize that this is a significant milestone in this woman's life and will show that we wish her well by clapping." The public's participation in games acts as a cultural affirmation that society accepts marriage as an institution and the buildup to marriage as a time when certain behaviors, normally not tolerated, are licensed. Jenna offers her own communication: "I feel uncomfortable, but I realize I have to go along with this with good grace."

The private group message was more complex; indeed, it could be summed up as the message of hen parties in general: "Jenna is getting married. She is moving from being a single woman to being married. She is leaving us. She needs to suffer a degree of 'punishment' for this. We will embarrass her both privately (with Pin the Willie) and publicly (making her wear a silly costume in front of strangers in a place where this would normally not be acceptable)." Of course, this is merely a symbolic message, since Jenna has been cohabiting with the groom-to-be for years, therefore effectively already living a "married" life. Also, in comparison to her grandmother and, to a lesser extent, her mother, she could continue to have contact with her friendship group, since both the husband and the wife in Scottish couples now tend to work, share housework and childcare, and generally have more free time. The hen party ritual, then, takes place in a liminal space, not between childhood and adulthood but between relative freedom and responsibility. That transition is suggestive of an enabled move from a hedonistic, narcissistic lifestyle to a more committed one. Rather than a coming-of-age ritual, it should be thought of as a "coming-of-(st)age ritual" (Young 2019, 151), where the "stage" is prepared for marriage following the trial period of cohabitation and the couple should be ready for the next phase in life's journey, which for many is to start a family. The difference between being married and cohabiting is blurry. Marriage may have less social status than it previously had, but it is clearly still desirable. In Cele Otnes and Elizabeth Pleck's (2003, 4, original emphasis) seminal work on the contemporary "lavish wedding" in America, they argue that it has become "*the* major ritual of the entire life span" and is now as much a "rite" as a "right." The marriage ritual can be thought of as a rite of confirmation and conformation: *confirmation* that the couple views marriage as the next stage in their life journey and *conformation* because the couple is conforming to social mores by opting to follow convention and get married (Young 2019, 150). It is also a rite of *clarification*: the power of married status is that there is no ambiguity; the relationship is clear to society. It is intended to be permanent.

NAUGHTY AND NICE

The hen party contains an interesting mix of "naughty" and "nice" games and activities. Communal happiness, or the "mutual delight of our minds being in harmony together with one another" (Blackburn 2014, 129), is one of the chief aims of the hen party. While Jenna was made to feel extremely uncomfortable on several occasions, at other times she was made to feel loved. Each member of the group was asked to bring a small gift, which she had to present to Jenna explaining the reason behind the gift. Personalized activities such as this (along with quizzes, treasure hunts, and riddles) carried the message that the bride was valued by her friends because they were willing to invest time into their production. For this particular activity, the group sat in a circle, with Jenna both part of the group and apart from the group, standing out as she did from the rest with her "bride-to-be" sash and tiara. As each told her own particular story, Jenna recalled feeling "ever more emotional" and being "quite tearful." The explicit message from each participant was that she valued Jenna's friendship, while the implicit message was that she expected this relationship to continue into the future and reciprocity (Mauss 1954) to take place when it was her turn to marry.

Jenna's gift-giving activity is an example of how the players experienced the "intensity of moments" (Shapiro 2020, 209). This polarization between "naughty" and "nice" activities is a play feature (Drewal 1992).

Both have their own intensity—some pleasant, some unpleasant. The message this gives the bride is "don't get too comfortable; you don't know what else we've got in store for you." Jenna said that while she enjoyed her hen party, she wasn't able to totally relax. Brides in general anticipate this "ritual playground" (Handelman 1984) with a mix of pleasure and dread. For the bride, the hen party is both a magical fairground ride *and* a carnival of horrors. She does not know, at any given point, what is about to jump out at her. Will it be naughty, or will it be nice?

FRIENDSHIP AND TRUST

Simply being invited to a hen party communicates to the invitees that they are part of the bride's inner circle. Jenna's mother-in-law-to-be recalled "I felt privileged to be asked" (EI 2012.030), and she clearly regarded this as a sign that Jenna liked her. Friendship lies at the root of all hen parties, and one of the principal worries of both bride and organizer is whether members of the group—often disparate, with guests from different areas of the bride's life—will get along. Organizers are conscious that the success of a hen party depends very much on how well the group gels. As a result, many hen parties start with an icebreaker—generally a team game, a drinking game, or a quiz—so members of the group can mix and get to know one another. Participants recognized that these types of games were chosen to help the group bond.

Drinking games are used to "create a therapeutic context whereby participants loosen up" (Zamboanga et al. 2007), as alcohol is considered to be confidence boosting and empowering (Rudolfsdottir and Morgan 2009; Wilson 2005). Alcohol, combined with specific games, encourages lewd conversation (Tye and Powers 1998). At another hen party, the group was asked to make a sculpture of the groom's penis with modeling clay. When asked if she could have done this without the aid of alcohol, one participant replied "no! I think everyone would have been like 'what's going on here?' Some people made quite graphic ones. It was quite weird" (EI 2012.030). Normally taboo topics are tackled while intoxicated. This also helps to create a sense of intimacy and bonding.

Finally, like the weddings that follow them, hen parties are reviewed and judged on their relative success. One hen party I attended ended in a physical fight between a bridesmaid and one of the guests. The atmosphere from the beginning was palpably unpleasant, so much so that the bride left before the party was finished. When I talked with her several days later, she told me she was now presented with a dilemma. She would have to "uninvite" one of the two, as she could not risk them fighting and spoiling her wedding. They had already ruined her hen party. Jenna's hen party, in contrast, was a great success, and several participants said it had made them look forward to the wedding even more. I argue that the hen party is both a training run and a metonym for the wedding (Young 2019, 168). A successful hen party communicates to the bride that the wedding should be equally successful. Organizing a hen party, although not of the same magnitude as organizing the wedding, is still a major exercise in planning, and expectations of the bride and the organizers to produce a successful event are huge. A well-run hen party communicates to the bride how exceptional her bridesmaid's organizational skills are, a sure sign that choosing her bridesmaid to be at her side on her wedding day was the correct decision.

CONCLUSION

The hen party is a consumption-oriented ritual that is regarded by those who take part as simply "a fun event" or a rite of passage in the modern sense of "something you have to do." It draws heavily on the children's party, containing as it does games, playgrounds, party food, party treats, dressing up, and sleepovers. It has thrived because it is both ritual and commodity. It continues because we still turn to rituals at critical points in the life cycle. It is ubiquitous because it is fun, and that is in no small part due to its ludic nature. Games and activities are an important part of the hen party ritual, since they are used to regulate the ritual event and to communicate a range of complex emotions. Beneath the surface of this event, which appears at first to be simple fun, complex cultural messages are given and received.

REFERENCES

Archival and Unprinted Sources

Interviews recorded during research fieldwork. Archival institution: Elphinstone Institute Archive, University of Aberdeen, Scotland. Archival codes: EI 2011.014, EI 2014.093, EI 2012.077, EI 2012.030.

Literature

Allan, John R. 1954. *The North East Lowlands of Scotland*. London: Robert Hale Limited.

Avedon, Elliot, and Brian Sutton-Smith. 1971. *The Study of Games*. New York: Wiley.

Bell, Catherine. 2009. *Ritual: Perspectives and Dimensions*. Revised ed. Oxford: Oxford University Press.

Bennett, Margaret. 2004. *Scottish Customs*. Edinburgh, UK: Birlinn.

Blackburn, Simon. 2014. *Mirror, Mirror: The Uses and Abuses of Self-Love*. Princeton, NJ: Princeton University Press.

Boden, Sharon. 2003. *Consumerism, Romance, and the Wedding Experience*. Basingstoke: Palgrave Macmillan.

Bouissac, Paul. 1990. "The Profanation of the Sacred in Circus Clown Performances." In *By Means of Performance*, edited by Richard Schechner and Willa Appel, 194–207. Cambridge: Cambridge University Press.

Bromley, Catherine, and Rachel Ormston. 2005. *Part of the Scottish Way of Life? Attitudes towards Drinking and Smoking in Scotland*. Edinburgh, UK: Scottish Executive.

Bronner, Simon J. 1999. "Material Folk Culture of Children." In *Children's Folklore: A Source Book*, 2nd ed., edited by Brian Sutton-Smith, Jay Mechling, Thomas W. Johnson, and Felicia R. McMahon, 251–71. Logan: Utah State University Press.

Caillois, Roger. 1961. *Man, Play, and Games*. New York: Free Press of Glencoe.

Charsley, Simon. 1991. *The Rites of Marrying: The Wedding Industry in Scotland*. Manchester, UK: Manchester University Press.

Clarke, Alison. 2007. "Consuming Children and Making Mothers: Birthday Parties, Gifts, and the Pursuit of Sameness." *Norizontes Antropológicos* 13 (28): 263–87.

Drewal, Margaret Thompson. 1992. *Yoruba Ritual*. Bloomington: Indiana University Press.

Dyer, George A. 1979. "Wedding Customs in the Office: A Note." *Lore and Language* 3 (1) part A: 73–74.

Geertz, Clifford. 1973. "Thick Description: Toward an Intepretive Theory of Culture." In *The Interpretation of Cultures: Selected Essays*, 3–30. New York: Basic Books.
van Gennep, Arnold. 1960 [1909]. *The Rites of Passage*. Chicago: University of Chicago Press.
Gillis, John R. 1985. *For Better, for Worse: British Marriages 1600 to Present Day*. New York: Oxford University Press.
Glaser, Barney G., and Anselm L. Strauss. 1971. *Status Passage*. London: Routledge.
Gomme, Alice. 1894. *The Traditional Games of England, Scotland, and Ireland*. London: Thames and Hudson.
Handelman, Don. 1984. "Inside-Out, Outside-In: Concealment and Revelation in Newfoundland Christmas Mumming." In *Text, Play, and Story*, edited by Edward M. Bruner, 247–77. Prospect Heights, IL: Waveland.
Hobbs, Dick, Simon Winlow, Phillip Hadfield, and Stuart Lister. 2005. "Violent Hypocrisy: Governance and the Nighttime Economy." *European Journal of Criminology* 2 (2): 161–83.
Huizinga, Johan. 1949. *Homo Ludens*. London: Routledge and Kegan Paul.
Jackson, Carolyn, and Penny Tinkler. 2007. "Ladettes and Modern Girls: 'Troublesome' Young Femininities." *Sociological Review* 55: 251–72.
Lewis, J. Lowell. 2013. *The Anthropology of Cultural Performance*. New York: Palgrave Macmillan.
Livingstone, Sheila. 1996. *Scottish Customs*. New York: Barnes and Noble.
Martin, Neill. 2007. *The Form and Function of Ritual Dialogue in the Marriage Traditions of Celtic-Language Cultures*. Lampeter, Wales: Edward Mellen.
Mauss, Marcel. 1954. *The Gift*. London: Coehn and West.
Measham, Fiona, and Kevin Brain. 2005. "Binge Drinking, British Alcohol Policy, and the New Culture of Intoxification." *Crime, Media, Culture* 1: 262–83.
Monger, George P. 1996. "Pre-marriage Ceremonies: A Study of Custom and Function." *Lore and Language* 14 (2): 143–55.
Montemurro, Beth. 2006. *Something Old, Something Bold: Bridal Showers and Bachelorette Parties*. New Brunswick, NJ: Rutgers University Press.
Myerhoff, Barbara. 1977. "We Don't Wrap Herring in a Printed Page: Fusion, Fictions, and Continuity in Secular Ritual." In *Secular Ritual*, edited by Sally F. Moore and Barbara Myerhoff, 199–224. Assen, The Netherlands: Van Gorkum.
Opie, Iona, and Peter Opie. 1969. *Children's Games in the Street and Playground*. Oxford: Oxford University Press.
Otnes, Cele, and Tina M. Lowrey. 1993. "'Til Debt Do Us Part': The Selection and Meaning of Artifacts in the American Wedding." *Advances in Consumer Research* 20: 325–29.
Otnes, Cele, and Elizabeth Pleck. 2003. *Cinderella Dreams: The Allure of the Lavish Wedding*. Los Angeles: University of California Press.

Rojek, Chris. 2000. *Leisure and Culture*. Basingstoke, UK: Palgrave MacMillan.
Rudolfsdottir, Annadis, and Philippa Morgan. 2009. "'Alcohol Is My Friend': Young Middle Class Women Discuss Their Relationship with Alcohol." *Journal of Community and Applied Social Psychology* 19: 492–505.
Santino, Jack. 1996. *New Old-Fashioned Ways: Holidays and Popular Culture*. Knoxville: University of Tennessee Press.
Schechner, Richard. 2002. *Performance Studies*. London: Routledge.
Shapiro, Matan. 2020. "Dynamics of Movement: Intensity, Ritualized Play, and the Cosmology of Kinship Relations in Northeast Brazil." *Anthropological Theory* 20 (2): 193–220.
Skeggs, Bev. 2004. *Class, Self, and Culture*. London: Routledge.
Stebbins, Robert. 1997. "Casual Leisure: A Conceptual Statement." *Leisure Studies* 16 (1): 17–25.
Sutton-Smith, Brian. 1959. "A Formal Analysis of Game Meaning." *Western Folklore* 18 (1): 13–24.
Thurnell-Read, Thomas. 2011. "Off the Leash and Out of Control: Masculinities and Embodiment in Eastern European Stag Tourism." *Sociology* 45 (6): 977–91.
Turner, Victor. 1982. *From Ritual to Theatre*. Baltimore, MD: Johns Hopkins University Press.
Tye, Diane, and Anne Marie Powers. 1998. "Gender, Resistance, and Play: Bachelorette Parties in Atlantic Canada." *Women's Studies International Forum* 21: 551–61.
Westwood, Sallie. 1984. *All Day, Every Day: Factory and Family in the Making of Women's Lives*. London: Pluto.
Whittaker, Gareth. 2012. "A Type Index for Children's Games." *Folklore* 123 (3): 269–92.
Wilson, Thomas. 2005. *Drinking Cultures*. Oxford: Berg.
Winlow, Simon, and Steven Hall. 2006. *Violent Night: Urban Leisure and Contemporary Culture*. Oxford: Berg.
Young, Sheila M. 2016. "The Hen Party." PhD dissertation, University of Aberdeen, UK.
Young, Sheila M. 2019. *Premarriage Rituals in Scotland*. Boulder: Lexington.
Zamboanga, Byron, Barbara Calvert, Siobhan O'Riordan, and Elan McCollum. 2007. "Ping-Pong, Endurance, Card, and Other Types of Drinking Games: Are These Games of the Same Feather?" *American Journal of Alcohol and Drug Education* 51 (2): 26–39.

3

The Big Question

Unwrapping the Modern Performative Marriage Proposal

AUDUN KJUS

In the early morning of December 13, 2001, in the dense woods north of Oslo, silhouettes of giant spruce trees are looming while the stars are shining down on a large timber building that looks like it has escaped from a fairy tale. Inside, a solitary figure is moving quietly, sneaking from room to room, trying to avoid squeaking floorboards, laying out items in a carefully planned pattern. Hours later, when Princess Märtha Louise of Norway wakes up, she starts following the signs and is drawn deeper and deeper into a love labyrinth made from photographs, puzzles, and Märtha-lilies. She comes to the end of the trail, to the room with a fireplace. Waiting on the fur of a great polar bear is her celebrity boyfriend, Ari Behn. He is holding a ring his grandfather has forged for this occasion. When the engagement was announced at a press conference the same afternoon, one of the journalists asked Ari if he had been nervous. He replied that he had been very nervous: "You never know ... Besides, it took a long time before she found me because of all the tasks I had laid out" (VG 13.12.2001).

This chapter studies the trend of large, dramatic marriage proposals that gained momentum in the early 2000s. Based on a selection of Norwegian proposal stories, I offer interpretations of the performative and visual aspects and consider recent customs in a historical context, drawing from a variety of sources. To conclude, I examine how framing is carried out and discuss how play elements are used to regulate interactions and produce messages about the actors.

THREE TRENDS

I work at a research institute where we aim to follow how social customs develop over time. We collected information about marriage proposals in 1959 in the project Youth Preparing for Marriage (NEG 71), which we followed up in 2014 with the project Proposal Stories (NEG S65). Judging from the collected materials, three consecutive trends characterized the second half of the twentieth century. The trends overlap, and old customs do not necessarily go away when new ones appear. Even so, the collected testimonies indicate that (1) proposals in the 1950s and 1960s were predominantly low-key; (2) a wave of culture-critical proposals followed in the 1970s; and (3) in the early 1990s, many proposal stories carried testimonies of a new current of romanticism, displaying the ideal of a surprising and overwhelming proposal.

Public proposals were not standard in the 1960s. A 1960 etiquette book stated that among present-day young and newly married couples, the couple was not likely to know where and when the proposal took place (Brøgger 1960, 520). The usual procedure seems to have been that an agreement was reached in a private and confidential manner; the big question may have been posed or, equally often, the couple may simply have talked about it and agreed to marry. The public announcement came later, when the couple went to the jeweler and bought rings. Then they were engaged and could show themselves in public as a couple. However, in most circles, it was not proper for them to live together or have children without getting married. If the couple wanted a romantic relationship to be a secure sexual relationship or if they wanted to share a household, they would usually get married:

> My husband and I had been friends for 15 years. We arranged to go fishing at his brother's cabin. When we went to collect the keys, I panicked. Should I be alone with . . . the whole evening? But we went fishing, cooked our catch in seawater, and had a good time. That evening we

became a couple. Three months later, we bought rings, and in December, we celebrated our wedding. (NEG S65/45491 woman 1937 Hareid)[1]

I was married in 1963, but I don't remember any proposal. We "had to" marry, as they said. The marriage did not last long—he found another. I have also asked my parents, who cannot remember anything special. Other than that my mother's parents got furious when she told them that she was pregnant. They were told to marry. I was born a month after their wedding. (NEG S65/45309 woman 1945 Grue)

I proposed in June 1967. During the summer holidays, we travelled to Copenhagen with the ferry "Holger Danske," with backpacks and tent. Kirsten Kimer's Camping was our address for nearly two weeks. On Saturday evening, we decided to treat ourselves to a nice dinner. After dessert, I proposed, and the Monday after, we went and bought rings. (NEG S65/45073 man 1946 Kongsvinger)

In the 1970s, this system came under pressure. Many members of the new generation considered marriage a bourgeois and paternalistic institution, unsuitable for free, independent young people. The 1970s marriage *en passant*—a morning at the Registry Office, wedding pictures out of focus, a newspaper sticking out of the groom's pocket—is connected to the nonchalant proposal, perhaps posed as a stray thought while walking down the street:

In 1970, a boyfriend asked me nonchalantly—on the street—if I thought we should get married. I would very much have liked to marry him, but I answered casually "not for a couple of years, at least," which he responded was a cool reply. A tough and independent woman, you know. Not the clingy sort. A few months later, he made another woman pregnant. After that, he broke up with me and married her. (NEG S65/45090 woman 1949 Trondheim)

I have not proposed with a direct question, and I have not been proposed to, but at one stage, we agreed to marry, though this cannot be dated more exact than spring 1972. We paid for the marriage ourselves, and as students, we had to limit the celebration to the closest family and best man and woman. A friend acted as a photographer, but the pictures do not hold the expected standard. This is the one thing I would have done

---

[1] All quotes from questionnaire responses have been translated from Norwegian by the author.

differently: to have a decent photograph. (NEG S65/45128 woman 1948 Bergen)

People of this generation note the differences between how they handled the proposal and how young people do it today. Some marvel at how sober and demonstratively un-romantic they were. Others fear that young people today are going astray. While they themselves challenged and broke with suppressive customs that have largely been abandoned, they see young women dressing up like princesses, eager to walk down the aisle to Mendelssohn's accompaniment with rosy cheeks and stars in their eyes—while young men fall on their knees, offering the ring after asking the father for "his daughter's hand."

PROPOSALS FROM THE THIRD MILLENNIUM

The most recent group of proposal stories shows a variety of approaches. What do they still have in common with earlier approaches? Moreover, how are they different from previous trends? Some things are similar. Many proposals still take place during vacations. In accounts from the 1960s and 1970s, we heard about cabins and camping. In the early 2000s, the destinations for the proposal are often more exotic, such as Dubai, Greece, or New York, and the gestures are often more dramatic and spectacular. The big question is posed at the edge of the world's deepest canyon (the Grand Canyon, 1,600 meters deep) or the top of the world's tallest tower (Burj Khalifa in Dubai, 828 meters tall). It may demand weeks of preparations. The person proposed to is astonished, really taken aback. The sabering of champagne bottles and multitudes of lit candles are popular features. When young women explain how a person could or should propose, there are some common, predictable elements:

> If he chooses to kneel, I think the suitor should go down on one knee, but I am not sure about this logic. I am a bit old-fashioned, and I think the most ideal and romantic is for the man to propose. It is nice if he is inventive and spontaneous. (NEG S65/45068 woman 1982 Oslo)

> I like the traditional proposal, where the man kneels—nevertheless, there are many other surprising and fun ways to do it. (NEG S65/45097 woman 1989 Hordaland)

A proposal with minimal romance: Kneel in a spontaneous setting. Middle romance: make some effort to find a romantic setting and kneel. Max romance: Find a unique setting for the woman—that she appreciates aesthetically, personally, or emotionally. Lay down some time and energy in the arrangement so that the woman sees and feels he has done some real work. (NEG S65/45113 woman 1980 Østfold)

For young people, what the informants often called a traditional or old-fashioned proposal, with a kneeling suitor in front of an overwhelmed beloved, is the apparent ideal. However, neither their parents nor their grandparents would have regarded this as usual. I have found that kneeling suitors were not common in Norway until recently.

The rural customs for proposal and marriage have been well documented (Frimannslund 1949; Sundt 1968 [1857]; Visted and Stigum 1951, 323–55). The official proposal was a formal affair carried out through an intermediary (figure 3.1).

Most often, the bride- and groom-to-be had already decided that they wished to marry. The custom of nightly visits gave eligible young men and women an opportunity to make their match. During the summer, grown girls took their nightly rest in outhouses, and local suitors visited them on Saturday evenings. Generally, when the suitor and his intermediary presented the formal offer, he had reason to believe that both the girl and her parents would say yes. If not, he risked becoming a comical figure: the rejected suitor. No kneeling is mentioned in the nightly visits or the formal proposals.

The customs of the upper classes are less well documented. However, I have studied some literary examples—proposals described by writers Camilla Collett, Bjørnstjerne Bjørnson, Henrik Ibsen, and Alexander Kielland. In the books by Ibsen and Kielland, the suitors do not kneel. Collet and Bjørnson have some kneeling suitors, but the practice seems dubious when the cases are inspected.

The novel *The District Governor's Daughters* (1855) by Camilla Collett reads like a manual on how not to propose to a lady. On the one hand, you have the self-absorbed art bum who throws himself on his knees with no regard for anything but his passions. On the other hand, you have the humorless, dry stick, who poses the question directly to the woman's parents. Finally, between these two, you have the man who should have

FIGURE 3.1. Textile box from Telemark, painted in 1805 by Ola Hansson. The cover shows a proposal scene. The suitor is standing to the left. He is turned away from the negotiations between the intermediary and the girl's father. The spokesman stands ready to toast the agreement, but the father is severe. The girl is only present through the decorated mittens held by the suitor. She has probably made and given them to him to show she wanted to marry him. The arrangement with an intermediary eases the fall for the suitor if his offer is refused. Photo by Anne-Lise Reinsfelt / Norsk Folkemuseum.

proposed, but only almost does it, in a mutual conversation about art, music, and aesthetics.

In the play *Mary Stuart in Scotland* (1864), Bjørnstjerne Bjørnson lets the Earl of Bothwell kneel when proposing to his queen, but this is a historical drama set in royal circles. It is a fair guess that kneeling suitors may have been displayed on the theater stage even when the actual kneeling was not mentioned in the text. Onstage, to make the acts visible, they

FIGURE 3.2. Kneeling for one's lady when receiving a knighthood is a stock motif in medieval chivalrous literature. The illustration is from a collection of love poems from the Codex Manesse (1305–40 Zürich). The manuscript contains 137 portraits of the poets posing as idealized knights. In this picture, der Schenke von Limburg is kneeling for his lady while he receives his knight's helmet.

must be done with large gestures. In the more mature and realistic novel *In God's Way* (1889), Bjørnson lets the main character kneel for his lady when he is in a moral crisis. It is remarked that he is doing something he never thought he would do, for he had always despised lovers in novels and plays who throw themselves on their knees.

In these texts, the kneeling suitor appears more like a literary cliché than a social custom. And it is an old cliché, already expertly mocked by Miguel de Cervantes in his novel *Don Quijote* (1605) about the imaginary lovesick defender of virgins and widows. Then, more than 400 years had passed since Crétien de Troyes (1986 [1177–1181], 73–76), in full earnest, could write with passion and effect about the noble knight Yvain falling on his knees while courting the wonderful Laudine (figure 3.2).

In nineteenth-century plays and novels, the kneeling suitor is not an obvious ideal. If there are no special circumstances, chances are that the kneeling suitor is a dubious or comical figure. The question remains: from where do present-day young people get the idea that this is the proper and traditional way to do it? Bjørnson mentioned novels and plays. Today we must add films and television series. I suspect there has been an inflation of kneeling suitors in historical dramas. Take, for instance, the cinema adaption of Jane Austen's novel *Pride and Prejudice* (2005), with Keira Knightley as Miss Elizabeth Bennet. Here, both Mr. Darcy and Mr. Bigley bend a knee, while in the 1813 novel they remain upright.

The new trend of compulsory kneeling has many followers, but another trait distinguishes the modern traditional marriage proposal even more: the expectation that the proposal should be surprising and overwhelming. This expectation is commonplace today but absent from older material. On the surface, it seems like a paradox that young women say they want a surprise proposal, while at the same time they say—and sometimes it is the very same women—that a surprise proposal is the worst type of proposal they can imagine. Upon closer examination the paradox dissolves, as even today most couples have figured out that they want to live together and have agreed that they wish to marry before a proposal takes place. Most often, it is no surprise that a proposal is under way. The elements of surprise are when, where, and how the proposal takes place.

THE PROPOSAL AS A RITE OF PASSAGE

The marriage proposal belongs to the group of acts that Arnold van Gennep (1960 [1909], 26) described as rites of passage: formal and symbolic procedures that both display and cause social change. He pointed out that biological death alone does not make a person socially dead. For a person to be included in the dead part of society, an intricate system of death rites must be carried out (146–64). For the critical changes in human life—such as birth and death—rites of passage carry out cultural processing of a natural process, at the same time expressing emotional and cognitive messages and producing social rights and obligations. The marriage proposal initiates a series of acts that ideally lead to the formation of a new, permanent couple. The suitor who receives the answer "yes" and is able to present his bride at the altar or the Registry Office is a culture hero.

A successful courtship is a glorious event that affirms and re-creates social institutions. The failed suitor is a pitiful creature, perhaps threatening and always ridiculous.

Bronislaw Malinowski (1948 [1922], 59; 1984, 413) observed that rites were used to regulate dangerous and uncertain situations. The suitor puts himself in an uncertain position. As one respondent said, "You declare your wishes and emotions—with no guarantee that you will get the answer you hope for. It demands courage and sincerity" (NEG S65/45125 man 1954). Even with the best preparations, the proposal may fail, and the fall will be brutal. It is like giving a gift that does not demonstrate that you have understood the other person, but rather the opposite. You may have misread the signs. It is yourself that you offer. If you are rejected, it is actually *you* who are rejected.

With the proposal, the suitor wants to break the frame provided by the already established relationship. It is the suitor's challenge to find or create a situation where such a question can be posed. Seen in this light, it should not be surprising that proposals are often performed in situations where the frames of the everyday have already been broken (see Handelman 1980), such as public holidays, vacations, or Saturday evenings. I proposed to my wife on New Year's Eve, just before midnight. I thought of it as a spontaneous act, but in hindsight, I understand that I was following a cultural pattern.

PLAYFUL ELEMENTS IN COURTSHIP CUSTOMS

As mentioned, many people think of the new performative marriage proposals as returning to previous customs. However, an examination of the playful elements in both the older and more recent customs will highlight the differences.

Rural courtship customs in the nineteenth century featured many aspects of play. The nightly visits have been described as "night-running and night-swarming, with noise and commotion" (Sundt 1968 [1857], 100). Other writers mention wild rides on stolen horses (Visted and Stigum 1951, 326). This sounds like what play-theorist Roger Caillois would characterize as *ilinx*, or vertigo. According to Caillois (2001 [1961], 23), this is one of the main branches of play, where the point is "to momentarily destroy the stability of perception and inflict a kind of voluptuous panic upon an otherwise lucid mind." Role-play—the play form Caillois calls *mimicry*—was also part of the nightly scenes. During the negotiations, when the boys asked for admission to the girls' chamber, they could, for instance, copy the voices of other boys (Visted and Stigum 1951, 326). Elements of competition—the play form Caillois called *agon*—were very much to the fore. Courtship quickly assumed the form of a sport, in which the participants aimed to capture symbolic points. The boys competed to be let into the girls' rooms. The girls competed to have the most and the best suitors (see Wolff 2014, 90–103).

In summary, it seems that the serious matter of future marriage was bargained in a playful atmosphere. Perhaps other aspects of the nightly visits, like the girls serving food and drink and the boys offering courtship gifts, also were carried out with a playful attitude? Nevertheless, while the preliminary courtship was playful, the formal proposals, in contrast, were very serious affairs. With the modern proposal, it is the actual posing of *the big question* that attracts playful elements. Here are a few examples:

> My daughter-in-law told me they were out on a hike to a tall mountain top. It was a warm day, but my son was carrying a large backpack. When they reached the top, he covered the moss with a tablecloth. He laid out food, roses inside a glass bell, glasses, and a bottle of bubbles and prepared his camera on a stand. Then he knelt for her and asked her to marry him. It could not be more romantic. When he received her "Yes," the camera went clicking. They have a large picture of this on their bedroom wall, with glorious weather and a spectacular view. (NEG S65/45285 woman 1935 Volda)

> A friend of mine wanted a special proposal, but she was sure her boyfriend would not come up with anything. She had herself wrapped in a cardboard box and delivered to his workplace, where she proposed. (NEG S65/45078 woman 1973 Stokke)

> I sent him an invitation to a meeting with his boss. When he arrived at the hotel where the meeting should take place, he could not find his boss, so he went looking for her. I had left a card for him at the reception desk . . . It was a playing card—the king of spades—with lots of gold and sparkle. On it, I had written: "Hey, my King of Spades. Can I be your Queen of Spades? Come up to the summit." He still did not get it, but he took the elevator to the top-floor bar. I had arranged that we would be

served champagne when I got company at my table. He came over with the card, asking what this was all about. I was not very confident and asked, somewhat clumsily, if he wanted to marry me? At that moment, two glasses of champagne fell onto his lap. There was some commotion, and the waiter was sorry. We had to change tables. In the middle of all this, I felt I had not finished what I started and asked, "Well, what about it?" He answered, "Well, I said yes." Then we had more champagne. (NEG S65/45086 woman 1970 Oslo)

These proposals have aspects that can be characterized as playful. They have unexpected and imaginative features. Out of the backpack, roses and champagne appear. There are elements of deceit. You think you are going to a job meeting—and suddenly you are engaged to be married. Margaret Thompson Drewal (1992) has studied the uses of play in the ritual culture of the Yoruba people. She points out that the ability to play appears to be the prerequisite for creating transformations. Eye-catching exaggeration and unexpected changes attract the public attention that provides the ritual efficiency (73). More fundamentally, through playful interventions, set procedures can be disturbed—allowing for surprise, disorientation, and results that were not initially obvious (197).

ABRUPT SCENE CHANGES

A swift transformation of the scene is an apt summary of the modern performative marriage proposal, and one that can be used to identify play elements. For example, one strategy for asking the big question is to construct a kind of labyrinth that, when entered, will lead to the proposal—like the woman in the previous example or Ari Behn in the introduction to this chapter. Another strategy is to prepare a swift, profound transformation, like the mountaintop suddenly clothed for a feast. Here is another example: "A friend from Morocco brought his girlfriend to his home country. He took her out to a place in the desert, where he had lit an abundance of candles, and proposed beneath the stars, with bare feet in the desert sand" (NEG S65/45080 woman 1971 Sørum).

Both the exaggeration and the surprise—the sheer number of burning candles suddenly revealed—contribute to a change of scene. A similar trap was reported from the city of Bergen. At a secluded vantage point, the suitor had worked several hours to prepare "a vast number of candles, carpets, pillows, a well-stocked picnic basket, and roses. Between the trees, he arranged photographs, and he had made a giant collage of their life together so far" (NEG S65/45114 woman 1987 Hovsherad). The amount of work required is part of the overwhelming effect when you stroll into this scene on your regular evening walk.

It can also have a good effect if you are able to exploit a scene that spontaneously offers itself, showing the ability to improvise:

> I was on a date with my boyfriend, and we were walking through the botanical gardens in Oslo. We were sitting on a bench by a pond, watching the ducks. Then we noticed a couple laying out a picnic carpet, and we remarked to each other that it was not allowed to picnic on that spot. It did not take long before a guard appeared. He addressed the man—a little to the side—and downcast, he returned to the woman, and they started packing up. While she was standing and he was gathering things from a kneeling position, he suddenly sat forth his right foot and stretched his arm towards her. We saw her reach for her mouth, and he stood up, and then they were embracing. A marriage proposal! (NEG S65/45105 woman 1984 Oslo)

The suitor noticed that his posture required only marginal adjustments to enter proposal mode, and his sweetheart recognized the new frame he had created for their interaction. For the situation to be played this way, the prerequisite was that they were both familiar with the kneeling suitor as a meta-communicative signal. Gregory Bateson (2000 [1972], 189) coined this term for signs that regulate or frame the relation between those who communicate. The examples discussed by Bateson are signs offering the message *this is play* as a frame for interaction. When the suitor is kneeling, holding out the ring, and asking "Will you marry me?" these signs show the wish to enter a particular mode of interaction. The modern "traditional" marriage proposal is an explicitly framed act. In addition, many of the examples show the use of double framing.

DOUBLE FRAMING

Don Handelman explained the phenomenon of double framing by considering the effort and energy demanded to create a framed situation. First, he reasoned that it will be more demanding to establish frames that permanently change social rights and obligations than to establish frames that only suspend ordinary reality. In other words, it should be easier to create portals to play than to create portals to ritual. Next, he assumed that it will be less demanding to attach an extra frame to an already framed situation than to arrange for the initial departure from the ordinary situational understanding (Handelman 1980, 66–70). For example, Christmas dinner is already a framed situation, and our collected proposal stories reveal that many also find it to be a suitable setting for a marriage proposal. Sports events and music concerts are less frequent, but they do occur:

> My sister was proposed to on Christmas Eve. It was carefully planned. My brother-in-law had asked my father for "his daughter's hand." Naturally, the decision was entirely up to my sister, but it was part of the arrangement to do it the old-fashioned way. He knelt for her and proposed. My parents knew about it in advance, but I knew nothing and was as eager as the bride-to-be. (NEG S65/45046 woman 1972 Oslo)

> A friend proposed to her sweetheart on the big screen at the Extreme Sports Week at Voss. She was tired of waiting for him. (NEG S65/45130 woman 1982 Ullensvang)

Ari Behn's proposal is an example of triple framing. December 13 is Saint Lucy's Day—a day for lit candles and family values. Onto this, the labyrinth of love, with small tasks and Märtha-lilies, established a play frame. Finally, the kneeling Ari, with his ring and question, reveals the formal proposal. In other cases, the establishment of the play frame and the posing of the question come in close sequence, as with the woman at her sweetheart's workplace, jumping out of a box and posing the question. I earlier referred to this kind of proposal as a trap, and there is a structural similarity with the practical joke. When the other party unknowingly wanders into the play frame and gets "caught" in the joke, the person also gets "caught" into marriage. At least this would be the suitor's plan.

When the proposal is acted out as an intervention in a public situation, for instance, on the big screen at Extreme Sports Week, the negotiated change of social status and the public announcement happen simultaneously. In the 1960s, the standard procedure was that the question about marriage was first settled in a private conversation. The status change was announced only later when the couple showed themselves wearing rings and holding hands in public.

DOUBLE PLAY

Gregory Bateson wrote that play is built on paradox, since it is recognized that the figures and acts performed within the play frame at the same time *are* and *are not* the figures and acts they portray. The current performative marriage proposal contains paradoxes not known from previous customs. The element of surprise is essential, but this is most often an agreed-upon game. The partners know that a proposal is expected. Some young women wrote that they expected to be surprised. In several of the stories, we learn that the suitor had asked the father for "his daughter's hand," but it is clear to all parties that the father cannot actually refuse. If he could, the suitor would not likely ask. When a significant portion of young men choose to ask for the father's blessing, this can be seen as an element in establishing the imagined "good old days" as a play world in which the proposal is taking place. This also strengthens the logic of proposing during Christmas because "the good old days" are already established as the play world in which Norwegian Christmas celebrations occur (Haugen 2016, 224–28; Kjus 1997).

The perspective of the play-ritual continuum allows for recognition of the polysemy of this kind of performance. Some participants may understand "the good old days" as an unreality, while others may see them as a super-reality. A participant may also be ambivalent in this regard—the frame can be understood as make-believe and serious at the same time. Lotten Gustafsson (2002, 201) has pointed out how performances acted out in settings understood as historical often allow for this kind of polysemy. This significant ambivalence also sheds light on the standardized visual expression of the modern "traditional" proposal: kneel, produce the ring, pose the question. The cliché of the kneeling suitor can be both played and meant.

Drewal (1992, 17, 75) argued that play elements can be used to regulate a ritual and adapt it to the situation at hand. The modern performative proposal follows two rules that create tension and invite playfulness. On the one hand, the proposal has a strictly standardized form. Everybody knows what the "traditional" suitor must do: bend the knee and so on. On the other hand, until it has been carried out, it is uncertain where, when, and how the proposal will take place. Thus, the performative proposal is a formula that is varied in countless ways, large and small. And when a play frame is evoked, this will invite participants and spectators to pay close attention to all such variations.

TO SHOW YOUR TRUE COLORS

According to ethologist Robert Fagen (1995, 35, 37), several species use play to assess other group members' physical and mental capabilities. It is an aspect of the performative proposal that suitors, in one way or another, show what they are made of. Even if the suitor does not make the proposal memorable or if the proposal fails, the story about it can be interpreted as one about the suitor's character. The strategy of using play elements to check out the opposite party has been noted in other, somewhat similar circumstances. For instance, in some business circles, you have to go through several rounds of karaoke and vodka drinking to show your character before a contract of any importance can be signed. The suitor should demonstrate an apt understanding of the person at the recieving end of the proposal. As one respondent wrote: "It is important that the suitor know his bride and know what she does and does not like. This is a must. He should know her preferences, for instance, if she will enjoy a public declaration or if she will find it embarrassing" (NEG S65/45113 woman 1980 Østfold).

If play, as Drewal (1992, 17) suggests, is about the ability to change a situation, then the suitor's challenge is to understand how the situation can be changed. To do this, the suitor must make realistic assessments of not only himself, but also of the other party and of the social setting. It will be to the suitor's advantage to apply a flexible, probing, and playful approach to solving this task. Then he may not end up like the person in the following example: "A former colleague was 55 years old when her equally old partner knelt for her and proposed in the middle of a Christmas party they hosted. With ring and all. She was severely affected, sparking anger inside, but she joked it away in a manner that did not ruin the party. They continued to be partners, but they never married" (NEG S65/45089 woman 1949 Oslo).

The performance of a proposal invites the partners to evaluate each other. The story about a proposal invites the listeners to evaluate the main characters. Such an evaluation can be taken further, to an interpretation of the proposal as a drama with a message. Thus, it is possible to read the proposal as an allegory for the future marriage. For instance, you can imagine that an entertaining and engaging proposal will lead to a fun and fulfilling marriage.

The notion that a great endeavor demands a proper start is a well-known idea in folklore. This goes for fishing excursions, house building, and marriage proposals: it is crucial that the beginning sets you on the right course (Storaker 1921, 36–44, 239–34). Among the collected proposal stories, interpretations of this kind appear mainly in the negative form: "I must admit that I made him propose—partly as a game—with fake rings. I can still see his face when he was going for it. We were sitting on a bench by a lake, both students. We were very much in love. By God, I was in such a hurry. Of course, I answered *Yes*, it was my idea. The phony proposal led to marriage, divorce a couple of years later, and two beautiful children" (NEG S65/45109 kvinne 1967 Stavanger). The story can be understood in different ways, but one interpretation is that an unfortunate proposal led to a marriage that did not last.

MNEMOTECHNICS

An optimistic view often expressed is that a good and memorable proposal becomes an important event in the story of one's life. In the next example, this is stated by a woman who has never been proposed to: "If you put some extra effort into the proposal, you can remember it with affection for the rest of your life, which I would have appreciated. It does not have to be extravagant, but tailor it to what your loved one loves" (NEG S65/45043 woman 1977 Bergen).

Many share this view, hinting that the marriage proposal should also be seen as an exercise in mnemotechnics. In contrast, the book on etiquette from 1960, mentioned earlier, stated that young couples often could not tell when the proposal occurred. Collected stories from the 1960s support this claim: "Since I was married for 39 years (until my husband's death), I must have been proposed to. I do not remember how, and this puzzles me. However, I clearly remember that we went and bought the rings" (NEG S65/45137 woman 1945 Førde).

If nothing out of the ordinary makes the event stand out, there is no guarantee that it will be kept in your memory. The way memory works, proceedings from ordinary weekdays are stored on top of each other; and without specific markers, it will be hard to separate one day from the other. Making the marriage proposal visibly different (e.g., by kneeling), adding elements of surprise, including an audience, and doing it at a particular time and in a special place—all of these measures can be effective markers, and all of them can be developed and refined. Extraordinary proposals have the added quality that they become stories. If an event has become a story that people around you know and tell, this strongly contributes to a lasting memory. Just like the practical joke, the performance and the subsequent narrative are two sides of the same coin, as the performance is planned with the story in mind (Bauman 1986, 35).

The current performative marriage proposal can also illustrate another path to lasting memory, as strong sensory impressions—for instance, those provided by exaggerations (oceans of roses and lit candles), vertigo (standing on a tall building or a mountaintop), or beautiful scenery (the sunset over the ocean)—may trigger the creation of so-called flashbulb memories. Likewise, a swift change in the situational frame, when a person is suddenly exposed to a rupture in the presupposed situational logic, creates an experience of absurdity, and the absurd profoundly impacts memory. As a parallel, Sara Iles Johnston (2018, 177) has pointed out how violation of categories and other absurdities were permeating the stories of Greek myths, and she sees this as a strategy to create memorable and attractive pieces of narration.

Many couples aim for the marriage proposal to become a good memory and a nexus in their shared life histories. When you take the serious step to promise and publicly announce that from now you should be considered a permanent couple, you make a conjuncture that has many uncertain consequences. A marriage proposal that is burned into the memories of both parties, as a shared mnemonic structure, can be seen as both a symbolic expression and a first realization of such a promise.

COURAGE AND DESPAIR

My friend was proposed to when she and her boyfriend were having a Sunday walk. He had been carrying the ring in his pocket for a long time, but he did not dare to ask before that day when they were walking along the beach. (NEG S65/45060 woman 1990 Bærum)

Drewal (1992) argued that play elements are used to regulate ritual proceedings, adapting them to the situations at hand and opening opportunities for change. I have found that play elements have corresponding functions in the current performative marriage proposal. Unexpected scene changes and overwhelming impressions can draw the other person into the exchange. The play frame opens for a joint performance in which the two parties show their colors and it invites close examination and interpretation of the nuances in the acts performed.

However, the play frame does not necessarily reduce the risks the suitor is taking. There are many ways in which a proposal may fail. The other person's preferences and expectations may not have been clearly expressed. What one person finds brilliant is another's total misery. Even a thorough and thoughtful plan can misfire. One would think suitors would make plans that allowed for strategic retreat—and in other settings, this is something the play frame makes room for. For instance, in cases of playground bullying, aspects of play can allow the bullies to argue that it was just a game. This is contrary to how modern performative proposals function.

When the social frame is swiftly and dramatically changed, the drop height is in fact increased, as there can be no way of denying what you have attempted. Fortunately, there are other options. You do not have to put all your money into a grand and carefully staged production. The ability to exploit a situation that suddenly presents itself can offer equally good results. Because of this there will, at any given moment, be a number of persons walking about, carrying rings in their pockets, waiting for the right moment to act impulsively.

REFERENCES

Archival and Unprinted Sources

Responses to a qualitative questionnaire on marriage proposals, issued 2014. Archive institution: Norsk etnologisk gransking / Norsk Folkemuseum (NEG) [Norwegian Ethnological Research Institute / Norwegian Museum of Cultural History]. Archival code: NEG S65 Frierhistorier.

Online newspaper article. VG 13.12.2001 kl. 15:27. https://www.vg.no/nyheter/innenriks/i/oRROxo/fridde-paa-kongsseteren, accessed August 1, 2020.

Literature

Bateson, Gregory. 2000 [1972]. *Steps to an Ecology of Mind*. Chicago: University of Chicago Press.

Bauman, Richard. 1986. *Story, Performance, and Event: Contextual Studies of Oral Narrative*. Cambridge: Cambridge University Press.

Bjørnson, Bjørnstjerne. 1864. *Mary Stuart i Skotland* [Mary Stuart in Scotland]. Kjøbenhavn, Denmark: Gyldendal.

Bjørnson, Bjørnstjerne. 1889. *Paa Guds Veje* [In God's Way]. Kjøbenhavn, Denmark: Gyldendal.

Brøgger, Waldemar, ed. 1960. *Skikk og bruk*. Oslo: Cappelen.

Caillois, Roger. 2001 [1961]. *Man, Play, and Games*. Chicago: University of Illinois Press.

Collett, Camilla. 1855. *Amtmannens døtre* [The District Governor's Daughters]. Christiania, Norway: Johan Dahl.

Drewal, Margaret Thompson. 1992. *Yoruba Ritual: Performers, Play, Agency*. Bloomington: Indiana University Press.

Fagen, Robert. 1995. "Animal Play, Games of Angels, Biology, and Brian." In *The Future of Play Theory: A Multidisciplinary Inquiry into the Contributions of Brian Sutton-Smith*, edited by Anthony D. Pellegrini, 23–44. Albany: State University of New York Press.

Frimannslund, Rigmor. 1949. "Skikk og tro ved friing og bryllup." In *Livets högtider*, edited by Karl Robert Villehad Wikman, 41–87. Nordisk kultur, vol. 20. Oslo: Aschehoug.

van Gennep, Arnold. 1960 [1909]. *The Rites of Passage*. Chicago: University of Chicago Press.

Gustafsson, Lotten. 2002. *Den förtrollade zonen: Lekar med tid, rum och identitet under Medeltidsveckan på Gotland*. Nora, Sweden: Nya Doxa.

Handelman, Don. 1980. "Re-thinking Naven: Play and Identity." In *The Ritual Dimensions of Play: Structure and Perspective, Play and Culture*, edited by Helen B. Schwartzman, 58–70. 1978 Proceedings of the Association for the Anthropological Study of Play. New York: Leisure Press.

Haugen, Bjørn Sverre Hol. 2016. "Kristoffer Visted: museumsmann og kulturhistoriker." In *Jul i gamle dager: Tekster av Kristoffer Visted*, edited by Gudmund Harildstad, 193–229. Norsk folkeminnelags skrifter 171. Oslo: Scandinavian Academic Press.

Johnston, Sarah Iles. 2018. *The Story of Myth*. London: Harward University Press.

Kjus, Audun. 1997. "Historien om hvordan julen ble feiret i Norge i gamle dager." *Folk, et folkloristisk forum* 17: 12–16.

Malinowski, Bronislaw. 1948. *Magic Science and Religion and Other Essays*. Boston: Beacon.

Malinowski, Bronislaw. 1984 [1922]. *Argonauts of the Western Pacific*. Prospect Heigths, IL: Waveland.
Storaker, Johan Theodor. 1921. *Tiden i den norske folketro*. Norsk folkeminnelags skrifter 21. Edited by Nils Lid. Kristiania: Norsk folkeminnelag.
Sundt, Eilert. 1968 [1857]. *Om sædelighetstilstanden i Norge*. Volume 1. Oslo: Pax.
de Troyes, Chrétien. 1986 [1177–1181]. *Yvain: Løveridderen*. Translated by Olaug Berdal. Oslo: Aschehoug.
Visted, Kristofer, and Hilmar Stigum. 1951. *Vår gamle bondekultur*. Volume 1. Oslo: Cappelen.
Wolff, Simon Olaus. 2014. *Riarhammeren eller Spøgeriet og to andre sagnfortellinger*. Norsk folkeminnelags skrifter 168. Edited by Ørnulf Hodne. Oslo: Scandinavian Academic Press.

4

Inventive Ash Scatterings in the Swedish Archipelago

HANNA JANSSON

It is a sunny Midsummer's Eve, and the bay in the archipelago is filled with boats carrying families and revelers. A family is fishing from one small boat, or at least so it would seem. They do have nets and buckets with them, and the floats hanging from the rods are bobbing up and down in the waves. But something else is apparently going on as well. With nervous glances at the other parties in the bay, the family members surreptitiously place an urn in the water and watch it float away. Then the ceremony begins to get out of hand, as we will see later.

Ash scattering is a form of disposal of remains in which the ashes are scattered in nature, outside of established cemeteries. In Sweden, where more than 80 percent of the dead are cremated, this alternative has tripled in frequency in past decades and now constitutes 3–4 percent of all funerals (Sveriges kyrkogårds- och krematorieförbund 2022). The practice is strictly regulated by Swedish law, yet mourners are, in the end, entrusted with full control over the disposal of the remains and can organize the scattering act to their liking. This opens up the possibility for individualization, invention, and improvisation, as mourners are free to create their own death rituals (cf. Jansson 2021a, 2021b, 2021c).

https://doi.org/10.7330/9781646426751.c004

Play is perhaps not what one immediately associates with such rituals, and it was surely not what I expected to hear about when I interviewed relatives who had scattered the ashes of a loved one at sea. The interviewees mostly spoke of grief, their dead relatives' love for the sea, and their own feeling of satisfaction at choosing a form of ceremony in line with the deceased's personality and life history. Yet two of the accounts, which I explore here, also included descriptions of what can surely be described as examples of play in relation to the funerary acts. The examples illustrate how play elements such as pretense, make-believe, and games become part of the ritual processes of funerals and how they can both enhance and disrupt mourners' experiences of these processes.

The balance between play and ritual is a delicate and complicated one, as they share many distinguishing traits but may also be dominated by vastly different moods. This makes the interrelationship of play- and funeral-related rituals particularly fruitful to investigate, to understand the interconnected practices in relation to changing cultural perceptions of death. The scattering acts and secular memorials discussed in this study can be described as informal, partly improvised, and loosely formed rituals of death, as the mourners combined familiar elements from established funerary customs with personal details to reflect the taste and personality of the deceased (cf. Grimes 2000; Jansson 2021b; cf. Myerhoff 1977). Rituals are understood here as special occasions, characterized by role taking, special moods, and symbolic actions that set them apart from the mundane flow of everyday life (Blehr 2009; Klein 1995). Although generally characterized by established orders and styles, they may also include spontaneity, creativity, and improvisation (Gerholm 1988; Klein 1995; Myerhoff 1977).

However, this could also be said about play. In my analysis here of the two women's accounts, I have therefore found it productive to emphasize one vital difference: rituals are dramas of persuasion (Meyerhof 1977, 222). Their symbols, evocative styles, music, wordings, movements, and objects may evoke particular moods and feelings in the participants and convince them of the rituals' authenticity and legitimacy (Klein 1995; Myerhoff 1977). Play instead requires players to be aware that the play is partly *not* for real. For as Gregory Bateson (1999) notes in his classical observation, play can be regarded as meta-communicative acts of pretense. In play, participants make the paradoxical agreement that what is said and done is simultaneously real and unreal. Play thus imitates actions, yet the imitation does not mean the same thing as that which is imitated and carries different intentions and effects (Bateson 1999; Gustafsson 1995).

REGULATED AND PERSONAL

Practices and rituals of death have become increasingly individualized and life-centered in contemporary Western society; obituaries, funeral ceremonies, and gravestones are now frequently designed with the deceased's personality and life history in mind (Walter 1994, 2019; Wanseele and Jacobsen 2009). This is also true for ash scatterings. The choice is often motivated by the deceased's strong affection for, or relation to, a specific place, a coastal region, or the sea (cf. Høeg 2021; cf. Kellaher, Hockey, and Prendergast 2010). Due to the emphasis on individuality, ash scatterings are generally characterized by a strong do-it-yourself ideal (cf. Jacobsen 2016; Walter 1994, 174; cf. Wanseele and Jacobsen 2009). When existing rituals of death are found inadequate to suit mourners' needs or do not conform to the deceased's requests, mourners may adapt or (re)invent their own (Grimes 2000; Jansson 2021b). Relatives are free to plan the scattering act according to their own wishes. Of the fourteen scatterings I documented, thirteen were planned and carried out by the families themselves—without aid from clergy, funeral directors, or public officiants.

Yet since ash scattering is also strictly regulated, conflicts may arise between legal authorities and mourners as to where, when, and how ashes should be dispersed. The Western tradition to separate the remains of the dead from those of the living has had a great influence on legal and administrative regulations and may collide with changing ideals of what constitutes a good funeral or resting place (cf. Prendergast, Hockey, and Kellaher 2006; cf. Walter 2019). Before a scattering, an application must be approved by the county administrative board. According to the regulations, ashes should be scattered at least 300 meters from land or any settlement. Mountain and forest areas are considered appropriate, while ash disposal is not allowed in densely populated areas, hiking trails, or nature reserves, or on hiking trails or beaches. Urns cannot be stored in a home (Länsstyrelserna 2019). Regulations vary among the Nordic countries. In Finland, one needs only the landowner's permission, and ashes may also be scattered in some city centers (Mariehamns Församling 2020; Regionförvaltningsverket

2017). The legislations of Norway and Iceland are similar to those of Sweden. In Denmark, ashes can only be scattered at sea (Barne-og familiedepartementet 2019; Borger.dk 2020; Forssell 2016; Forststyrelsen n.d.). In other countries, such as the UK and the Netherlands, regulations differ vastly from those of the Nordic countries. Relatives may keep ashes permanently in their home or bury them in a private garden, on football pitches, or in public parks. Ashes may also be incorporated into jewelery or tattooed into the skin, enabling mourners to literally carry the remains on their own body (Heessels, Poots, and Venbrux 2012; Mathijssen 2017; Prendergast, Hockey, and Kellaher 2006).

As this and previous studies show, mourners might challenge existing or presumed regulations and secretly carry out funeral ceremonies according to their own wishes or the wishes of the deceased. This is what happened in the cases discussed here and what motivated the family in the opening example to disguise the ceremony as a fishing excursion. Other participants in my study have, without permission, split the ashes and buried parts of them in secrecy in an existing family grave, kept ashes at home without permission for several years before scattering them, or scattered ashes in un-permitted places (Jansson 2021a). Similarly, Leonie Kellaher, Jenny Hockey, and David Prendergast (2010), in their British study, interviewed a woman who distributed tiny portions of her father's ashes into the carpets and furniture of his favorite pubs and a man who covertly scattered his gay friend's ashes in a public area where the friend used to meet other men. In all these cases, the mourners expressed satisfaction over acts they felt corresponded with the concerns or biographies of the deceased (cf. Clark and Franzmann 2006).

FOOTBALL AND BUTTERFLY FUNERARY RITES

Ash scattering is generally one of several ritual acts following a person's death. Judging from my material, it is most often preceded by a religious or secular funeral or memorial ceremony and is often followed by years of commemorative acts, as relatives, for example, lay down flowers or pastries or pour alcohol into rivers, lakes, and seas so these objects can travel with the water to the deceased's resting place. Funerary rites are thus seen to stretch beyond the singular acts, especially as the planning and preparing can also be vital parts of them, as can subsequent retellings (Blehr

2000, 20–21). Consequently, the interviewed relatives frequently spoke in great detail about the processes leading up to the scattering, as well as the planning and enactment of preceding ceremonies. In what follows, we meet Eva and Ellen, whose accounts of ash disposal at sea share many similarities while also being vastly different from each other—particularly when it comes to how the play elements functioned in their ritual contexts.

Eva's husband, Anders,[1] passed away in his mid-sixties after several years of illness. Her grief is apparent, both audibly and visibly. Yet her description of how she and her family organized Anders's secular memorial service and later scattered his ashes includes expressions of satisfaction and humor—but also frustration. Sweden is often described as a secular country (Thurfjell 2015), but the majority of funerals are still supervised by the Swedish church. It can therefore be difficult, my interviewees argued, to know what to do if one is to organize a secular memorial service and funeral. The funeral director could not help, Eva says, or advise them on a place that could house several hundred guests and fit Anders's personality. She therefore decided to do all the work herself and finally chose a banqueting room in the part of the city where Anders had grown up. Together with her children, she strived to achieve the solemn atmosphere they wished for (cf. Klein 1995, 17; cf. Moore and Myerhoff 1977, 7–8; cf. Myerhoff 1977, 199). A relative who was used to public speaking was asked to function as an officiant. The guests were served Danish butter breads and Anders's favorite Danish beer, just as he had requested. The urn holding his ashes stood on a table together with his photograph, candles, and a bouquet of flowers from the couple's garden, in a vase bought during one of their trips. As Anders had wished, a Spotify play list with his favorite songs played in the background.

The memorial was thus an individual, partly improvised ritual, as the family strove to create a non-religious, more personal alternative to a church funeral. Yet it is still easily recognizable as a funerary rite—with the urn, candles, music, an officiant, and flowers. By combining personal and axiomatic symbols, Eva and her children reinvented what was for them a new but still familiar ritual of death (Jansson 2021b; Myerhoff 1977). The same can be said about the scattering of Anders's ashes, which took place the following day. The ashes were scattered from a rock close

---

[1] All quotes have been translated from Swedish by the author. Interviewees' names have been changed and other identifying details left out.

to their summer house on an island in the archipelago. As stated above, according to Swedish regulations, ashes should be scattered on the open sea. But Eva and her family lacked access to a boat, so she chose to disregard this. They brought a photograph of Anders, shared a drink of his favorite liquor, and played his favorite songs from a portable speaker as they watched their roses float away together with the ashes (cf. Kellaher, Hockey, and Prendergast 2010). When it started to rain, they went back to the house and shared a meal.

Eva goes on to describe how Anders and the children had a tradition in which they played football together in the garden. Hours after they scattered his ashes and due to the now pouring rain, his children and grandchildren stripped to their underwear and lined up inside the house, like elite football players about to enter the arena. To the chorus of the "UEFA Champions League Anthem," they marched out and began to play. Eva reads from a text she has written about that day: "The music is grand, it's ceremonial. I laugh. I almost wet myself. If Anders was here, he would laugh, too, and say 'you're crazy!' They play in the rain. Fight. Fall. Cry. Laugh."

The rainy football match is layered with intertwined elements of play and ritual. Following the informal yet recognizable funeral ritual—again with photographs, flowers, and music—the family members imitate the ritual of a spectacular sports game. They pretend they are professional players. They also play an actual game, a tribute to their football-playing father and a reminder of their previous games in the garden with him. The entanglement of play and ritual is also emphasized in the likewise interwoven emotions described by Eva—the tears of grief and loss, the children's tears from slipping while playing, and humor and laughter at the absurdity of the almost naked, soaked family members imitating professional football players. Play and humor are closely related, as they both tend to join seemingly incompatible phenomena, thereby challenging established categories or norms (Bateson 1999, 16; Engman 2014, 22; Jönsson and Nilsson 2014, 11; Norrick 2003; see also Denzin 1977, 173, for views on world or life construction through children's play). Positive emotions and expressions of humor, happiness, and laughter can also provide catharsis from grief and function as a coping strategy for mourners (Lund et al. 2008; Wilson et al. 2022).

One year later, Eva's and Anders's grandchildren once again combined ritual and play, this time by reenacting a version of Anders's funeral. "We have plenty of butterflies in the garden," Eva says during the interview, and continues: "The children play with them. Then one of them died. And that butterfly was called Anders." For once during our conversation Eva laughs, even though her laughter is clearly marked by grief. "Then they arranged a funeral for it. They put out chairs in the living room and placement cards where everyone was to sit. There was one card for Anders too." She laughs again as she imitates the children's voices. The boy acting as officiant sounded a fanfare with a toy and asked in a grave voice, "does anyone wish to say something?" The four-year-old girl rose and dramatically exclaimed "I'm going to miss the butterfly Anders." The adults acted along and helped the children cremate the butterfly after the ceremony. Then the company set out down to the sea, the adults steering the children away from the site where they had scattered Anders's ashes, to another bay: "The children had built a small raft and poured the ashes onto it. And they wanted music to be played." Eva laughs again as she describes the thunderous music echoing over the bay. On the way home, they met their neighbors and told them they had just held a funeral for a dead butterfly. The neighbors, aware of the family's recent loss, nodded solemnly in comprehension.

THE MASQUERADE GOES WRONG

In Eva's example, humor, play, and games contributed to positive emotions and experiences in the midst of her process of mourning. However, in the second example, play and pretense instead threatened the desired mood of the ceremony. Ellen chose to describe her experiences from her grandfather's scattering in writing, during the first turbulent months of the restrictions of the Covid-19 pandemic. Ellen described the Christian funeral they held for him as perfectly in line with what he would have appreciated—respectful, tasteful, and personal. He had spent his professional life in the Swedish Navy and had a great love of sailing, so having his ashes scattered at sea suited him perfectly. The family was granted permission to scatter the ashes in one of Sweden's largest lakes, close to where he had lived and died. But the family lacked access to a boat, so the actual scattering was postponed. However, they submitted the required attestation to the authorities, stating that the ash disposal had been completed. For a year the urn was kept secretly in the basement of a family member's house. At one time it fell to the floor, and the ashes had to be swept up. "I guess it started to feel undignified and my dad and aunt felt it was time to do something about it," Ellen wrote.

The plan was to scatter the ashes in the archipelago off the Swedish east coast, where the family had a boat. As they now lacked the required permit, the challenge was to not be seen—a difficult task in the Swedish archipelago during the popular Midsummer holiday, when the area was filled with other boats and people fishing, bathing, and enjoying themselves. The family decided to disguise the ash scattering as their traditional Midsummer fishing excursion. "So on Midsummer morning, we filled the small boat with fishing gear, buckets, nets, kids, flowers, life jackets, and the urn," Ellen wrote. The result was confusing to her: "On the one hand, it was a beautiful midsummer day with romping kids in the boat. They were too small to fully understand death, or even to understand what we were about to do. They were really mainly there as an alibi. On the other hand, the rest of us were in a gloomy mood." One of the older children, old enough to grasp the true purpose of the excursion, was reluctant to touch the urn. Ellen noted that it was good for her to see her niece's discomfort, as it was a welcome reminder that the urn actually contained human remains, which called for respectful treatment.

The informal ritual is framed by play. Corresponding to Bateson's (1999) criteria, the fishing trip is at once real and unreal, as the family members—apart from the small children—know that their traditional Midsummer outing for once is not really about fishing. The rods, nets, and buckets are props; even the children are an alibi. It is this aspect of play as a form of concealment that in Ellen's description ruined the desired mood of the event: "It did not turn into a dignified ceremony. We anchored and brought out the fishing gear. There were other boats in the bay, but we placed ourselves so that they were not very close. Had we really been fishing, we would have anchored in a different way, so it did not actually fit well with our masquerade. But it would have to do." The family members began to fish or rather to imitate the act of fishing: "Someone placed the urn in the water. The plan was to let it sink to the bottom, to lay down our flowers and then sit there for a while." But disaster struck because the urn would not sink: "It bobbed on the waves, and the wind caught it and made it float away from the boat." The urn was likely of a cardboard variety that supposedly was later withdrawn from the market due to this very problem. The bobbing urn caused feverish activity in the small boat. "My brother tried to catch the urn with his fishing rod to pull it back without himself falling in, my dad struggled to get the anchor up so that we could go after the urn, my aunt splashed water towards it, and the rest of us pretended to fish so as not to draw attention to ourselves. The dignity was completely lost. As stubborn as my grandfather had been in life, just as stubbornly he now refused to sink," Ellen noted. Her next memory, she wrote, is of fading flowers floating in the water: "We had picked the few flowers we could find that still flowered at this time of year and had to make due with lanky stems and drooping blossoms, and it felt shabby. It was far from the departure my grandfather would have wanted."

It was not the aspect of play itself that Ellen found so disturbing because the pretense was intentional and pre-planned. Instead, it was the effects of the turn of events and the sudden lack of control that made her less content with the scattering act. Ash mishaps are a common theme in urban legends, jokes, and popular culture (Newall 1985). There, the ashes of the deceased tend to blow back in the mourners' faces, be spilled on slippery roads, or be eaten when mistaken for a cake mix, all for comic effect. Thus, the ceremony is reframed, and its mood shifts in an instant. Yet the way such a shift is interpreted can vary, as seen in some of the videos depicting real-life scatterings found online. One YouTube video from the US, for instance, shows three generations of women tenderly taking small handfuls of ashes to scatter in a river. The eldest looks into the camera and speaks lovingly to her deceased son. Then she solemnly opens her palm—and the ashes unexpectedly blow back over the other two. The youngest shrieks "oh my god, Grandma. It's in my mouth." Then she adds: "Does it look like I just ate a powdered doughnut?" All three of the women laugh before scattering the last of the ashes: "We had to have some humor." "It was fun." "It was the way it should have been" (YouTube 2018, cf. 2017).

The events described by Ellen could likely also be told in humorous ways. The scenario is surely absurd for an outsider: the beautiful summer day and the family pretending to fish while desperately trying to catch the stray urn before anyone understands what is actually going on. It amuses me every time I read her text, an uncommon reaction to empirical material that more often struck me with its tender sadness. Yet the tone of Ellen's written text is serious and subdued. The conflict between her grandfather's personality and what Ellen perceives as an undignified departure seems so great that it—in her text at least—outweighs any expression of mirth. But then the tone of Ellen's text shifts, as she describes how her disposition lightened on the way back to shore. She wanted to jump and laugh in the small boat while also realizing that doing so would be inappropriate and ill-timed. At the time she thought the bubbling sensation was a reaction to the excitement of the forbidden act. However, she later experienced the same feeling at other funerals, as the mourners gather after the ceremony, the mood gradually shifts, and laughter increasingly mingles with crying. "In that room, all emotions are allowed," she notes: "laughter, tears, gravity."

On Midsummer's Eve 2021, Ellen sent me a recent photograph of a wreath floating on waves. It is from her family's yearly outing to the spot where they scattered her grandfather's ashes that day ten years ago. Still they return, once a year, to fish. Actually fish. What was then an act of play to cover the surreptitious scattering has added to the already existing family tradition, as they now also remember her grandfather and mark the anniversary of his funeral. She no longer recognizes the exact spot at which the scattering took place, and the urn and flowers are obviously long gone. Instead, it is the memories of that day that make the excursions special.

PERSUASION, PLAY, AND RITUAL

The combination of laughter, tears, and grief that Ellen describes is a theme the two women's stories have in common, and it pinpoints the complicated interrelationships among play, playfulness, humor, and grief in the informal and individualized funerary rituals discussed here. What Eva's and Ellen's stories have in common is that they tell of ritual processes in which the families have strived to independently create personal rituals of death by combining familiar funerary symbols and orders with existing family traditions, places, objects, and acts deeply associated with the deceased. In both cases, play can be seen as one aspect of this, but the impacts of play on the overall experiences differ. For Eva, play seems to have enhanced her experience and contributed to the desired atmosphere of the events (cf. Lund et al. 2008; Moore and Myerhoff 1977, 7–8, 15; cf. Wilson et al. 2022). For Ellen, it was quite the opposite. Some key differences in the two women's accounts, combined, help explain this.

Despite the fact that it was mostly improvised, hastily put together that same day, Eva's and her family's scattering of Anders's ashes is an easily recognizable ritual, including equally easily recognizable funerary symbolic objects and deeply meaningful items of memory. The act is at once ceremonial and dignified, on the one hand, and informal and personal, on the other. The subsequent acts of play—the football match and the butterfly funeral—happened, respectively, hours and a year later and are thus certainly intimately linked to, yet also separated from, the actual scattering. This enables all three occasions—the scattering act, the football match, and the butterfly funeral—to follow their own orders and have their own moods and settings.

At the disposal of Ellen's grandfather's ashes, play and ritual instead took place simultaneously, to prevent the permit-less scattering from being discovered by potential witnesses. That which was not real—the fake fishing tour—was to appear real to conceal that which was actually real: the disposal of the remains. To the observer, the actions and objects were therefore those not of a funerary ritual but of a fishing trip. According to Ellen's description, there were no commemorative words uttered and no solemn markers apart from the flowers, which were faded and drooping and did not convey the desired dignity. The resulting incongruity is unwelcome, as the farcical escape of the urn collides with the insight that this is likely not what the proud grandfather would have appreciated.

The football match also includes incongruity, as its goofiness, exhilaration, and playfulness stand in contrast to the solemn memorial service the day before and the mournful scattering a few hours earlier. This shift in emotions, however, seems to be regarded as fitting by Eva and in line with Anders's personality (cf. Wilson et al. 2022). The match's significance appears to have been heightened for Eva by the imitation of the opening ritual, with its music and parade, marking the rainy game as out of the ordinary and an extension of the ceremony. The memorial, ash disposal, and subsequent acts of play thus appear to complement each other, as they, in different ways, enable the family members to express their grief, affection, and memories of their lost relative.

The engagement of the participants in the acts of play also differs. The adults in the fishing boat do not care for fishing; they are doing it only to keep up appearances. They are not playing for their own sake but for others. The footballers, in contrast, are invested in the parade and the match, as they pose, run, kick, laugh, fall, and cry. Their bodies become increasingly dirty and wet. The football match and the butterfly funeral also include the children in the rituals of death. The butterfly funeral is simultaneously an actual funeral for the dead insect and an act of play, as the children imitate Anders's memorial and scattering. The adults play along as the children display their remarkably observant re-staging of the emotions, moods, intonations, lamentations, settings, orders, sounds, and practical and symbolic actions of the original event (Klein 1995; Moore and Myerhoff 1977). At the same time, the adults clearly mark that the respective scatterings of a beloved family member and a butterfly are surely not the same thing, as they steer the children away from the scattering site to ensure that the butterfly has its resting place at another part of the shore. The exchanged nods between the adult family members and neighbors also seem to highlight their mutual understanding of the children's play as precisely that—the imitation of an act with altered meanings, intentions, and consequences (Bateson 1999).

This brings us back to the understanding of persuasion as the defining difference between ritual and play. Rituals have been described as ways of doing things with symbols—words, objects, songs, actions, and behaviors that mean something beyond themselves (Gerholm 1988, 198; Myerhoff 1977). Even when rituals are improvised or new, the recognition of such axiomatic symbols endows the rituals with authenticity and may convince participants of their legitimacy (Myerhoff 1977, 201). Their success resides in their capacity to move; how and in what ways will vary depending on the situation at hand. This capacity, however, presupposes that participants abstain from critical distance and allow themselves to be carried away: "Critical, analytical thought, the attitude which would pierce the illusion of reality, is anathema to ritual . . . The enemy of the ritual is one who is incapable of or unwilling to voluntarily suspend disbelief—the spoilsport" (199). For play in the Batesonian sense, the opposite is true. Play presupposes the maintaining of a certain critical distance, an underlying awareness that what is said and done in play does not mean what it usually means (Bateson 1999). For the fishing excursion to remain an act of play, it cannot turn into an authentic fishing trip; the family in the boat cannot be so absorbed by the task of catching a fish that it makes them loose their focus on the disposal of the urn.

In summary, for Eva, the acts of play appear to have contributed to her positive experience of her husband's memorial and ash disposal. Despite her apparent grief, she finds satisfaction in having independently brought about what she conceives to be a memorial and an ash disposal ceremony that fit Anders's personality and life history. In Ellen's case, the characterizing critical awareness of playing instead affected the ash disposal, hindered her engagement in the ritual, and gave rise to very different emotions and moods. The roles and conceptions of play in relation to funerary rituals are thus dependent on contextual and individual factors. Play, for example, would possibly be considered less appropriate in relation to more formal and formalized funerary rituals, where mourners feel more obligated to follow conventions. Depending on the personality and wishes of the deceased and the concerns and ideals of the mourners, elements of play can enable or, to the contrary, obstruct the achievement of the funerary rituals' desired effects and impressions. Humor or laughter may similarly be regarded by some as appreciated aspects of rituals of death and grief, while other mourners may perceive them as indicating a lack of decorum.

With changing attitudes toward death, conceptions of what constitutes appropriate or meaningful funerary rituals also change. The studied rituals are the results of intertwined processes of imitation, reinvention, improvisation, and individualization (Grimes 2000; Jansson 2021b; cf. Myerhoff 1977; Walter 1994), as the mourners compose personalized rituals of death by combining elements that carry biographical meaning with familiar, established funerary structures and objects. In these processes, play, ritual, humor, and solemnity may exist side by side and are interwoven—sometimes in cooperation, sometimes in contrast, and sometimes in conflict—showing the complex and multifaceted significations of death and grief.

REFERENCES

Unprinted Sources

Interviews recorded during research fieldwork, author's collection.

Barne-og familiedepartementet. 2019. "Om askespredning." regjeringen.no. Accessed April 2, 2020. https://www.regjeringen.no/no/tema/tro-og-livssyn/gravferd/innsiktsartikler/om-askespredning/id445138/.

Borger.dk. 2020. "Begravelse eller bisættelse." Accessed May 12, 2020. https://www.borger.dk/sundhed-og-sygdom/doedsfald-og-begravelse/begravelse.

Forssell, Monica. 2016. "Nya ställen för askspridning i Åbo." Svenska Yle. December 5. Accessed October 22, 2020. https://svenska.yle.fi/artikel/2016/05/12/nya-stallen-askspridning-i-abo.

Forststyrelsen. n.d. "Forststyrelsens samtycke till spridande av askan efter en avliden." Accessed October 28, 2020. https://www.metsa.fi/sv/jord-och-vatten/tillstand/spridande-av-askan-efter-en-avliden/.

Länsstyrelserna. 2019. "Gemensamma riktlinjer för askspridning." Unpublished document, County Administrative Boards.

Mariehamns Församling. 2020. "Vägledning vid dödsfall." Accessed May 12, 2020. https://www.mariehamnsforsamling.fi/begravningsplats/vagledning-vid-dodsfall.

Regionförvaltningsverket. 2017. "Den avlidnes aska." Accessed May 12, 2020. https://www.avi.fi/sv/web/avi/vainajan-tuhka.

Sveriges kyrkogårds- och krematorieförbund. 2022. "Kremationsstatistik 2021." Accessed May 18, 2022. https://skkf.se/krematorieverksamheten/statistik/.

YouTube. 2017. "Spreading Moms Ashes Gone Wrong." Accessed May 19, 2020. https://www.youtube.com/watch?v=p6qdGg9irCo.

YouTube. 2018. "Spreading Uncles Ashes Gone Wrong." Accessed May 19, 2020. https://www.youtube.com/watch?v=IXLLlwSxy_Q.

Literature

Bateson, Gregory. 1999. *Steps to an Ecology of Mind: Collected Essays in Anthropology, Psychiatry, Evolution, and Epistemology*. Chicago: University of Chicago Press.

Blehr, Barbro. 2000. *En norsk besvärjelse: 17 maj-firande vid 1900-talets slut*. Nora, Sweeden: Nya Doxa.

Blehr, Barbro. 2009. "Working, Moving, Visiting: On the Quality of Everyday Rituals." *Journal of Nordic Archaeological Science* 16: 33–38.

Clark, Jennifer, and Majella Franzmann. 2006. "Authority from Grief, Presence, and Place in the Making of Roadside Memorials." *Death Studies* 30 (6): 579–99.

Denzin, Norman K. 1977. *Childhood Socialization*. San Francisco: Jossey Bass.

Engman, Jonas. 2014. "Den skrattande löjtnanten: Parad, karneval och humor." In *Skratt som fastnar: Kulturella perspektiv på skratt och humor*, edited by Lars-Eric Jönsson and Fredrik Nilsson, 19–38. Lund, Sweden: Lunds universitet.

Gerholm, Tomas. 1988. "On Ritual: A Postmodernist View." *Ethnos* 53 (3–4): 190–203.

Grimes, Ronald L. 2000. *Deeply into the Bone: Re-Inventing Rites of Passage*. Berkeley: University of California Press.

Gustafsson, Lotten. 1995. "Den förtrollade zonen: Leken som möjlighet och fara under Medeltidsveckan i Visby." *Kulturella Perspektiv* 4 (2): 2–12.

Heessels, Meike, Fleur Poots, and Eric Venbrux. 2012. "In Touch with the Deceased: Animate Objects and Human Ashes." *Material Religion* 8 (4): 466–88.

Høeg, Ida Marie. 2021. "Solid and Floating Burial Places: Ash Disposal and the Constituting of Spaces of Disposal." *Mortality* (March): 1–20. Accessed November 22, 2022. https://doi.org/10.1080/13576275.2020.1869707.

Jacobsen, Michael Hviid. 2016. "Spectacular Death: Proposing a New Fifth Phase to Philippe Ariès's Admirable History of Death." *Humanities* 5 (19). Accessed November 22, 2022. https://doi.org/10.3390/h5020019.

Jansson, Hanna. 2021a. "Ashes, Law, and (Dis)Order: Negotiating Authority in Ash Scattering Rituals." *Ethnologia Scandinavica* 51: 171–87.

Jansson, Hanna. 2021b. "Grankvistar, äppelkaka och improvisation: Erfarenheter av arbetet bakom personliga begravningsritualer." *Tidsskrift for Kulturforskning* 20 (2): 59–77.

Jansson, Hanna. 2021c. "Here, There, and Everywhere: Ash Disposal at Sea and the Construction of a Maritime Memory Landscape." In *Facing the Sea: Essays in Swedish Maritime Studies*, edited by Simon Ekström and Leos Müller, 263–82. Lund, Sweden: Nordic Academic Press.

Jönsson, Lars-Eric, and Fredrik Nilsson. 2014. "Skratt som fastnar." In *Skratt som fastnar: Kulturella perspektiv på skratt och humor*, edited by Lars-Eric Jönsson and Fredrik Nilsson, 7–18. Lund, Sweden: Lund Studies in Arts and Cultural Science, Lunds universitet.

Kellaher, Leonie, Jenny Hockey, and David Prendergast. 2010. "Wandering Lines and Cul-de-Sacs: Trajectories of Ashes in the United Kingdom." In *The Matter of Death: Space, Place, and Materiality*, edited by Jenny Hockey, Carol Komaromy, and Kate Woodthorpe, 133–47. London: Palgrave Macmillan UK.

Klein, Barbro. 1995. "Inledning." In *Gatan är vår! Ritualer på offentliga platser*, edited by Barbro Klein, 7–42. Stockholm: Carlsson.

Lund, Dale A., Rebecca Utz, Michael S. Caserta, and Brian de Vries. 2008. "Humor, Laughter, and Happiness in the Daily Lives of Recently Bereaved Spouses." *OMEGA: Journal of Death and Dying* 58 (2): 87–105.

Mathijssen, Brenda. 2017. "The Ambiguity of Human Ashes: Exploring Encounters with Cremated Remains in the Netherlands." *Death Studies* 41 (1): 34–41.

Moore, Sally F., and Barbara G. Myerhoff. 1977. "Introduction: Secular Ritual; Forms and Meanings." In *Secular Ritual*, edited by Sally F. Moore and Barbara G. Myerhoff, 3–24. Assen, The Netherlands: Van Gorcum.

Myerhoff, Barbara G. 1977. "We Don't Wrap Herring in a Printed Page: Fusion, Fictions, and Continuity in Secular Ritual." In *Secular Ritual*, edited by Sally F. Moore and Barbara G. Myerhoff, 199–224. Assen, The Netherlands: Van Gorcum.

Newall, Venetia. 1985. "Folklore and Cremation." *Folklore* 96 (2): 139–55.

Norrick, Neal R. 2003. "Issues in Conversational Joking." *Journal of Pragmatics* 35 (9): 1333–59.

Prendergast, David, Jenny Hockey, and Leonie Kellaher. 2006. "Blowing in the Wind? Identity, Materiality, and the Destinations of Human Ashes." *Journal of the Royal Anthropological Institute* 12 (4): 881–98.

Thurfjell, David. 2015. *Det gudlösa folket: de postkristna svenskarna och religionen.* Stockholm: Molin and Sorgenfrei.

Walter, Tony. 1994. *The Revival of Death*. London: Routledge.

Walter, Tony. 2019. "The Pervasive Dead." *Mortality* 24 (4): 389–404.

Wanseele, Janet Ferrari, and Michael Hviid Jacobsen. 2009. "I Did It My Way? En sociologisk samtidsdiagnose over den senmoderne/postmoderne død." *Dansk Sociologi* 20 (4): 9–34.

Wilson, Donna M., Michelle Knox, Gilbert Banamwana, Cary A. Brown, and Begoña Errasi-Ibarrondo. 2022. "Humor: A Grief Trigger and Also a Way to Manage or Live with Your Grief." *OMEGA: Journal of Death and Dying*, 1–16. Accessed November 30, 2022. https://doi.org/10.1177/00302228221075276.

5

The Play and Ritual of Extreme Sports Races

Exploring the Cultural Logic of Endurance Events

KARIN S. LINDELÖF AND ANNIE WOUBE

Imagine a twenty-five–obstacle terrain race with the object of running at least thirty miles in less than twenty-four hours and a difference in altitude of 600 meters in each five-mile lap. Then add a number of burpees as penalty for missed obstacles and a complicated set of rules. There you have the Spartan Ultra World Championship arranged by the American company Spartan, a leading platform in obstacle course racing (OCR). The race was held November 9–10, 2019, at the Swedish mountain resort Åre, in snowy terrain and a temperature of -10°C, largely in darkness (figure 5.1). The motto of the arrangement was "the goal is not to win but to be a finisher."

This would seem unusual and extreme for almost anybody, even for us researchers doing our first ethnographic fieldwork—including interviews and observations—with the purpose of studying extreme sports races as a cultural phenomenon. In our study, we included extremely long sports races in open-water swimming, cross-country skiing, trail running, mountain bike and road cycling, as well as triathlons from Ironman distance and further, in addition to long and complicated obstacle races. Many of these races take more than twenty-four hours to accomplish, and they challenge the body's endurance in extreme environments. They are also

https://doi.org/10.7330/9781646426751.c005

FIGURE 5.1. Participants at the start of the Spartan Ultra World Championship, Åre, Sweden, November 2019. Photo by Karin S. Lindelöf.

seen as hyper-masculine activities (Robinson 2008). In this chapter, we explore athletes' reasons for participating in extreme sports races, the cultural logic that foregrounds such races, and how the extreme nature of the races constructs elements of play and ritual.

The race is headquartered at a hotel, which houses the race office, a race area called the transit area, and vendors. A mandatory meeting is held at the hotel the night before the race, during which the American organizers explain the general rules for Spartan and specifically the rules for this year's race. They describe the course rules: the transit area allowing two–three square meters for each participant must be passed during every lap of the race in accordance with specific instructions. Athletes enter through a particular door and leave through another, with a set time for rest before they must decide whether to leave the race or complete another lap. There is also obligatory equipment that everyone must carry with them during the race and certain sections of the track where shoe spikes are permitted. Finally, the system of "penalties" is explained, in which participants who miss obstacles are assigned punishment burpees. Athletes do their burpees in the transit area and must complete all burpees before they can finish the race or start a new lap (figure 5.2).

A local race official has allowed the two of us to join in the meeting. We are obvious outsiders, barely understanding anything. What is this? It

FIGURE 5.2. Sign with instructions for the correct burpee: a press-up followed by a leap into the air. Spartan Ultra World Championship, Åre, Sweden, November 2019. Photo by Karin S. Lindelöf.

is nothing like any traditional sporting event; it is more like some kind of complicated and ritualized game, with a multitude of confusing rules. We cannot understand how the participants can grasp what they should or should not do during the race. The major challenge of a Spartan race is not—as we had imagined beforehand—the physical achievement but rather the ability to follow the rules and to think clearly when you are physically and mentally exhausted, freezing and dehydrated, and deprived of nourishment and sleep.

Our goal is to understand the cultural logic of these events, both from an inside perspective and in their relation to the surrounding world. What are the functions of extreme races? How can it seem reasonable to spend twenty-four hours running lap after lap up and down a mountain, doing burpees, climbing over obstacles, following a complicated set of rules—and, on top of it all, doing this in the cold and darkness? We want to understand the extreme nature of these races. Why do they have to be so extreme? Since the events are unlike other sporting events and instead seem to be about something different, we want to test whether theories of play and ritual might help us understand what these races are all about.

BACKGROUND: EXTREME SPORTS RACES IN SOCIOLOGICAL TERMS

Before we dive into the fieldwork material, we want to relate these races to some of the general trends of sporting events in late modernity. The extreme sports races of today should be seen in relation to the general workout and exercise trend that has been going on in the Western world since at least the end of the 1970s. Today, physical exercise has become a common leisure activity for people from many backgrounds, even becoming a moral imperative for the good citizen. Around the turn of the millennium in Sweden, long-distance racing was a high-status hobby worth noting on one's CV. Since then, participation in long-distance races has trickled down from a hegemonic elite to a broad level of society. Consequently, in a time when "all" people train for participation in "ordinary" races, a more exceptional aspect has become necessary if long-distance racing is still to be regarded as high status.

This has paved the way for extreme sports races, such as Spartan in Åre. In addition to covering a long distance and demanding a long time, the race is set in a cold, dark, and slippery terrain traversing a mountain covered in snow. Conditions are snowy and windy, and the course presents tough obstacles, punishment laps, punishment burpees, and complicated race rules that involve the use of specific and mandatory equipment—along with rules on when and when not to use that equipment. Athletes are deprived of sleep and meals and are potentially dehydrated.

Competitiveness and achievement are major social motivations in late modern society in general (Rosa 2010, 2014). At an individual level, it is a case of forming one's life and lifestyle according to one's own ideas. Extreme sports athletes want to stand out in a crowd and to be noticeable and unique (cf. Giddens 1991). Furthermore, participation in extreme sports races ensures that this uniqueness is recognized by one's peers as exclusive and status-enhancing (cf. Honneth 2003). Today, a general agreement appears to be that expansion and development are highly valued. Success is often described in terms of more amazing experiences, greater income, more material assets. Consequently, we can no longer count on our achievements and performances to guarantee social recognition that lasts a lifetime (Rosa 2010). Hartmut Rosa states that societal changes occur rapidly today, and achievements that used to be sufficient

FIGURE 5.3. One of twenty-five obstacles at the Spartan Ultra World Championship, Åre, Sweden, November 2019. Photo by Karin S. Lindelöf.

to maintain the respected exclusivity of a social position are no longer enough. New challenges must continually be conquered if individuals want to uphold their social status. Taking part in an extreme sports race can be understood as an important means to maintain or strengthen one's position.

SPARTAN: A GAME FOR ADULTS IN LATE MODERNITY

Playfulness is a significant part of Spartan events. The obstacles often look like an ordinary playground for children but hugely oversized (figure 5.3). The point is to clamber, climb, crawl, jump, and swing on monkey bars—similar to what playing children do. Spartan thus appears to offer participants the opportunity to play in an organized form. However, in other extreme races, the element of playfulness is not as distinct as it is in obstacle races like Spartan.

Playfulness is also present in the Spartan merchandise for sale during the event. These items are characterized by a kind of war game aesthetic that references ancient Greece, beginning with the name of the race. An example is a long cloak with the Spartan logo on the back, depicting an ancient warrior helmet in red. In their marketing, presentation, and merchandise, the organizers have tailored an aggressive, violent, and

FIGURE 5.4. Warrior "mascot" at the Spartan Ultra World Championship, Åre, Sweden, November 2019. Photo by Karin S. Lindelöf.

dramatically masculine participant archetype—it is hard to tell the difference between play and seriousness in this gendered image of a Spartan participant. In their aggressive marketing of this archetype, the organizers seem to imply that finishers in a Spartan event are not just anybody; they are hyper-masculine *he-man* types who performatively represent the true heirs of ancient Greek warriors (cf. Burstyn 1999, 22). At the start of the race, this archetype is celebrated explicitly. A muscular Spartan warrior mascot—wearing a plumed helmet, mantle, and leather trunks—whips up the atmosphere, bellowing in a deep voice "history will know your names," and the participants shout back in loud guttural voices, "arooo" (figure 5.4).

With a playful approach like this, the event can be understood as a type of outdoor playground for grownups. But when adults play, things do not seem to be simple but tend to be complicated and serious (cf. Huizinga

1950). In the case of Spartan, this means an intricate set of rules only comprehensible to those already involved. Significant in all this is that participation is very expensive, giving the race an air of exclusivity. Procedures for qualification are also extensive, which creates a recurrent ritualized structure for those who want to take part in the event. A parade through the village was also arranged prior to the Spartan event in Åre. Participants and their supporting teams from around forty countries, mainly from the Global North, marched in a long procession with their national flags to the sound of music and loud shouting. Through this ritualized process, Spartan athletes established themselves in the geographic location as if this were an opening ceremony of the Olympic Games.

The ritualized setting of the event, in which the exclusive and complicated procedure of playing is governed by intricate race rules and repetition, makes this phenomenon appear to be important by creating an aura of seriousness that has little external basis. The necessity for participants to have a support team to assist them during the race is another factor that enhances the activity's significance, culturally transforming it into *serious leisure* (Stebbins 2006). Participants cannot manage the race on their own; they need people to support them so they are able to go through with the race. The teams ensure efficient intake of nutrients and fluids, as well as adequate sleep, and keep participants motivated and pacing so they do not withdraw from the race for the wrong reasons, such as tiredness (cf. Finn 2019).

The playful and ritual aspects of these races are distinct. In anthropological literature, play and ritual as cultural phenomena are considered to be closely associated (see Handelman 1998 [1990]; Turner 1982). Our purpose, therefore, is to study the cultural logic of Spartan events by applying theories of play and ritual/ritualization. We have applied an explorative approach to try to understand if, and possibly how, these theoretical tools can assist the analysis of what is involved in the cultural logic of the races, what this logic does, and its potential for participants, as well as how the participants themselves relate to it.

When it comes to ritual theory, we rely on classical texts by Arnold van Gennep (1960 [1909]), Victor Turner (1969, 1982), Sally Falk Moore and Barbara G. Myerhoff (1977), and Don Handelman (1998 [1990]). Significant theoretical works that inform our understanding of play include Johan Huizinga (1950), Gregory Bateson (2000 [1972]), and Brian

Sutton-Smith (2001 [1997]). In the Western cultural sphere, there is an implicit idea that play is a leisure activity and the opposite of seriousness. Play is seen in Western culture as voluntary, fun, and exiting and is engaged in for its own sake (Huizinga 1950, 5–8). Play therefore has a special relation to notions about work and duty: we play because it is pleasurable, and we play in our spare time, consistent with the Protestant work ethic and the division of time in the European medieval calendar into weekdays and holy days. Work is associated with weekdays and is compulsory, sober, serious, and involving responsibility. Playing is the opposite: it is leisure, free time, pastime, non-productive, trivial, silly, pleasurable, and lighthearted (Sutton-Smith 2001 [1997], 202).

The division between pleasure and duty is somewhat blurred when it comes to training and taking part in races such as Spartan. This is in line with neoliberal trends in society where leisure activities are considered investments that lead to results that can be advantageous for the individual (Keinan and Kivertz 2011). Exercising and training as a way of playing follows this development and has become gradually more serious and professionalized and more like work (Peterson 2004). For example, ordinary adults often train as if they were training for an elite level of sport, spending considerable time and money and dedicating themselves to such a degree and with the same seriousness as if their sport were their main occupation (see, for example, Andreasson, Johansson, and Danielsson 2017). Carys Egan-Wyer (2019) has pointed out that ultra-running is characterized, by runners themselves, as a free and pleasurable hobby. However, it also includes strong elements of duty, control, and discipline based on cultural, social, economic, and political ideals and expectations. In praxis, running becomes a mandatory requirement to live up to standards as an achieving individual in the eyes of one's surroundings (cf. Rosa 2010).

A question that arises is this: are seriousness, importance, and a sense of duty implicit in the play in which adults engage? A general idea about play is that children (or kittens, or puppies) play as a way of preparing for life (Huizinga 1950). In these cases, we do not regard playing as just a waste of time without value but instead as an important and significant part of childhood and of youthful testing and practicing abilities that are vital for adult life. The cultural value of playing is high, and some parents and educators regard "proper" playing in an imagined world of one's own as much better for children than the world of a computer game created by somebody else. Play is thus distinctly positioned in childhood. By contrast, play among adults has not generally been a pronounced and self-evident aspect of modernity (Huizinga 1950).

So, what evidence is there to indicate that participation in Spartan can be placed in a ritualized framework of playing? According to Huizinga (1950, 9–10), playing takes place in a special time and space of its own—a *play zone*—which the player can enter and leave. The Spartan event constitutes such a play zone in two ways. First is the concrete physical place that is marked out along the race course and roped off, together with the obstacles, rest zones, and punishment zones. This material framework is built up for each race in the series, creating a standardized ritual structure that remains the same for each race. Since the race course is run in laps, it also displays repetition, a common characteristic of ritual. A transit zone is passed between each pair of laps, providing the recurrent option of leaving the play zone, of discontinuing the race, or of just resting for a short while.

Second, the play zone constitutes an imaginary world with a distinct beginning signaled and activated by the presence of the lightly dressed, muscular Spartan warrior and by a linguistic act ("history will know your names"), followed by the participants' loud answering shouts of "arooo." A starting signal also sounds for each starting group. The participants enter a special place, which in fact is an imaginary world in their own minds where they confront themselves in the extreme conditions of the race. Entering the play zone, the participants let go of reality and the everyday life of the outside world, which ceases to be relevant for those who are playing, there and then (cf. Gustafsson 2002). The play zone becomes a specific place with its own rules, perspectives, and inner logic. In the Spartan event, "arooo" marks the separation from ordinary life—the play zone becomes a liminal space. Within the liminal structure of the race, the participant encounters a different order. It can be described as inverted space in which things, relationships, and secular processes are canceled and rearranged. Participants lose their social standing when they enter this phase, becoming athletes among other athletes—all participants share a similar, structurally invisible, and anonymous position (cf. Turner 1982, 23–25).

According to Turner (1982), in liminal space, culturally comprehensible and ordinary components are recombined, enlarged, and exaggerated—frequently in a grotesque way—which amplifies their meaning. Further, he writes that the grotesque is derived from what is possible and imaginable rather than the already experienced (27). Within the imaginable framework of extreme races, it is thus possible to create races that are more, bigger, longer, higher, and heavier and that have a greater number of obstacles. The essence of these races is to magnify and amplify. This desire to reach the horizon—to be first, best, biggest, and the like—is well-known in several fields: in "ordinary" sports and racing, in adventure and lifestyle sports, among explorers and expeditions. It is a central characteristic of modernity. To combine components such as long distances, extreme weather conditions, and inaccessible terrain in a playful yet unexpected way constitutes what is new, enlarged, and extreme in the races we are studying. This is one of the keys to these races' cultural logic.

Another element of the logic is the tension that arises between security and uncertainty. While the social structure in the rest of society is predictable, safe, and secure, liminality stands for the opposite: ambivalence, contradiction, and uncertainty. Birgitta Olofsson (1993) emphasizes that both humans and animals play when they feel secure; this creates the necessary conditions for seeking the excitement involved in play. The popularity of extreme races appears to spring from the same feeling of security: "because we have such a nice home," as one sixty-year-old male ultra-runner exclaimed to his wife when she rhetorically questioned why they were painfully negotiating a North African desert on foot instead of enjoying their pleasant home (Finn 2019, 18). Participation seems to be a response to a predictable and comfortable modern life, full of everyday routines and without real challenges. Sutton-Smith (2001 [1997], 231) considers that one point of playing is to create stylized existential conditions that mimic danger and insecurity. In late modern Western existence, where many desires and dreams can be fulfilled and are within reach, it appears as if the participants in extreme sports races seek resistance and difficulties "to really feel that they are alive" (Kvist 2017, 85, authors' translation).

The frustration and despair of the liminal experience involved in the race sap one's strength at the same time as they are liberating; the experience is more destructive but also more creative than ordinary life (Turner 1982, 46–47). Moreover, there is space for a new order to arise; after the liminal phase comes an incorporating phase when the individual returns to society, often with an improved social position (van Gennep 1960 [1909]). *Liminoid phenomena* is the term Turner (1982, 52) uses for leisure activities such as games, races, sports, and dance; he states that in modern society, the liminoid aspects are particularly expressed in playing. In contrast to the collective objective of "primitive" *rites de passage*, leisure-time play relates to an individual's potential, though it may have a collective effect when practiced together with other participants (Turner 1982). This can be related to the phenomenon of extreme races, where the participants' individual development and the testing of their physical endurance are central—which, in turn, influences collective and cultural views concerning sports and human beings' physical capacity.

RULES AND COMPANIONSHIP

According to Huizinga (1950), even if play is often represented as free, it is usually kept within the bounds of distinct rules. The game creates order through its rules, and participants must know the rules to be able to take part in the companionship and to uphold the actual play zone. This is highly applicable to the Spartan events; apart from following the race rules, it is significant to master them in a skillful way. Those who do not follow the rules or respect the limits of the play zone spoil the game (11–12). A basic but unspoken agreement or rule among the participants is not to quit prematurely for the "wrong" reasons. One of the tasks of the supporter team is to make sure this norm is followed. Wrong reasons include exhaustion, hallucinations, pain, and feelings of tediousness and resignation. Such reasons do not count in the extreme races; only serious injury and total collapse are good enough reasons to quit the race and leave the play zone. Sometimes participants still must leave the race when they cannot live up to its extremeness. When this happens, athletes often compensate by returning to try again on another occasion. This way, their initial withdrawal does not mean they have spoiled the game; they have just taken a break and can then return.

Another unspoken rule among the majority of race participants is that the real opponent is not any of the other participants; it is the race itself that is to be conquered. This is the fundamental reason for taking part in these races: to find one's own physical and mental limits and to find out if one can manage such a race. The race is conquered together with, or with help from, the other participants, which creates a strong companionship, or *communitas* in Turner's terminology (1969, 1982). Ultra-marathon runner Molly Sheridan (Sheridan and Marquis 2014, 111) describes the companionship of a race: "There were very few runners around me, but when Pierre from France passed me, I got in behind him and followed his footsteps. This was something that I loved about this race. You would run with someone—in front, behind, or next to them—for significant distances and not even exchange a single word. It was silent companionship. The sense of security provided in a foreign environment under extreme conditions was not to be underestimated."

Further, as Huizinga (1950, 12) expressed, "the feeling of being 'apart together' in an exceptional situation, of sharing something important, of mutually withdrawing from the rest of the world and rejecting the usual norms, retains its magic beyond the duration of the individual game." The participants know they are doing something out of the ordinary—possibly even something unachievable—and the actual accomplishment of it is a victory; those who do manage to accomplish the goal constitute a "club of winners" (Wellington 2013, 6). A strong sense of community develops from the players' experience of feeling different and sharing something that is not attainable for most people. This camaraderie arises during the game but can also continue outside the playing field.

One of the essential key words in the Spartan event is "arooo." It starts the game but is also continued afterward and is a way of reestablishing the common experience—for example, in social media. The word is used frequently and knits together the community, the club, the "secret" society that includes Spartan participants from all over the world. Our interviews with race participants show that the companionship and community of the race participants figures prominently in their social lives, and they rarely talk about the training and events with people outside this community. As Huizinga (1950, 12, original emphasis) states: "This is for *us*, not for the 'others.' What the 'others' do 'outside' is no concern of ours at the moment. Inside the circle of the game the laws and customs of ordinary life no longer count. We are different and do things differently."

Playing can bridge social conflicts and can be used to point out, challenge, and change power relations in real life; carnivals and festivals have often had this function in a historical perspective (e.g., Ehrenreich 2009; Turner 1969). Furthermore, power positions in games often reflect power positions in society—or vice versa—in the form of winners/losers, rulers/subordinates, power struggles, heroic deeds, and honor. In a pre-industrial context, this was understood in terms of collectiveness. The identities that were born out of power struggles would be for the common good, and a more equal society would be created through the breakdown of hierarchies. Today, however, individuals' own development, self-fulfillment, and status development—both within the game and outside it—are most significant (Sutton-Smith 2001 [1997], 78). This idea was referenced by many of the race participants we interviewed.

Consequently, the study of play forms can be a means of analyzing the society in question at a certain point in time (Geertz 1973). Much can be understood about a society, its culture, and general trends by studying a variety of current games. According to Janet Johansson (2017), serious exercising and sports participation, including extreme racing, are significant for a privileged group; this is no mass phenomenon of our times. Nevertheless, an athletic elite influences society and the spirit of the times in a broad sense, since its members inhabit a hegemonic position and their activities and actions set the standard for a wider sphere of people (Johansson 2017).

Generally, play belongs to the world of children, and play is seen as having a low status unless the purpose is educational. In certain institutionalized settings, play can attain a high status, typically when performed by a certain type of participants. In our society, this would, for instance, imply participants who are white, heteronormative, and physically normative adult men (and sometimes women) from the upper classes of society. Not only does play come to have a high status through its participants, but the participants themselves attain recognition and high status through their participation. In turn, status and recognition add seriousness to the activity in question. The Spartan games are described by participants and organizers as epic and monumental—the descriptions include experiences of nature, as well as the adventurous, imaginative, and heroically inspired elements of the races. The participants are described in Spartan events' social media content as "superhuman males" and "superhuman females." This brings to mind the paradox of play as described by Bateson (2000 [1972]). According to him, play is a fiction that does not actually exist but still leads to consequences; a virtual reality is created that both is and is not what it represents. Using Bateson's terminology, we can describe the Spartan events as containing a tension between intensified super-reality and distinct unreality (Kjus, chapter

1, this volume). The participants *are* heroes in an epic adventure, and at the same time they *are not* heroes, even if this varies for different people during the various parts of the race.

WHAT DOES THE CULTURAL LOGIC OF EXTREME RACES DO FOR PARTICIPANTS?

These races stand out as unusual and illogical to the majority of outsiders, which is why they are considered extreme. Despite the popularity of sports training in our time, these races remain culturally incomprehensible, primarily because the inner logic of the races exceeds "normality" and culturally shared ideas about what a human body is expected to manage. When we have told people about our research, most say spontaneously "that can't be healthy." Our interviewees affirm a similar response to their activities. Such reactions suggest that the phenomenon we are studying is positioned on the edge of what people generally consider possible. Even so, the concept of extreme races also impresses people, since this is a difficult type of training in a cultural context where physical exercise in general is considered high status (cf. Johansson 2017).

Jesper Andreasson and colleagues (2017) have studied how participants in triathlon races organize their family life. In line with our conclusions, they write: "Triathlon is extreme in the sense that its participants are challenging and breaking societal perceptions of what is regarded as being possible to achieve in terms of physical training, and bodily development, which also relates to normative gender configurations within the organized sport" (2).

Participants in extreme races relate to the races' inner logic in different ways. Some of the participants are deeply dedicated to keeping to the rules of the race and following its logic while at the same time regarding their participation from the detached view of an outsider. In the interviews, it is evident that they do not always tell their relatives, friends, and workmates about the races in detail. The interviewees told us that they want to give the impression that they are "training in an ordinary kind of way" and are "more than just extreme race participants." They certainly do not want to be regarded as unusual in the eyes of others. For training and races, they meet with a small group of like-minded people, but they have other friends who are "spared" the details (so as not to seem boastful, puffed up, or freak-like). At the same time, these participants are obviously aware that their achievements are out of the ordinary and may imply a high social value. The participant becomes the type of person who endures, who does not give up, who is resolute: a hero of a kind.

In contrast, plenty of participants tell all and sundry about their participation in extreme sporting events (and about the great amount of training). Not only have they adopted the full extent of extreme race logic, but they also identify with it and relate primarily to other like-minded people. These participants are part of an explicit extreme race culture and community with which they strongly identify, regardless of whether they are everyday athletes or professionals with sponsor contracts. They could not care less what "ordinary people" think, since their everyday lives fully support this particular lifestyle. The important people in their lives, who provide them with recognition and status, may also be part of the extreme sports world. These participants said they like to stand out and reported enjoying excelling in relation to others.

EXTREME RACE LOGIC

In the introduction to this chapter, we asked why these races have to be so extreme. The purpose of this study has been to understand the cultural logic of extreme sports races, both from an inside perspective and in relation to their surroundings. We have also examined the benefits participants glean from these races and how they relate to the logic undergirding the races. The Spartan event was our first fieldwork outing in this study, and it differed distinctly from "ordinary" sports events in its extreme nature as well as in its ritualized and imaginative setting characterized by playfulness. Consequently, we wanted to test whether we could apply theory on play and ritual in our attempt to understand the cultural logic of extreme races. This turned out to be tremendously useful, increasing our understanding for this cultural phenomenon in several ways.

The theories have helped us discover several patterns. The event is set in a framework of ritualized playfulness in the form of a marked play zone. In the play zone, participants shed their "normal" social roles and become athletes among other athletes. They are expected to take part and to be able to follow the rules. Physical activity is central; the actual achievement of the race is paramount.

The importance of the game is amplified by complicated rules and qualification procedures. The race's seriousness is further amplified by the involvement of supporting teams that help participants carry out the race. Exercising and training as ways of playing have become more serious, professionalized, and work-like (Peterson 2004).

The essence of extreme races is to magnify and amplify the activity by playfully combining various components in new and unexpected ways—more, longer, higher, faster, and worse—all at the same time.

The relation between security/safety and insecurity/uncertainty is challenged. In the races, participants, who otherwise live comfortable lives, can challenge their physical and mental limits. This creates a shift both in participants' individual perceptions of their own abilities and in the collective social perceptions of sports and the physical capacity of human beings in society in general.

The main antagonists in the races are not the other participants. Rather, it is the race itself that is to be conquered. A strong sense of community is created with the other participants when they are all exceeding their physical and mental limits. The companionship within the group is enhanced by engaging in an activity most people cannot manage. This amplifies status and recognition.

The cultural logic of extreme races provides the opportunity for participants to create companionship and individual status within the subculture of the races. By understanding the logic, being capable of acting successfully in accordance with that logic, and becoming proficient in the rules of the game, individual participants can create, maintain, and improve their position within the community and to some extent in the surrounding world. They are nevertheless aware of the skepticism of the surrounding society, since the activities are somewhat beyond the sphere of the culturally comprehensible; participants noted in interviews that they therefore sometimes avoid speaking of this leisure-time activity to others.

We have shown that race events such as Spartan benefit from a complicated set of rules when legitimizing this activity as play for adults (figure 5.5). The intricate rules are a way of adding importance to the game, turning recreational exercise and childish play into serious leisure. However, a paradox of the Spartan event is that the participant archetype, the Spartan warrior—who is such an important and central part of the setting

FIGURE 5.5. Instruction sign at barbed-wire obstacle, Spartan Ultra World Championship, Åre, Sweden, November 2019. Photo by Karin S. Lindelöf.

and marketing—turned out to be absent during the actual race. Instead of hard-boiled men in warrior clothing, the race was performed by subdued, slowly trudging participants of various ages and genders, dressed in outdoor clothing with a head torch to light up the snowy night. The promised imagery of superhuman heroic feats was decidedly absent. The clash between the tough, cool, and complicated—seen from the outside—and the slow inner practice constitutes the essence of many extreme sports races. Participants are both extreme and moderate at the same time. The participants are not even particularly competitive, apart from a few of the very top athletes. As the race motto states, "the goal is not to win but to be a finisher." While the cultural logic of these races is set in a regulated, ritualized, and elevated play zone, in practice participants appear to be able to carry out the race with their unique own mentalities and approaches.

REFERENCES

Unprinted Sources

The chapter is based on fieldwork observations and interviews, authors' collection.

Literature

Andreasson, Jesper, Thomas Johansson, and Erik Danielsson. 2017. "Becoming an Ironman Triathlete: Extreme Exercise, Gender Equality, and the Family Puzzle." *Sport in Society* 21 (9): 1351–63.

Bateson, Gregory. 2000 [1972]. *Steps to an Ecology of Mind*. Chicago: University of Chicago Press.

Burstyn, Varda. 1999. *The Rites of Men: Manhood, Politics, and the Culture of Sport*. Toronto: University of Toronto Press.

Egan-Wyer, Carys. 2019. "The Sellable Self: Exploring Endurance Running as an Extraordinary Consumption Experience." PhD dissertation, Lunds universitet, Lund, Sweden.

Ehrenreich, Barbara. 2009. *Karnevalsyra: Den kollektiva glädjens historia*. Stockholm: Leopard.

Finn, Adharanand. 2019. *The Rise of the Ultra Runners: A Journey to the Edge of Human Endurance*. London: Guardian Faber.

Geertz, Clifford. 1973. *The Interpretation of Cultures: Selected Essays*. New York: Basic Books.

van Gennep, Arnold. 1960 [1909]. *The Rites of Passage*. Chicago: University of Chicago Press.

Giddens, Anthony. 1991. *Modernity and Self-Identity: Self and Society in the Late Modern Age*. Redwood, CA: Polity.

Gustafsson, Lotten. 2002. *Den förtrollade zonen: Lekar med tid, rum och identitet under Medeltidsveckan på Gotland*. Nora, Sweden: Nya Doxa.

Handelman, Don. 1998 [1990]. *Models and Mirrors: Towards an Anthropology of Public Events*. New York: Berghahn Books.

Honneth, Axel. 2003. *Erkännande: Praktisk-filosofiska studier*. Göteborg, Sweden: Daidalos.

Huizinga, Johan. 1950. *Homo Ludens: A Study of the Play-Element in Culture*. New York: Roy.

Johansson, Janet. 2017. "'Sweat Is Weakness Leaving the Body': A Study on the Self-Presentational Practices of Sporty Top Managers in Sweden." PhD dissertation, Stockholm University, Stockholm.

Keinan, Anat, and Ran Kivertz. 2011. "Productivity Orientation and the Consumption of Collectable Experiences." *Journal of Consumer Research* 37 (6): 935–50.

Kvist, Miranda. 2017. *Naturkraft*. Stockholm: Louise Bäckelin Förlag.

Moore, Sally Falk, and Barbara G. Myerhoff, eds. 1977. *Secular Ritual*. Assen, The Netherlands: Van Gorcum.

Olofsson, Birgitta. 1993. *I lekens verden*. Oslo: Pedagogisk forum.

Peterson, Tomas. 2004. "Idrotten och samhället." In *Perspektiv på sport management*, edited by Ingela Broberg, 14–37. Stockholm: SISU Idrottsböcker.

Robinson, Victoria. 2008. *Everyday Masculinities and Extreme Sport*. Oxford: Berg.
Rosa, Hartmut. 2010. *Alienation and Acceleration: Towards a Critical Theory of Late-Modern Temporality*. Malmö, Sweden: Nordic Summer University Press.
Rosa, Hartmut. 2014. *Acceleration, modernitet och identitet: Tre essäer*. Göteborg, Sweden: Daidalos.
Sheridan, Molly, and Al Marquis. 2014. *Running Past Midnight: A Woman's Ultra Marathon Adventure*. USA: Molly LLC.
Sutton-Smith, Brian. 2001 [1997]. *The Ambiguity of Play*. Cambridge, MA: Harvard University Press.
Stebbins, Robert A. 2006. *Serious Leisure: A Perspective for Our Time*. New Brunswick, NJ: Transaction.
Turner, Victor. 1969. *The Ritual Process*. London: Routledge and Kegan Paul.
Turner, Victor. 1982. *From Ritual to Theatre: The Human Seriousness of Play*. New York: Performing Arts Journal Publication.
Wellington, Chrissie. 2013. *Life without Limits: A World Champions Journey*. London: Constable and Robinson.

6

Rules of Play, Playing with the Rules

Challenge and Cooperation between Security Forces and Football Fans in Sweden

KATARZYNA HERD

Football is based on play, both on and off the pitch. The interaction between the audience and the police is tense, especially in the active, confrontational stands. However, this is not just about a conflict. It is more nuanced than that, because fans and police must be able to "play" together. They depend on each other to perform their roles through rituals and rely on mutual understanding of what behavior in the situation is to be considered sensible and what is perceived as inappropriate. This chapter focuses on how supporters and security staff (police and stewards) construct ritualistic play while interpreting and "reading" the football context. I will discuss the interaction between supporters and the police and focus on play and ritualistic elements in play. Psychologist Chris Oakley (2007, 47) analyzed group behavior in arenas and referred to both play and ritual in that context to explain its structure:

> But let us return to the idea of football as play. To resume the thesis that football is one of the ways in which it has been possible to retain elements of the "play forms," of the innocence so associated with childhood . . . Superficially it might seem that sport, and in particular football, has more than compensated for any loss of play forms in our

contemporary world. Football installs yet another place of ritual, of fun and festivity in our lives. And this is whether it be "when Saturday comes" and out come the boots, or the more casual but insistent quickening of the pulse when it is that time when our TVs are saturated with World Cup coverage.

A football match can be seen as a type of heterotopia (cf. Foucault 1967; Herd 2018b), a place that allows specific rituals to take place. By understanding the match as a heterotopic place, one can begin to understand the cultural expressions that occur in that place as a ritual. A match has rules, both on and off the field. Fans can, for example, express their feelings by shouting and swearing—something that would be considered strange in "ordinary life" but is accepted in a match context. Play can also be seen in the more serious exchanges of emotions between security staff and supporters that take place during a match. It should not be said that violent behavior has no consequences, but relations between fans and the police are often governed by a common understanding of the rules of the game. Or rather, they are governed by an understanding or misunderstanding of the game. Failure, by either side, to play the game can result in trouble. Chapter 8 (this volume) discusses the literary world of Sir Terry Pratchett. The Discworld universe includes a novel about a game of foot-a-ball. Wizards from the Unseen University want to understand the game, and a university kitchen worker tries to explain matches at a local ground referred to as "the Shove," finishing with: "There's a feeling I can't describe, but it's a bit like being a kid at Hogswatch, and you can't just buy it, sir, you can't write it down or organize it or make it shiny or make it tame . . . You must have known it, sir" (Pratchett 2010, 182–83). The rules are established there and then, somewhat organically, soaked in the emotional response of the crowd.

SO PLAYFUL THAT IT IS SERIOUS

Football is a social construction based on physical activity between two teams, but with a capacity for identity-creating processes. It has become an arena in which different societal relations are tested—for example, class issues or gender roles (e.g., Andersson 2002; Andersson and Radmann 1998; Lee 2008). Security staff became involved in confrontations with emotionally charged crowds early in the history of the sport. Historian Torbjörn Andersson (2001) describes unrest during matches as early as the beginning of the twentieth century and presents around 100 cases where spectators were regarded as those who created problems in the arenas.

Emotional commitment in a football context is nothing new. Sources from the nineteenth and twentieth centuries from different parts of the Nordic region show that football often caused strong reactions (Herd 2021). At the same time, commitment has become a matter of security. Oakley (2007) points out that strongly negative interpretations of football fans are often linked to the fear of large groups—especially large groups of men who show emotions, because men are often regarded as rational, as opposed to emotional, which "belongs" to women. The debates around football are many and complicated, and discussions often have a serious tone (e.g., Bairner 2001; Green 2009), but the context of football is filled with humor and irony as well (Herd 2018b; Herd and Löfgren 2020).

Linked to this are discussions about security, violence, and hooliganism (Andersson and Radmann 1998; Green 2009; Radmann 2013, 2015). Contacts between police and supporters have a long history and their own rules. I will use two examples of how play takes place in arenas through established rituals. The first comes from a media debate on masking and pyrotechnics (flares) in 2017, and the second is from an ethnographic observation the same year. The theories I use are Susan Stewart's concept of sense and nonsense (1989), Michel Foucault's *heterotopia* (1967), and Johan Huizinga's *homo ludens* (1944 [1932]). The playful aspects of football can be linked to the process of creating sense or nonsense, as analyzed by Stewart (1989). She comments on the construction of "common sense" as follows: "The common-sense construction of reality takes place in contexts of everyday life situations. Common sense underlies and is an outcome of the interpretations created in and by these situations; it is rooted in the reality of this everyday world. These interpretations depend upon the immediate situational context, on such features of the interaction as 'settings, participants, ends, act sequences, keys, instrumentalities, norms and genres'" (27)

Stewart points out that a game is an example of how different discourses can be mixed and how they can build new discourses based on our intertextual reading. Stewart (1989, 199) refers to repetition as a marker of play: "Repetition, for example, seems to be a marker for play performance whenever its threat of infinity is recognized." Repetition is linked to rites and rituals. Much research on ritual and many definitions exist that one can relate to. I use the term *ritual* in the sense described by anthropologist Stanley J. Tambiah (1996 [1981]). He emphasizes repetition and the need for repetitive behaviors: "Ritual is not a 'free expression of emotions,' but a disciplined rehearsal of 'right attitudes'" (500). Both Stewart and Tambiah link their texts to Huizinga's (1944 [1932]) study of *homo ludens*, the playing man.

Repetition and established routines make it possible to accept behavior that would not be acceptable in other contexts. Football relies on boundaries, in time and place, that seclude participants from everyday life. Stewart (1989, 171) bases her argument on nonsense creation, with discussion of a "playground" and the delimitation of time and place that Huizinga discussed. A concept that encompasses both place and boundaries is Foucault's (1967) heterotopia, which he describes as a place outside normal life that has its own rules. He offers a boat as an example. On a boat, you have to distance yourself from the logic that applies on land and act according to a different set of rules so the boat and crew can function.

The material in this chapter comes from an ethnographic study that took place between 2014 and 2018. During the fieldwork, in addition to observing the stands and interviewing supporters, I talked to police officers and stewards. The material used here consists of three interviews (from 2015 and 2017), two observations of matches, and media material from 2017. Interviews were anonymized and names replaced with pseudonyms. There is more material from the supporters' point of view than from that of the police. Opportunities to work with the police on these issues were limited, and security personnel were cautious about participating. The two examples chosen concern three top football clubs from Sweden—AIK and Djurgårdens IF from Stockholm and Malmö FF (MFF) from southern Sweden.

The police officers interviewed pointed out that they liked football and emphasized that it was important to learn the context. One officer, Albin, said the most problematic aspect of working as a police officer if you had not experienced football matches was believing you could apply the same policing procedures inside the football ground as you did outside. This would not work in the arenas but instead would create more problems (interview with Albin, August 15, 2017). He stressed the situational understanding and awareness police officers needed to take part in the game they had to play with supporters. One can question whether it is really play from the perspective of the police. Supporters' contacts with police in arenas can have serious consequences. Huizinga (1944 [1932], 6) discusses how play should be categorized and emphasizes that "examined more closely, however, the contrast between play and seriousness proves to be neither conclusive nor fixed." At the same time, Huizinga points out in his analysis that law and order also have their starting point in play and rituals (6).

"IT IS NOT A WALK IN THE PARK"

The quote in the subhead above comes from a supporter who discussed police work during the matches (interview with Martin, January 25, 2015). Martin was well aware that supporters do not want to cooperate with the police and that security forces have a bad reputation. A police officer from Stockholm commented, "We don't make for comfortable bedfellows" (interview with Kaspar, May 27, 2017). He later talked about "a match within a match against supporters." Police officers are well aware that they are in the game. They (the police) play and are being played with. There was an instance where supporters from two separate clubs ganged up against the police. In 2018 the police tried to introduce a so-called Conditional Ladder to have more control over the fans in standing sections and aimed against pyrotechnics. This sparked resentment and protests, open letters from some clubs, blamed leveled against politicians, and so on. During a match in Helsingborg in 2018, supporters from both the home and visiting teams began to chant "cop bastards—football killers" (*snutjävlar—fotbolls mördare* in Swedish) loud and long. The different stands continued with the exchange for about fifteen minutes; when the match became more interesting, they went back to challenging and criticizing each other (match observations, HIF-AIK, May 15, 2019). Although many words and expressions in the arenas can be seen as rude or serious and threatening, the chant signals a shifting focus. "The enemy" is a fluid category in the world of football play. Security forces are there to guarantee a safe space during matches, even if their behavior can be questioned (cf. Herd 2018a). They need to understand the rationality of the context.

A policeman who has worked with supporters from many different clubs said: "I personally think that the police should not be there. That's not our thing. MFF arranges it so that they can see that it is safe. So we tell them that you need so many security guards, etc. . . . We should be visible before a match, in town and then after, but not during a match. And you know, the police are there to protect the third party. So that the third party is not harmed" (interview with Albin, August 15, 2017).

Although Albin was used to working and being at the matches, he was not convinced that the police needed to be there at all, although they are aware of risks and undesirable situations that can occur. Kaspar, who was quoted earlier, also talked about a "violence capital" that some supporters bring to the arena (interview with Kaspar, May 27, 2017). Such a history of violence is obviously problematic, and there is a fear that something will go wrong, that people will not respect the boundaries—the limit security forces must be able to read to understand and react in relation to the situation. Albin further commented: "You have to ignore certain things sometimes, react another time. It is difficult with emotions, you have to be patient. Some policemen are very surprised and amazed, but if you do that . . . then you can be amazed every day. Some things you have to accept, that this is exactly what they do here" (interview with Albin, August 15, 2017).

Albin explains why some events during matches can feel strange or incomprehensible, but sometimes the police have to accept them and negotiate with supporters. The limits of what happens in the stands are not set just because of legislation. Rehearsal and knowledge of the context are needed for the play to continue. The performative structure seen during football matches becomes ritual in that it has an established sequence and established characteristics, symbols, and rites. Tambiah (1996 [1981], 501) sees the ritual as a performance, similar to a dramatic actualization, the special structure of which promotes a sort of communication. At the same time, it is a game, a complicated and multidimensional game that shows its ritualistic character: "Gradually the significance of a sacred act permeates the playing. Ritual grafts itself upon it; but the primary thing is and remains play" (Huizinga 1944 [1932], 18).

Albin's earlier statement reflects Huizinga's elements of play, which concern chaos and order. Although the order during a football match is somewhat different from what one would observe in "normal life" (Foucault

1967, 3–4), it is precise (for its context) and must be respected; otherwise, the game does not work. Play can create order: "Into an imperfect world and into the confusion of life it brings a temporary, a limited perfection. Play demands order absolute and supreme. The least deviation from it 'spoils the game,' robs it of its character and makes it worthless" (Huizinga 1944 [1932], 10).

It is not only supporters or players who can play; the police are also an important factor in the game. If they refuse to follow the rules demanded by the situation, there will be no order. Sometimes the police and official authorities try to control the "nonsense" in football through the "sense" that exists outside football.

MASKING BAN 2017

One of the top questions regarding football in Sweden concerns the use of pyrotechnics (flares) and smoke bombs during matches. They are banned in the arenas, but individuals who want some fire usually manage to smuggle them in, despite the frisk search and sniffer dogs. Smuggling in and lighting flares has become a game within a game, when supporters and police seek to outdo each other and be one step ahead of the other in a game of cat and mouse. Many outside the football context have criticized flares and young people who are fixated with fire. The game is about a different understanding of rules, however—it is about what is considered "sense." The ritual can seem brutal or senseless, perhaps terrifying to onlookers, but it keeps its festive nature through the rite that is recognizable to participants (Huizinga 1944 [1932], 21).

Supporters who come with pyrotechnics use masks (e.g., balaclavas) because the police often try to film and identify them. Starting in 2013, different masking bans were discussed (Käck 2017). After some attempts to stop pyrotechnics, a new law came into force in March 2017 that forbade people from covering their faces during sports events, punishable by up to six months in prison. There were, however, exceptions, such as for religious beliefs. The ban did not apply if you covered your face because of your faith ("Maskeringsförbud vid idrottsarrangemang" ["Decision on a ban on masking"], January 25, 2017).

In April 2017, supporters of the Stockholm team AIK lit flares while wearing the *niqab*—a Muslim face veil for women—during a match. The press had a field day. A digital article from Dagen.se was titled "AIK Fans Defied Masking Ban with Niqab" (Ottestig 2017). Another newspaper, *Aftonbladet*, had a picture of young men with black "masks" and a banner that said "AIK ultras [fan groups associated with the use of flares and smoke bombs] mean well, now we disguise ourselves for religious reasons. Freedom for ultras is the ultimate goal, thank you Ygeman for the loophole" (Käck 2017). Anders Ygeman was minister of interior affairs from 2014 to 2017. When asked by *Aftonbladet* for comment, Ygeman "just laughed off the event: 'Honestly, I think the banner was quite funny. This indicates that the AIKs have a bit of humour,' says Ygeman" (Käck 2017).

A serious effort to counter what the police considered dangerous behavior was met with ridicule and laughter. Stewart (1989, 38) points out that one can receive a humorous response when an intellectual contradiction arises. By acknowledging that supporters are funny, Ygeman's statement makes both sense and no sense. The supporters are right, while the actions of the police become strange and nonsensical. By being funny, supporters make the police a laughingstock; through this, nonsense and common sense change places.

The pyrotechnics law was introduced after investigation and research and with good intentions, but supporters saw it only as an attack on what they do best and are known for—pyrotechnics. The protest was marked by following the rules literally. The result was comical, with young men posing as Muslim women and with burning fires on the football field. Those elements do not go together to formulate "sense" in everyday life. The situation could be considered comical because supporters did what the law said. They used loopholes and could laugh at the government's proposal and the attempt to stop them. Football is a good modern example of how folklore is practical and how people construct and use their lore (Herd 2018b). As Stewart (1989, 39) puts it: "Ludic genres present a critique not only of conceptual classifications, but on the level of nonsense, of classification itself. This is the point where metaphor becomes the norm and is therefore literal again. In any of these forms—riddles, pranks, puns, jokes—multiple levels of order are played with, and are played against each other."

However, the supporters' reaction is only part of the incident. It can be argued that their actions would be the first things they would do—a kind of logical, "rational" way of acting in the context of pyrotechnics conflict in Swedish football. One could guess that something would happen and that fire-loving individuals would not refrain from using pyrotechnics solely because of a new law. In an informal telephone conversation, a police officer stated that flares have become a symbol of struggle against the authorities. However, he did not see a direct connection between police work and the supporters' reasoning. The behavior was ritualized. It started with a game but ended (at least for the moment) with an almost ideological discussion about freedom, security, emotional commitment, and identity (e.g., Bromberger 1995; Herd 2018b, 195–205; Jones 2019). Huizinga (1944 [1932], 5) designated ritual as something that comes from playing and a playing ritual as something that builds a framework for many aspects of society, law and order included. The "forces of civilized life" had their origin in the ritualistic, primeval soil of play.

Sport has always been positioned between play and seriousness. Many were against professionalization in the early twentieth century, and amateurism was idealized. Then came a period marked by fear of hooliganism and unrest and proposals to make football games more of a family-friendly event. Attending a game would be just a pleasant experience, according to those who wanted to see football as an "experience economy" (van Uden 2005), but it has become an arena for competition between the state and its citizens. You can see that the game is actually serious and, interestingly, that it can maintain its playful character due to serious commitment. AIK supporters not only went against the law banning flares, they also took on appropriated religious symbols. They treated the niqab as fancy dress that could be used in the play. A mix of the two serious elements (religiously loaded attire and security issues) led to comic results. The minister of interior affairs was amused. He interpreted it as a game because the mix of football, niqab, and flares did not make sense when actually put together.

In the 2017 events, supporters fought against the law on police terms, and I would say they gained the upper hand. By mixing religion, fire, and sports, they showed that you can see the law as a game, that it is possible to play with both the law and the police. The press was also involved in the process of creating nonsense from this situation. This is especially evident in the use of a quote from the person who did the investigation into flares to make arenas safer. He did not want to comment but said "you just get so tired" (Käck 2017). Ongoing play with the system can be tiring, and that may be the point supporters wanted to make. They have rites and well-established routines, so they can react quickly to the actions of police and authorities. For example, there are chants that start and end matches; there are songs about specific players or that are aimed at the police or different clubs. You can jump, scream, and wave scarves. Their play is well organized.

The mixing of serious and crazy elements often occurs in football. As Oakley (2007, 49) pointed out, for example, all the money and transactions can be so serious (very large sums) that the situation becomes crazy. One cannot consider the astonishing sums clubs pay for players as something serious. In an intriguing way, very serious elements in football build its playful character. The same structure appears in contact with the police. It is serious, so serious that it is a game. At the same time, the structure has serious consequences.

STOP LAUGHING

The second example comes from a match in Malmö, in April 2017, between Malmö FF (MFF) and Djurgårdens IF (DIF). I was with Djurgården fans in the stands for away supporters. A large net lay on the chairs and divided DIF fans from MFF's family section (figure 6.1). There were uniformed police, as well as police in civilian clothes and security guards, as a match against DIF from Stockholm is considered a high-risk game. Malmö FF scored early in the game, and its fans exploded with joy. Near the net on MFF's side sat four or five young boys. They turned toward the DIF supporters and antagonized them by simply smiling at them. In response, DIF fans, many in black clothes, began to move closer to the net. They uttered many swear words, pointed at the young people on MFF's side, and were generally angry. Big smiles provoked furious reactions, but no one tried to cross the net. The police and guards tried to calm the DIF group, who wanted the Malmö supporters to stop smiling. To my surprise, a policeman went over to MFF's side and said something to the boys, and they changed seats and stopped grinning. The result was that the DIF supporters calmed down (match observations, Malmö, April 24, 2017).

The situation during the MFF-DIF match was not lengthy or particularly dramatic. None of the supporters seemed to consider jumping over the chairs or attacking the smiling MFF teenagers. In addition, the security forces were visible and numerous. To create order, the police took on a role reminiscent of a mediator. One group did not want the other group to laugh at them.

Although the situation could have become serious and the police did not want it to escalate, in retrospect it sounds almost ridiculous—not just because fans reacted so strongly to a smile but because the police played along. Interpretation of boundaries took place, and the police helped establish a framework for the game (Stewart 1989, 91). To keep the balance and maintain order, the police agreed to the rules of the game established by supporters; they constructed rules together with supporters. The police needed to participate and act in a way that would be accepted in the game (between MFF and DIF fans) that was going on. Adult (mostly) males did not want to be laughed at, and the police agreed to cooperate. The relationship was not broken, and the sense of football prevailed. As Huizinga (1944 [1932], 8) writes:

> Play is not "ordinary" or "real" life. It is rather a stepping out of "real" life into a temporary sphere of activity with a disposition all of its own. Every child knows perfectly well that he is "only pretending," or that it was "only for fun" . . . Nevertheless, as we have already pointed out, the consciousness of play being "only a pretend" does not by any means prevent it from proceeding with the utmost seriousness, with an absorption, a devotion that passes into rapture and, temporarily at least, completely abolishes that troublesome "only" feeling. Any game can at any time wholly run away with the players . . . Play turns to seriousness and seriousness to play.

Even if it is "just" a game, it must be taken seriously. The opponents' laughter was considered too much: too much of a joke. The reaction from Djurgården's supporters warned of the limits of "sense." The result depended on how the police would position themselves. How should they react to laughing young men?

At that moment, the security forces assumed a role as mediator. They needed to be serious in the situation, which initially was rather unserious with regard to everyday rules but which was made serious by play. Police tried to pacify supporters by warning them not to laugh too much. We see here that the roles in the play were not totally fixed but were ritualized in that everyone had their positions. An interviewed police officer commented on supporters' behavior: "They dare to do more because the police are there. They start throwing things because they see the police are already there. So they are tough because the police are there. Because they know, the police will take care of it. They feel safe . . . And then if they cannot fight against each other, they're gonna fight the police. We become the bad guy" (interview with Albin, August 15, 2017).

According to Albin, the police can be positioned with regard to different roles supporters can use. They can be enemies or protectors. Supporters know the police have the capacity to end their game because "the police will take care of it." If necessary, the police can use "everyday logic" and create order. This means that someone in the game has the power to navigate in and out by design. Perhaps that is why supporters find it difficult to communicate with the police, to interpret their behavior and react. You cannot always guess which rules security forces will follow—football rules or ordinary-society rules.

In the match between MFF and DIF, the police were in the middle of a ritualized conflict. The same situation is repeated thirty times a year in each club. DIF comes to Malmö every year and plays what is usually a tough match. After two or three times in the arena, you know the rites, how the crowd acts, how to be happy or disappointed. Yet, every match can come with some surprises. As discussed here, at one game there was laughter that was seen as a challenge that both police and away supporters responded to, in a way that was both rehearsed and spontaneous. Rites in football are not fixed; constant play with the rules occurs. If the police had ignored the DIF fans and given orders to keep quiet, they would not have accepted the fact that the laughter by some MFF fans was more than laughter. It would have made the DIF supporters look stupid, as if they did not understand that laughter is not serious. But the police accepted the premise. It was possible to continue playing due to previous, established, and ritualized behaviors. To an onlooker it was a *nonsense* response, opposed to the common sense of everyday life. We have to build on *common sense* that works for everyone involved. Stewart (1989, 88) comments on nonsense as a construction outside of everyday life: "Because nonsense has no everyday life context dominated by social structural considerations, and because it is primarily a discourse about discoursing rather than about any 'real life' content, its anomalous position may be seen as a liminal one. To engage in nonsense is not only to engage in a state of transition, it is also to engage in exploration of the nature of transition."

The stage of transition Stewart calls *liminal* exemplifies Foucault's concept of heterotopia. Yet, it is not boundary-less or irregular. The existence of heterotopia shows that different thought processes work in different places. Events are structured and filled with (potential) meanings that give them a ritualistic character (Smith 1996 [1982]). Stewart (1989, 90–93) gives an example of a child playing and stating "here is my castle." One needs to consider a piece of a garden, a box, or sticks on the ground as a castle, otherwise one cannot participate. One has to let oneself be transformed into something else according to the rules that govern the game. Stewart comments that the boundary of a game has to be kept intact until the game ends (92). The action undertaken by the police helped keep the borders around the game.

Being able to ignore or build boundaries often means you can build or maintain different identities (cf. Tolgensbakk 2014). I reacted when I saw the police "play with" and tell a group of young men they should stop laughing, but their doing so was completely logical in the game. It was my gaze that related to the world outside the arena walls as "normal." If the police had chosen not to accept the game, it could have had serious consequences. The interpretation of sense and nonsense is ongoing and sometimes falls flat, revealing different logics in different social contexts.

Although football includes voluntary playful activity, the play acts involve rites that cannot be ignored. Football becomes a framework in which playfulness and seriousness interact. If you ignore the rite, you ignore the temporary common sense that prevails; if you act on the basis of everyday logic, then something unforeseen may happen. This can lead to the interruption of the game. A practical interpretation of the rules of the game, such as a reaction to laughing supporters, leads to a new situation that affects the entire game and how it ends, although the end can be the opening for a new game (cf. Drewal Thompson 1992; Olofsson and Vedung 1998).

FINAL REMARKS

I have discussed two events from a football context that exemplify how playfulness and ritualistic behavior work are intertwined. The social life in the stands is a game with its own rules, logic, and rituals. If the police do not share the understanding of supporters' play and the rites that surround it, order could break down. Both police and supporters try to assess when play becomes too much and how to get the game to continue without activating the rules and boundaries of "normal" life. Stewart (1989, 64) writes that when it goes too far, a prank can become a crime if the effects are not reversible.

The burning of flares may have no lasting consequences, but you can also burn yourself, damage the arena, and scare others. Laughter as such is not classified as something with serious consequences, but it could end in physical violence and broken bones. Supporters depend on the understanding of the police, because the game in the arena can take different forms. The police have to read the game and play along to protect the "football logic." In the first example in this chapter, a protest against the police took the form of a joke while involving lawful obedience and religious practices associated with Muslim women. It was regarded by the authorities as play, in part because of its seriousness, which became ridiculous. What made sense in a legislative ruling became nonsense in the stands.

In the second event, the laughter of the MFF supporters became serious, and the police had to point out during the match that they should stop laughing. Joy could have had serious consequences. A nonsensical situation in which adults could not stand the laughter of others was made to make sense when the police accepted this line of reasoning. These are interpretations of situations based on a common understanding of rituals linked to a specific place. Negotiations like these make it possible to remain in the borderland between sense and nonsense, thus making sure the game continues. The arena and its boundaries allow for various rituals and build not only a sacred place but also a playground, as Huizinga (1944 [1932], 10) put it: "Just as there is no formal difference between play and ritual, so the 'consecrated spot' cannot be formally distinguished from the playground. All are temporary worlds within the ordinary world, dedicated to the performance of an act apart."

Temporality is another crucial element of football. Everyone perceives the actions as "here and now." Ruptures and transgressions are bound to the playground and are left when football's heterotopia ends after a match (Foucault 1967, 5). The rituals that govern how to go in and out of the game are many, and you must know them to be able to decide who plays, when, and how.

On one occasion, as I carried out an interview with a police officer, he greeted a passing supporter. The policeman told me that the supporter was a hooligan and that they had previously met in the woods during a fight. However, this time he came with his child and watched the match calmly. The policeman stated that in that situation, he would not consider a known hooligan to be a hooligan (interview with Kaspar, May 27, 2017). Previous experience made it possible to turn off the police-and-hooligan game. The policeman and the hooligan classified each other in categories that were not in direct opposition. The situation was not as serious as it could have been, as each interpreted the other in a certain way, within the framework of the arena.

The football context appears similar to a playground, with rules you can play with. You can say that within the supporter-ship, you play according to rules and then you have a game. In contrast, you can play with rules, break them, or try to challenge the regulations. Then it becomes another game, a game that can be more serious. The AIK supporters came masked (in female Muslim clothes) and with burning sticks just as the police announced again that both were banned. They played with sense and turned it into nonsense—it became a game instead of a serious situation.

The serious elements of the game are important and are emphasized through the use of various rituals. To be able to play by the rules or play with the rules, you must know the boundaries and know how and if you can cross them. Supporters challenge the police by pushing boundaries, trying to get more space for play, which would also mean more power. The borderland, however, is often the most exciting arena. Huizinga (1944 [1932], 11) commented on people who are spoilsports or fake players and emphasized that there are two different categories of such: "The player who trespasses against the rules or ignores them is a 'spoil-sport.' The spoil-sport is not the same as the false player, the cheat; for the latter pretends to be playing the game and, on the face of it, still acknowledges the magic circle . . . He robs play of its illusion–a pregnant word which means literally 'in-play' (from inlusio, illudere or inludere)."

Some theorists highlight the seriousness of the ritual as an important aspect. Football shows that it can also be the other way around. How to laugh, when to laugh, how to mock and write ironic/funny banners, how and when to sing sarcastic chants constitute learned, trained, and repeated behavior. In other words, it is behavior that is ritualized and that has a purpose—to lift one's own club/team and laugh at/mock the opponent. The fact that it is ritualized also means it is done "the right way." There is an established pattern for being spontaneous. To be able to do so, you need to agree that the ritual is a game. Then you can hate another city for ninety minutes or shout that the police officer is a hooligan without the consequences you would expect in everyday situations. It can be stated that football is a game in everyday life. The game uses everyday rules that can be questioned and broken. It balances everyday understandings of sense and nonsense. Excessive antagonism and interplay between supporters and police, as well as openness to variations, make it possible to have a game that can end in different ways. At the same time, it is the ritual framework that enables repetition and thereby recognition of the game. The contrast between established performances and interpretive possibilities attracts and nourishes identity-building processes, which thrive in the margins between sense and nonsense. Remember that the primary reason for this play is a football match. Fans are there to see it. Yet, this entangled social context allows them to have games of their own, which makes it even more exciting.

REFERENCES

Unprinted Sources

Interviews and observations recorded during research fieldwork, author's collection: Interview with Albin, August 15, 2017. Interview with Kaspar, May 27, 2017. Interview with Martin, January 25, 2015. Observations, HIF–AIK match, Helsingborg, May 15, 2019. Observations, MFF–DIF match, Malmo, April 24, 2017.

Käck, Andreas. April 2, 2017. "Tyder på humour från AIK-fansen." *Aftonbladet*. Accessed August 24, 2020. https://www.aftonbladet.se/sportbladet/fotboll/a/3a2VL/tyder-pa-humour-fran-aik-fansen.

"Maskeringsforbud vid idrottsarrangemang." January 25, 2017. Accessed July 14, 2020. https://www.riksdagen.se/sv/dokument-lagar/arende/betankande/maskeringsforbud-vid-idrottsarrangemang_H401JuU8.

Ottestig, Johannes. May 2, 2017. "AIK fans trotsade maskeringsforbud med niqab." Accessed July 18, 2020. https://www.dagen.se/aik-fans-trotsade-maskeringsforbud-med-niqab-1.947627?paywall=true.

Literature

Andersson, Torbjörn. 2001. "Swedish Football Hooliganism 1900–39." *Soccer and Society* 2 (1): 1–18. Accessed February 24, 2022. https://doi.org/10.1080/714004833.

Andersson, Torbjörn. 2002. *Kung Fotboll: Den Svenska fotbollens kulturhistoria från 1800-talets slut till 1950*. Malmö, Sweden: ARX Förlag.

Andersson, Torbjörn, and Aage Radmann. 1998. *Från gentleman till huligan? Svensk fotbollskultur förr och nu*. Stockholm: Brutus Östlings Bokförlag Symposion.

Bairner, Alan. 2001. *Sport, Nationalism, and Globalization: European and North American Perspectives*. Albany: State University of New York Press.

Bromberger, Christian. 1995. "Football as Worldview and as Ritual." *French Cultural Studies* 6 (18): 293–311. Accessed March 10, 2022. https://doi.org/10.1177/095715589500601803.

Drewal Thompson, Margaret. 1992. *Yoruba Ritual: Performers, Play, Agency*. Bloomington: Indiana University Press.

Foucault, Michel. 1967. *Of Other Spaces: Heterotopias*. Accessed November 14, 2021. http://foucault.info/documents/heteroTopia/foucault.heteroTopia.en.html.

Green, Anders. 2009. *Fotboll och huliganism: Utveckling, problem och åtgärdsarbete i England och Skandinavien*. Stockholm: Universitetsservice US-AB, Stockholms universitet.

Herd, Katarzyna. 2018a. "That Little Football Girl: Swedish Club Football and Gender Expectations." *Ethnologia Scandinavica: A Journal of Nordic Ethnology* 48: 123–38.

Herd, Katarzyna. 2018b. "'We Can Make New History Here': Rituals of Producing History in Swedish Football Clubs." *Lund Studies in Arts and Cultural Sciences* 19. PhD dissertation, Lund University, Lund, Sweden.

Herd, Katarzyna. 2021. "Fotboll i Finland på Svenska: Berättelser från början av 1900-talet." *Idrott, Historia and Samhället* 12 (14): 101–21.

Herd, Katarzyna, and Jakob Löfgren 2020. "Mocking Others, Parodying Ourselves: Chants and Songs Used in Swedish Football Musicultures." *Journal of the Canadian Society for Traditional Music* 74: 11–33.

Huizinga, Johan. 1944 [1932]. *Homo Ludens: A Study of the Play Element in Culture*. London: Routledge and Kegan Paul.

Jones, Tobias. 2019. *Ultra: The Underworld of Italian Football*. London: Head of Zeus.

Lee, James F. 2008. *The Lady Footballers: Struggling to Play in Victorian Britain*. London: Routledge.

Oakley, Chris. 2007. *Football Delirium*. London: Kadnac Books.

Olofsson, Patrik, and Evert Vedung. 1998. *Samspel och motspel i beslutsprocessen: Striderna 1993 i Storuman, Malå och Överkalix om kärnkraftens avfall.* Uppsala: Statsvetenskapliga institutionen, Uppsala universitet.

Pratchett, Terry. 2010. *Unseen Academicals.* London: Transworld.

Radmann, Aage. 2013. "Huliganlandskapet: Media, våld, och maskuliniteter." Studies in Sport Sciences 13. PhD dissertation, Malmö högskola, Malmö, Sweden.

Radmann, Aage. 2015. "Hit and Tell—Swedish Hooligan Narratives." *Sport in Society* 18 (2): 202–18.

Smith, Jonathan Z. 1996. "The Bare Facts of Ritual." In *Readings in Ritual Studies*, edited by Roland L. Grimes, 473–83. Upper Saddle River, NJ: Prentice-Hall.

Stewart, Susan. 1989. *Nonsense: Aspects of Intertextuality in Folklore and Literature.* Baltimore: Johns Hopkins University Press.

Tambiah, Stanley J. 1996 [1981]. "A Performative Approach to Ritual." In *Readings in Ritual Studies*, edited by Roland L. Grimes, 495–511. Upper Saddle River, NJ: Prentice-Hall.

Tolgensbakk, Ida. 2014. "Partysvensker; GO HARD: En narratologisk studie av unge svenske arbeidsmigranters nærvær i Oslo." PhD dissertation, University of Oslo, Oslo, Norway.

van Uden, Jacko. 2005. "Transforming a Football Club into a 'Total Experience' Entertainment Company: Implications for Management." *Managing Sport and Leisure* 10 (3): 184–98.

7

Playing in the In-Between

Practices of Play, Ritual, and Beyond at Computer Game Festivals

RUTH DOROTHEA EGGEL

Thousands of people gather regularly to celebrate video and computer games at numerous events throughout Europe. Gamers travel far to meet their otherwise digital communities in face-to-face settings. These gaming festivals are secular rituals (Malaby 2009, 212; Moore and Myerhoff 1977), building on repetition and consistent processes, including preformed procedures to produce meanings (Sutton-Smith 1997, 169). Simultaneously, they are dedicated to digital games as a form and frame of play (Malaby 2009). Beyond formal game playing, there also exists a more open-ended mode of acting, maintaining, and celebrating a playful disposition. Open-ended playfulness breaks game rules and frames but equally produces paradoxical states of reality (Bateson 2000 [1971]), for the sake of play itself (Csikszentmihalyi and Bennett 1971). Through a selection of ethnographic examples, this chapter explores the ways the practices at gaming events produce ritual, game, and play in reciprocal, alternating, and ambiguous forms.

First, I will trace how these events dedicated to computer games include excessive practices of play both online and offline, and I present my multisite and multimodal (Dicks, Soyinka, and Coffey 2006) ethnographic approach to follow the hybrid practices of in-person play and online gaming. Second, I will elaborate on how digital games display a more rigid, institutionalized form of play (Csikszentmihalyi and Bennett 1971). However, the events not only facilitate practices of gaming but simultaneously encourage open-ended and explorative forms of play as a mode of interaction. Strategies such as declaring that something is a quest introduce meta-communicative play frames (Bateson 2000 [1972]), transforming the meaning of the given situation.

However, play is not always confined to a distinctive frame, so I will examine how play can be conceptualized as a disposition (Malaby 2009). At gaming events, a playful attitude becomes a general stance and a mode of interaction that can be both the consequence of and the requirement for a play frame. I will explore how the disposition of play is characterized by its open-endedness and continually draws on indeterminacy to create lucky chances (Hamayon 2016). The relationship to indeterminacy can be further understood as a liminal quality that both ritual and play share (Handelman 1977).

Nevertheless, as Audun Kjus (chapter 1, this volume) points out, not everything played is a ritual, and not all ritual is played. The annual repetition of events, with extensive preparation and repeated procedures, displays many ritual qualities. Moreover, as players get more deeply involved, they take on roles with a sacred seriousness that becomes obligatory.

At the same time, unlike ritual, play is often detached from affecting social orders outside the play frame (Hamayon 2016, 299). To further understand the practices of ritual and play at gaming events, this chapter shows how ludic practices attempt to reach beyond play toward transcendence, lingering *in-between* ritual and play.

EMBODYING GAMING: TRACING DIGITAL PLAY AT GAMING EVENTS

The name and object of these events indicate their dedication to digital games. The rise of video games makes *games* and *play* a part of the everyday lives of many people in the twenty-first century (Hamayon 2016, 301). Digital games became a popular media practice and games became ubiquitous in digital environments (Dippel and Fizek 2017, 277). Virtual games, play, and ludic practices have also become a popular and growing field of research in anthropology and other disciplines (Malaby 2009, 209), leading to the advent of the interdisciplinary research area of game studies (Boellstorff 2006, 30). Digital games are what Thomas M. Malaby (2009) calls a *cultural form* of ludic practice, and rules are often assumed to be an essential characteristic of such games (Boellstorff 2006, 31). Thus, many accounts of ludic practices focus on game activities, with absolute orders (rules), temporal and spatial limits, and a detachment from ordinary life (see Huizinga 1980 [1949]; Malaby 2007, 103). With Roberte Hamayon (2016, 301), I understand digital games as an institutionalized form of play, often organized in competitive environments (Bareither 2020, 26).

My dissertation project (Eggel 2024), uses ethnographic methods to explore events, festivals, and conventions that attract up to 400,000 visitors and millions of followers online. These hybrid events in Central and Northern Europe combine commercial exhibitions, e-sports, local area network (LAN) parties, game developer conferences, and business events. The main attraction is playing games. The expo offers opportunities to test games and play game demos. The e-sports stages allow attendees to watch other people play digital games. LAN parties and bring-your-own-device (BYOD) areas offer a space to play computer games on one's own computer, with or without other participants, for the duration of the convention. Apart from digital games, the events offer a multitude of small games and competitions that involve players' physical presence. That includes competitions of muscle strength, such as doing push-ups to win a prize or running races through inflatable obstacle courses.

While there are many specific games to be observed, more open-ended forms of play are at the same time a widespread mode of interaction at the events. As Malaby (2009, 207) pointed out, these open-ended ludic practices are of anthropological interest, because everyday life shares the same open-endedness. Hamayon (2016, 15) argues that "more significantly than games, the notion of play is really what anthropology has neglected," and the notion of playing also opens up an exciting perspective on ludic practices at gaming events. Anthropology can use its ethnographic methods to explore game culture or cultures of gaming (Boellstorff 2006, 33) and is specially equipped to study more ambiguous forms of play, including its relation to the digital. The strength of ethnography lies in its ability to study digital gaming as an embedded and embodied practice (Hine 2015) and to look for the digital as a de-centred experience in which digital media are inseparably linked with other experiences (Postill and Pink 2012, 129). Gaming events embody digital gaming in physically manifested settings that, in turn, invite and afford the intensive use of digital media, so that *online* and *offline* practices cannot be understood as binary and separated fields (Taylor 2009, 153).

My ethnographic research followed this multi-site assemblage of various digital and non-digital practices. Twenty-one semi-structured interviews were combined with more than 900 hours of ethnographic participation at sixteen events in four European countries. As the events attract international crowds, English was the primary conversational language, in both online and offline interactions. In the occasional use of local languages (e.g., some interviews with German interlocuters), English terms like *gaming*, doing *quests*, and creating *lucky chances* were borrowed into gamers' native language speech. My participant observation-based multimodal approach included research on a variety of digital platforms such as chats, games, and event apps, which allowed me to achieve not only a physical co-location but also a co-presence in digital worlds (Pink et al. 2016, 33; Postill 2015). My participant-observation at events also included taking on different roles and ways of being present, like participating in the construction and deconstruction of events and assuming different event roles as a visitor, volunteer, and assistant to vendors and exhibitors. This approach allowed me to achieve a perspective on ludic practices at gaming events that spread beyond the few days the events themselves lasted.

QUEST DECLARATION: GAME/PLAY AND META-COMMUNICATIVE FRAMING

An ethnographic vignette allows a closer look at the distinctions and ambiguous entanglements of game as a form and play as a practice or mode. My experiences in the field follow practices of play, particularly the processes of turning tasks into games. Such behavior is a popular strategy at gaming events, creating and emerging from affordances of playfulness. In fact, the processes exceed the public event duration and start even before the event opens:

> It is my first event as a volunteer crew member to participate in the construction of an event. Heipol,[1] our team leader, whose name is printed in large letters on the back of his hoody, assigns me as a *minion* to a tall, slender teenager named Takelz. Our job is to bring twelve gaming

---

[1] All names used in this paper are pseudonyms.

chairs to the stream zone. "Come, we have a quest now," says Takelz as he walks through the halls aimlessly, asking everybody we meet if they had seen any gaming chairs. Eventually, we find a bunch of them standing in a hallway. "You know they are 6,000 kronor each,"[2] Takelz says, nodding reverently, gently stroking a headrest. A second later, he jumps on a chair, pushing it forward with his legs, dragging a second chair along, and shouts "come on, minion, we shall have a glorious race." I join, and we race through a hall, down the elevator and another two halls. As we pass, people stop working and start cheering for us. We go back and forth a few times; the cheering crowd gets bigger every time we pass. On our fifth run, Heipol has plugged in some loudspeakers and is playing techno on full volume. As he sees us approaching, he starts to dance in the middle of a scaffolding arch he had just built. His stretched arms with clenched fists are moving in opposite directions to his hips, alternating the movement in front and behind his body. This *flossdance* is increased to higher and higher speeds as we move through the arch as our finishing line. (Transcript of observations on June 15, 2018, at Dreamhack Summer, Jönköping, Sweden)

The adventures of play start with a work task that is declared to be a *quest*, a widespread practice at gaming events. Any given situation, any minor or more serious task, can be declared a quest that can subsequently be playfully approached and solved. Such *quest declarations* are numerous at gaming events and are a popular strategy to frame a situation as *play*.

This play declaration can be analyzed with Gregory Bateson's concept of meta-communication. While observing monkeys playfully biting each other in a zoo, Bateson (2000, 185) noticed that the playful bite denoted something different than another kind of bite would. The playful bite is at the same time both a bite and not a bite. For this kind of communication to take place, Bateson argued that three kinds of sign had to exist: (1) signs that express certain intentions, (2) signs that imitate signs of the first order, and (3) signs that allow observers and subjects to differentiate between the two (189). The latter *communication about communication* offers cues for identifying messages of the second order, signaling, for instance, that *this is play*.

An uttered quest declaration communicates that this is play to oneself and others involved. As such, a quest declaration serves as a

---

[2] 6,000 kronor refers to the currency of Swedish krona. The amount equaled approximately 650 USD at the time.

meta-communicative frame that suspends or alters what would otherwise be indicated by the action. While a work task is a serious action with obligatory and normative qualities, it becomes a pleasurable and fun experience by declaring it to be play. To frame something as a quest thus opens the possibility to approach it eagerly, with bolstered spirits and ready to have a playful adventure. The term *quest* in this context comes from digital games, mainly MMOs (Massively Multiplayer Online Games) and RPGs (Role-Playing Games), and describes in-game tasks or missions that can be completed to advance in the game. The chosen term *to be in quest of something* also includes a symbolic meaning and points toward a practice of seeking, frequently for a higher goal, thus giving mundane practices added importance.

However, the notion of play in this example is more ambiguous. Declaring an unpleasurable task to be a quest enables the participants to turn it into a positive emotional experience. The task is approached *as if* it were voluntary and exciting and is equipped with the characteristics of play. While a quest declaration allows the task to become play experientially, it does so by acting as if the obligation would be reduced. This strategy of equipping tasks or obligations with game-like features to make them more pleasurable can frequently be observed in gamification. However, in this process, games are often not played for the sake of playing but are instrumentalized and commercialized (Dippel and Fizek 2017, 280–81). The strategy of a quest declaration is complementary to gamification, as it is a bottom-up strategy to curate one's own experience and give a task a more appealing form *for the sake of playing*.

The ethnographic example includes a second meta-communicative frame of *this is play*. *We shall have a race* suggests not only any frame of play but a specific form: a game. A playful competition is a play form that is less open-ended but follows specific rules. Mihaly Csikszentmihalyi and Stith Bennett (1971, 46) argued that games as institutionalized play forms try to enable a ludic experience through different boundaries and limitations. Similarly, Margaret Boden (2004 [1990], 58) discussed how constraints can help us mentally explore and play around with given rules. She argues that restrictions invite the creativity of modifying and transforming things within the specified limits. As such, limiting the relevant objects, choices, and time frames through rule sets creates an affordance to explore the potential options of action within those boundaries. A game declaration serves as a play frame that encourages a play experience for the involved players. Giving actions such a formalized play form by declaring them a game allows one to create what Johan Huizinga (1980 [1949], 13) described as the "magic circle of play," where ordinary rules of interactions are suspended and replaced by the rules and realities of play. Game declarations at gaming events thus serve as a meta-communicative frame that allows players to slip in and out of a magic circle of play.

To understand the relations between a game declaration as a play frame and the ludic practices of playing, in the race above, the formalized rules of a race were never enforced. Nobody was keeping count, and what was declared a formalized game turned into a more open-ended form of play that other people joined, taking on additional roles by cheering or dancing. The meta-communicative frame here is not *this is a competitive racing game* but rather *this is playing as if this was a racing game*. The ludic actions turn a work task into an experience of play by playfully imitating a racing game. The more open-ended ludic practices are, the more ambiguous they get. To turn work into play in this manner is described by Takelz as a solicited practice, to do the chairs (as objects for play) and the events (dedicated to games) justice (transcript of conversation, June 15, 2018). Playing becomes the desired and encouraged mode of interaction at events. While *games* are declared and played, their cultural form, including their rules, are often not taken seriously but are replaced by more open-ended forms of *play*.

A PLAYFUL ATTITUDE: PRACTICING PLAY AS DISPOSITION OR MOOD

A declaration of play (or game) can encourage ludic practices and thus allow different forms of play to develop. However, the structure or frame of a situation is not enough. Play can only emerge when the players allow it to do so (Hamayon 2016, 65). Don Handelman (1977, 185) argued that play refers not to a particular *set of activities* but rather to *a way of organizing activities*. A *game* as a form of activity does not always include *play* as a mode of practice. As Malaby (2009, 212) pointed out, "A game may prompt a playful disposition, but then again, it may not." So, what does it take to prompt *play* at gaming events?

A look at the game declaration *let's race* reveals the knowledge and experience necessary to participate in this game. To frame a situation as a racing game implies an agreement on a set of rules. There is no explicit rule clarification in the situation; instead, it is assumed that the players know which rules such a race implies. It draws on knowledge about competitive games, specifically races, as a common form of game we frequently find in institutionalized settings such as sports (Hamayon 2016, 292; Malaby 2007, 101). These implicit rule agreements are common at gaming events, drawing on previous play experiences. People are frequently assumed to be familiar with different forms of *game play* and various *game mechanics*. Csikszentmihalyi and Bennett (1971, 46) argued that play is "a state of experience in which the actor's ability to act matches the requirements for action in his environment." I would argue that playing and taking part in a game is a particular *skill* that is practiced continually and is required if one is to be able to interact in play at gaming events.

To declare something to be a game or to answer a playful offer with a playful response includes a disposition that allows there to be play. At gaming events, I observed a readiness to engage in play in almost any given situation. My interlocutors explicitly called this disposition *a gaming attitude*, the core skill that makes someone *a gamer*. As this attitude includes not only games but also open-ended forms of play, I will call it *a playful attitude* that describes a very open and experimental disposition. This relates to Malaby's (2009, 206) proposal to look at play as an "attitude characterized by a readiness to improvise." He advocates an understanding of play as "a mode of cultural experience (a playful disposition towards activities no matter how game-like)" (209) as opposed to games as "a cultural form (a game-like activity, no matter how playfully engaged in)" (209). At gaming events, on the one hand, a *playful disposition* is enabled through the celebrated presence of games, as frames that encourage ludic interaction and offer affordances to react with a playful attitude (see Csikszentmihalyi and Bennett 1971, 46). On the other hand, this playful attitude precedes game as form, as it is the disposition necessary to engage in play or spontaneously declare something to be a game. Thus, the play frame encourages the same disposition from which it emerges.

In her ethnography of the Burning Man festival, Megan Heller (2013, 2) takes the idea of *play as a disposition* one step further and conceptualizes play as a *mood*. She thinks of "play as a contagious mood, something that can be caught through communication, and framing acts as a container that can help or hinder the spread of that mood" (5). Nevertheless, the disposition of play at gaming events is a stance actively taken and continually (re)produced in action; thus, I find the notion of an attitude more fitting than that of a mood. A playful attitude is something people are *doing*. Moreover, this activity allows play to spread through interaction. The specific qualities of this attitude include the power to transform the meaning of the entire surrounding and open up ways of (inter)acting that would not be considered a course of action outside of the play frame, as the following observation shows:

> "Your quest is to find the sign in the trunk of the car that is parked on the upper deck," says our boss on my first day working for an indie game exhibitor at a German event, as he is tossing us his car keys. My coworker Clemens and I reach the upper deck, but we forgot to ask what kind of car we are looking for. We stroll along each row, using the electric key, hoping to see the lights on some car flashing. No success. We start searching for the right city code on the number plates. After a long search, we find a car with the sign visible through the back window. Pressing the key, nothing happens. No lights, no unlock. Moreover, there is no keyhole at the door to use the physical key. Confusion. Clemens and I, neither of whom own cars, are clueless. I inspect the handle further and notice a small gap at the bottom. Oddly, it would be just enough for the tip of the key to fit. "Maybe putting the key in there will do something?" I say. "I don't think this works in real life," Clemens says. However, I'm in quest mode. I want to solve this. I push the key in, and with a little blop, the handle cover comes off and reveals a keyhole. I'm excited. It feels like the successful completion of this quest. "At least it was an adventure," Clemens smiles on our way back. (Transcript of observations on August 20, 2019, at Gamescom, Cologne, Germany)

This example highlights the specific quality of a playful attitude as a disposition that is a *mode of doing*. It is a disposition that allows one to relate to objects, time, space, and people differently than in a non-play frame. This becomes most apparent when faced with unforeseen trouble. The playful attitude changes the kind of solution that makes sense in a situation. While choices in ordinary life often try to evaluate the possible consequences of action (Csikszentmihalyi and Bennett 1971, 45), a playful mood reduces the perceived seriousness of such consequences. It allows a more experimental approach, in which social order, material value, and possible repercussions of actions have less influence over the decision-making process. It re-defines things so that a small gap becomes an invitation for experimental interaction. Playfully approached, the tiny slit holds the potential to reveal something hidden, something unexpected. A playful attitude thus fosters a notion of separating the act from potential negative consequences and instead turns it into an invitation of the unexpected.

Ludic practices at gaming events may reveal some of the existential aspects of play. Csikszentmihalyi and Bennett (1971) argued that choices and dilemmas can lead to frustration or boredom in everyday life. Limiting the possible choices for actions in institutionalized games reduces fear and anxieties and enables acting to become exciting (46). The example of a playful attitude shows how the opposite can also be observed in free play. It is a disposition that is not limiting but rather that expands participants' options. I would argue that in play, both the expansion and the limitation of choices enable players to react comfortably, in new and experimental ways, without fear of repercussions. Play at gaming events is often an invitation that allows for an improvised response. The playful attitude encourages people to find new ways to respond in a given situation. Thus, play as a disposition increases the players' *response-ability*. The concept of response-ability describes the process of rendering each other capable (Haraway 2016, 34). Open-ended play as disposition or mode of experience renders players *response-able*.

GETTING LUCKY: PLAYING AS AN INVITATION FOR INDETERMINACY

The notion of play as a disposition "marked by a readiness to improvise" (Malaby 2009, 211) or play as "a feeling of unlimited possibilities" (Heller 2013, 6) brings another aspect of play into focus. Indeterminacy is welcomed and embraced within the suspended realities of play. This stance toward the uncertain and unexpected marks a distinctive quality of playful interactions, games, and ritual.

The potential for something unexpected or unknown to happen is the intended outcome of play at gaming events. Malaby (2009, 211) stresses that the first feature of play as disposition is the stance toward contingencies and the notion that the same actions might not always have the same consequences. There is always the chance of an unexpected outcome (Malaby 2007, 107). A playful attitude in practice means doing things without being certain of the consequences. In addition, a particular outcome is frequently not accepted as a determined or permanent state. What would be considered a dead end outside of play is not accepted as a dead end in play. Instead, doing things with a playful attitude draws on the idea that there can always be another try, another chance to produce a different consequence. In her ethnographic work on play and ritual, Hamayon (2016, 208) explains that "playing is always a means of drawing on 'luck' and 'happiness,' but without it being necessarily specified in which field, or in which form this luck is expected." Furthermore, she says, "the indeterminacy of luck encourages the players to play and play again" (209). According to Hamayon (206), this is related to an *unproducibility* of play and luck. While institutionalized games are countable, *wild game* is uncountable, she argues: "Game and luck is considered eminently variable, and thought of not on an all-or-nothing basis, but on an enough-or-not-enough, better-or-worse, more-or-less basis" (206). A playful attitude at gaming events draws on luck to create lucky chances. Drawing on luck in such a way makes it something that cannot be lost (permanently). Instead, luck is something one could always have more of through another act of playing. Every action taken, every quest, every offer to play, and every obstacle is treated as a chance to get lucky. This exemplifies how indeterminacy of play makes it exciting (Kjus, chapter 1, this volume) and encourages it to continue.

While game and ritual in institutionalized forms include elements of indeterminacy, both often expect luck in a specific area or field (Hamayon 2016, 290). However, the playful practices of gaming events make indeterminacy in itself the desired effect, regardless of the form or field in which luck arises. One of my interlocutors described how the most magical moments occur when something unexpected happens: "Magical, strange, hilarious things happen. I think most of the fun is when you're actually at work, or you just get to meet people and come up with answers to problems that you didn't know existed, and then somehow magic happens, and things just work out" (interview with Tessa, she/her, twenty-nine years old, August 16, 2019).

The quote shows how indeterminacy can become an end in itself. Something unexpected happening, an unforeseen turn, becomes a chance to be lucky when approached with a playful attitude. Moments of indeterminacy, with unexpected problems and outcomes, may, within a playful frame, be understood as lucky moments. Malaby (2009, 208) argued that play as a disposition "allows us to see how games may be related to a particular mode of experience, a dispositional stance toward the indeterminate." The playful attitude at gaming events is a disposition to (re)act in a way that embraces, creates, and strives for indeterminacy. This is noteworthy, as indeterminacy outside of suspended realities of play (or ritual, for that matter) is often perceived as a threat to the status quo and treated as a source of insecurity for established social orders.

Hamayon (2016, 228) argues that, especially in Western games, randomness (as a form of indeterminacy) was something to be eliminated. Christianity played an essential role in efforts to contain the element of indeterminacy, as games of chance that draw on luck were perceived as ungodly (228). In anthropological research, the concept of liminality is pivotal in theorizing the indeterminacies of both ritual and play. Victor Turner (1991 [1969]) discusses liminality as a quality that is not exclusive to the liminal phase of transition rituals but can also be found outside ritual action. Through ritual or play, people enter a liminal mode, where time, space, and relationships are structured differently than they are outside (167). Society's rules and fixed structures are unstructured or restructured in such liminal phases (96).

Both ritual and play allow us to invert and change existing orders, as "liminality exists apart from 'structure,' which is roughly equivalent to the 'ordinary social order'" (Handelman 1977, 187). Social orders outside are suspended, making liminality a mode shared by both ritual and play. As Hamayon (2016, 265) argues, "Play is intrinsically liminal, and potentially transgressive; there can be no orthodoxy in playing." The importance of indeterminacy underlines the liminal quality present in play. However, Turner (1974, 64) differentiates between obligatory liminal states of ritual and voluntary forms of *in-between* that he calls *liminoid*, where the liminoid "resembles without being identical with [the] 'liminal.'" Gaming events with open-ended play that celebrates indeterminacy produce a voluntary liminoid mode.

SACRED SERIOUSNESS: WHEN GAME/PLAY BECOMES RITUAL

My ethnographic observations demonstrate that open-ended play is a popular mode of interaction at events dedicated to computer games. The play activities are both encouraged by and bring forth a playful attitude, characterized by improvisation and the invitation of indeterminacy to draw on luck. At the same time, the ritualistic qualities of these events cannot be overlooked. While gaming events do not serve a religious purpose, "scholars of ritual (many of them anthropologists) have recognized ritual as a cultural form irrespective of whether it brings about religious experience" (Malaby 2009, 212). To explore the continuum of ritual and play, I will look at the ritualistic qualities of gaming events, as "some play events are more highly ritualistic than others" (Sutton-Smith 1997, 169).

Ritual theorists point to repetition as one of the characteristics of ritual behavior (Kjus, chapter 1, this volume). The events I have documented are repetitive, mostly occurring once or twice a year, usually at a set date during the year. Many of my interlocutors return every year and view the annual occurrence as a prominent feature of the event. Moreover, the annual dates of events are often coordinated with other important dates or holidays. Some events happen during the first or last weekend of school holidays, some just before a national or religious holiday. Cultural festivals and holidays are considered markers of a temporal structure in the course of a year. The dates of the annual gaming events do indeed structure the time and life of many interlocutors. In addition, they align the date of a gaming festival with other relevant and auspicious dates (like vacation or holidays). Some extend the annual visit to a gaming event, adding another week of vacation. Two of my interlocutors got engaged at a gaming festival, so they could celebrate their anniversary at the event every year. In this way, the events are enriched with additional meaning that can either mark the date as an auspicious one or intensify the liminal quality of the festivals.

The repetitiveness of events is paired with a certain consistency in procedures and conventions, which characterizes a ritualistic process (Hamayon 2016, 290; Sutton-Smith 1997, 169). These procedures include elements like grand opening ceremonies and anticipation-boosting preparations. On the organizational level, a full year's work goes into preparing one specific event until it is repeated the following year. The construction of the events often starts days or even weeks before the event doors open. Many of my interlocutors started to do volunteer work at events after attending them for several years. But visitors, too, report various strategies of preparation. These include decoration of the body, such as dying hair in rainbow colors in reminiscence of digital characters or avatars and meticulously crafting and fitting clothing and costumes. The most drastic preparation goes into cosplays, for which months of manual work and often a considerable amount of money are used to embody a particular character during the few days of an event.

This brings us to the question of what kinds of roles are taken on during the event and with which levels of commitment. The decoration and costuming of bodies and the use of nicknames instead of given names emphasize the interplay between role(play) and identity. The decoration and costuming are what Hamayon (2016, 108–12) describes as playful imitation of doing *like* or *likewise* within a fictional frame of play, which she differentiates from acting *as-if*, where an additional identity is assumed for the time of the rite or play. However, unlike acting *likewise* in play, all my interlocutors agree that they are not playing a character at events. They instead stress that the events are a place to show their *true self*: "It doesn't matter who you are or how you see stuff outside of [the event]. But like, at [the event], you're accepted for who you really are" (interview with Takelz, he/him, nineteen years old, September 12, 2019).

The role taken on is a playful version of oneself rather than a role-play *like* or *as-if*. Most of my interlocutors stress that this version of their (true) selves is characterized by openness, being more outgoing, daring, and unafraid of repercussions. This matches the playful attitude that is prevalent in interactions. Unlike in ritual, the roles taken on are voluntary, yet simultaneously they can become a serious commitment for people. Some interlocutors report that participating in an event becomes obligatory, and their role within the event context becomes a vital part of their identity. One interview partner even described how the obligation to participate and volunteer at an event became so intense that he had to seek therapeutic help to escape it by going cold turkey. This normativity is a quality of rituals that "organize time, space, and social environments in ways that are obligatory and compulsory and even coercive" (Kjus, chapter 1, this volume). While some people temporarily take on the role of a player during events, the roles become a lasting and obligatory state in the life of others.

This closes the circle of the ambiguous continuum of ritual and play at gaming events, where elements of both are intertwined. Following Hamayon (2016, 292), it is "a continuum with no true border between play and rite, a continuum marked by a latent rituality of play." While Claude Lévi-Strauss (1996, 30) argued that "ritual is also 'played'" and play and ritual are complementary in how they relate to social order, scholars like Handelman (1977, 187) conceptualized them as mutually exclusive.

Hamayon (2016, 292) also disagrees with Lévi-Strauss, arguing: "While rite, like play, obviously appears to be structured as a metaphor, it opposes equally obviously the idea that its outcome could be unexpected... Quite the contrary, a rite of worship is defined by the observance of rules: the 'effect' expected from it is, in principle, subject to compliance with these rules." While these differentiations might hold true for some rites, ritual, like play—particularly in its secular form—is not static but changes with and alongside social and cultural transformations.

TRANSCENDING PLAY: IN-BETWEEN RITUAL AND PLAY EVENT?

While the frame explicitly communicated by gaming events, such as the festivals I have studied, is *let us play games*, I have shown how a playful attitude and play as a disposition become the general mode of interaction. This disposition celebrates and produces indeterminacy. While *game* and *play* always include the possibility of the unexpected, rituals may bring determinate outcomes (Malaby 2009, 214). Rituals, as opposed to games, try to contain contingencies and indeterminacy. As Hamayon (2016, 290) argues, "Ritual practices are supposed to influence realities only when they are performed according to prescribed gestures and the conventional props." Thus, the stance toward indeterminacy is related to the *effect* a play element or a ritual act should have and in which realm this effect is taking place.

Kjus (chapter 1, this volume) suggests that if players "perceive what they produce is unreal, then it could be play that we have witnessed, but if they perceive it as super-real, then it could be a ritual." *Play* is then something contained in itself, not purposefully trying to extend to life outside the play frame. As Csikszentmihalyi and Bennett (1971, 46) argued, "The cosmic duel on the board does not carry over to 'real' life; rarely does the competitive tension outlive the game." Contrastingly, "Ritual practices are supposed to influence realities" (Hamayon 2016, 278). According to Hamayon (299), the institutionalization of games in the West is what separated *play* from its potential effect: "This separation deprived these games, if not of all sacrality and rituality, then at least of any acknowledged sacrality and rituality" (300). Thus, one of the lines of differentiation between ritual and play is how they transcend their frame. While a ritual frame is striving for an *effect* on social order (reestablishing or renegotiating), play in the West is seemingly not, thus missing the aspect of sacredness or transcendence (beyond a play frame). While Hamayon (301) acknowledges new manifestations of playing in the virtual realm, she regrets the lack of interest in transcendental ideologies. For gaming events, the maneuvering between play and rituality poses the question of what effects the practices of play are aimed at producing.

As shown, the practices of playing embrace and create indeterminacy to draw on luck. The *effect* of such play is the *luck* created. *Getting lucky* at gaming events can refer to winning a game or a pleasurable playing experience without stretching beyond the play frame. However, my interlocutors describe lucky chances particularly as those situations that have a lasting effect on their lives. When indeterminate moments transcend the frame of play and even the event setting, they become *magic moments*. Such lucky chances and magic moments include finding soulmates, developing new social or technical skills, or being offered the job of one's dreams. The best indeterminate moments for my interlocutors are those that have a meaningful impact on life outside the frames of play. Even though the proclaimed purpose of events is to play games, for my interlocutors, social relationships are the main reason to attend. In particular, the lucky chances of meaningful social encounters are considered a unique feature of actualized events that virtual games are missing. While virtual games try to imitate indeterminacy through randomizations, digital technologies are based on discrete numbers and rely on determinacy. The human element of other players in a game adds some indeterminacies. However, the real-life encounters at gaming events, combined with a playful attitude, create an excess of indeterminacy, potentially leading from one lucky chance to another.

While indeterminacy as an end in itself can be interpreted as a lack of sacredness, it also adds a crucial quality: the unexpected. The unknown brings new perspectives, new potential actions, and new potentials for players to locate and imagine themselves. As one interview partner explained: "If our brain is usually working only on 15 percent of its capacity or something, then at [the event] my brain is working on 30 percent of its capacity. You're kind of yourself, but you're more. I'm myself but bigger. I'm not saying better. I'm just bigger" (interview with Yulianis, she/her, twenty-seven years old, September 14, 2019).

This reflects the ambiguous continuum between ritual and play at gaming events. Playing can remain self-contained, temporary, and situational, with no obligation outside the play frame. However, it is the transformative play that makes playing at events so valuable to participants, creating encounters that change their view of the world and experiences that let them move through life in new and different ways. Moments of indeterminacy become moments for potential change. However, this potential striving for transcendence remains ambiguous. The explicit frame remains *this is play*. The practices of playing move beyond *play* toward *ritual*. Yet, there is no commitment or acknowledgment of rituality or sacredness. The paradox of play allows one to decide in hindsight if a particular situation was only played or if it was reaching beyond; thus, the practices of playing at gaming events achieve their fullest potential when lingering in the in-betweens.

REFERENCES

Unprinted Sources

All fieldwork materials, including the interview transcripts and observation protocols cited in this chapter, were documented and anonymized during the period 2018–22 and are privately archived by the author.

Literature

Bareither, Christoph. 2020. *Playful Virtual Violence: An Ethnography of Emotional Practices in Video Games*. Elements in Histories of Emotions and the Senses. Cambridge: Cambridge University Press.

Bateson, Gregory. 2000 [1972]. *Steps to an Ecology of Mind*. Chicago: University of Chicago Press.

Boden, Margaret. 2004 [1990]. *The Creative Mind: Myths and Mechanisms*. London: Routledge.

Boellstorff, Tom. 2006. "A Ludicrous Discipline? Ethnography and Game Studies." *Games and Culture* 1 (1): 29–35.

Csikszentmihalyi, Mihaly, and Stith Bennett. 1971. "An Exploratory Model of Play." *American Anthropologist* 73 (1): 45–58.

Dicks, Bella, Bambo Soyinka, and Amanda Coffey. 2006. "Multimodal Ethnography." *Qualitative Research* 6 (1): 77–96.

Dippel, Anne, and Sonia Fizek. 2017. "Ludification of Culture: The Significance of Play and Games in Everyday Practices of the Digital Era." In *Digitisation: Theories and Concepts for Empirical Cultural Research*, edited by Getraud Koch, 276–92. London: Routledge.

Eggel, Ruth Dorothea. 2024. "Embodying Gaming: Enacting Playfulness and Spectacles of Actualising Virtual Worlds at Gaming Events." PhD dissertation, University of Bonn, Bonn, Germany.

Hamayon, Roberte. 2016. *Why We Play: An Anthropological Study*. Chicago: HAU Books.

Handelman, Don. 1977. "Play and Ritual: Complementary Frames of Metacommunication." In *It's a Funny Thing, Humor: Proceedings from the International Conference on Humor and Laughter, Cardiff 1976*, edited by Antony J. Chapman and Hugh C. Foot, 185–92. Oxford: Pergamon.

Haraway, Donna Jeanne. 2016. *Staying with the Trouble: Making Kin in the Chthulucene*. Durham, NC: Duke University Press.

Heller, Megan. 2013. "Sacred Playground: Adult Play and Transformation at Burning Man." PhD dissertation, University of California, Los Angeles.

Hine, Christine. 2015. *Ethnography for the Internet: Embedded, Embodied, and Everyday*. London: Bloomsbury.

Huizinga, Johan. 1980 [1949]. *Homo Ludens: A Study of the Play-Element in Culture*. New York: Routledge and Keegan Paul.

Lévi-Strauss, Claude. 1966 [1962]. *The Savage Mind*. Chicago: University of Chicago Press.

Malaby, Thomas M. 2007. "Beyond Play: A New Approach to Games." *Games and Culture* 2 (2): 95–113.

Malaby, Thomas M. 2009. "Anthropology and Play: The Contours of Playful Experience." *New Literary History* 40: 205–18.

Moore, Sally Falk, and Barbara Myerhoff, eds. 1977. *Secular Ritual*. Assen, The Netherlands: Van Gorcum.

Pink, Sarah, Heather A. Horst, John Postill, Larissa Hjorth, Tania Lewis, and Jo Tacchi. 2016. *Digital Ethnography: Principles and Practice*. London: Sage.

Postill, John. 2015. "Digital Ethnography: 'Being There' Physically, Remotely, Virtually, and Imaginatively." *Media/Anthropology*. Accessed June 10, 2022. http://johnpostill.com/2015/02/25/digital-ethnography-beingthere-physically-remotely-virtually-and-imaginatively/.

Postill, John, and Sarah Pink. 2012. "Social Media Ethnography: The Digital Researcher in a Messy Web." *Media International Australia* 145 (1): 123–34.

Sutton-Smith, Brian. 1997. *The Ambiguity of Play*. Cambridge, MA: Harvard University Press.

Taylor, T. L. 2009. *Play between Worlds: Exploring Online Gaming Culture*. Cambridge, MA: MIT Press.

Turner, Victor. 1974. "Liminal to Liminoid in Play, Flow, and Ritual: An Essay in Comparative Symbology." *Rice University Studies* 60 (3): 53–92.

Turner, Victor. 1991 [1969]. *The Ritual Process. Structure and Anti-Structure*. New York: Cornell Paperbacks.

8

To Leave a Receipt and Bang the Gavel

Play and Ceremony in Celebrations of Fandom

JAKOB LÖFGREN

I'm standing in a pub in a village in England. The year is 2010. Other fans and I have received papers indicating that we are members of the guild. The fact that the guild's rules include a stipulation that I promised to give away 15 percent of my income is self-evident, as is the rule to leave a receipt. The thieves' code of honor demands it. We who are in the room know that; we have all read Terry Pratchett's books. Seven years later I am sitting in a congress hall in Helsinki. WorldCon's toastmistress has just invited me and the other 6,000 people in the hall to go out and have fun. My friends and I go out to meet new friends. We all know what a magical party WorldCon is; maybe it's time for a beer.

AMONG PLAYING FANS AND CEREMONIES

Fandom constructs a place and a time for play. The purposes of my chapter are to show how the staging of ceremonies is part of what constitutes modern fandom and to study how play frames are applied and play elements are performed in the creation of these collective celebrations. While the theories of both play and ritual tend to be very general, I particularly want to point out traits that are characteristic of the uses of ceremonies

https://doi.org/10.7330/9781646426751.c008

within fan culture. By analyzing the use of ceremonies as a rational ritual (Chwe 2013) in the affective play of fandom (Hills 2002), I will shed light on how ceremonial elements in fandom are used.

In this chapter, I analyze ceremonies associated with two fandom events: (1) the annual celebration of Hogswatch in Wincanton, a celebration of the literary world of the English writer Terry Pratchett, and (2) the annual WorldCon convention, the world's largest international convention for fans of sci-fi, fantasy, and speculative fiction. Using ethnographic data collected between 2010 and 2017, I will consider two ceremonies: the initiation into Wincanton's Local Chapter of Ankh-Morpork's Guild of Thieves and the opening ceremony of WorldCon 75 in Helsinki. In this way, I wish to demonstrate the use of ceremonies in fandom, regardless of the size of the event.

HOGSWATCH

Pratchett is best known for his Discworld series (1985–2015). The books have been described as a mix of *The Lord of the Rings* and Monty Python (Butler 2001), and the book series and characters are immensely popular. During a period in the 1990s, Pratchett accounted for 1 percent of all books sold in the English language (Butler 2001). Pratchett died from Alzheimer's in his home in Wiltshire in 2015.

Since 2010, Hogswatch has been celebrated annually in November in the village of Wincanton in Somerset. Wincanton is a small town south of Bath, with approximately 3,000 inhabitants. Hogswatch is a term taken from the book *The Hogfather* (Pratchett 1997) and denotes Discworld's equivalent of Christmas. Hundreds of visiting fans take part in a three-day party, which includes an annual Hogswatch dinner and a variety of games with ritual and ceremonial elements, initiations into various guilds, the singing of Hogswatch carols, and a baking competition. Everything is imbued with Pratchettesque humor and satire. Fans from different parts of the world attend; because Wincanton is a small town, the Hogswatch celebration cannot grow beyond a maximum of 1,500 participants. Usually, the celebration is smaller than that (400–500 people).

WORLDCON

WorldCon is a much bigger event. It is an annual convention that gathers approximately 70,000 fans of fantasy, sci-fi, and speculative fiction for a week to socialize, listen to lectures, meet authors, and participate in the Hugo Awards ceremony. The event was founded in 1939 and has happened every year since 1946. WorldCon is an itinerant event that is organized after application by a host city. In 2017 the host city was Helsinki, and I was there to take part. The event can be described as a mixture of academic conference—with lectures and a book fair—and the Oscars, complete with opening ceremony, awards ceremony, and a gala dinner. During the week, the Hugo Awards are handed out, the most prestigious prize an author of sci-fi, fantasy, and speculative fiction can receive.

WorldCon is organized by a local committee, which competes to host the event. Organizing a WordCon means spending time and money on managing as good and attractive an event as possible and making sure to attract visiting high-profile writers. During the event, there are many ceremonial elements but also play activities on various levels and stages. Among other things, the event hosts cosplay and a games room with board games (worldcon.com).

"ALWAYS LEAVE A RECEIPT": A KICKOFF CEREMONY

Between 2010 and 2014, I attended the Hogswatch celebrations in Wincanton. During those years, the celebration's opening ceremony was formalized, making a specific skit a recurring element. The ceremony has both new and recurring participants (approximately 200 in number), and it is organized by a group of fans. The ceremony took place in the back hall of the Bear Pub on High Street in Wincanton (figures 8.1, 8.2):

> The chairman of the thieves' guild, Mr. Boggis and two lower ranking thieves take the stage. They are wearing black and white striped clothes and bowler hats. They also bear the insignia, and the emblem of the guild. Mr. Boggis starts talking, the speech is written as an inaugural speech of a principal who speaks to new students at a school. He asks everyone who has never been to Hogswatch to stand up.
>
> (Audience) Oooooooh! Laughing.

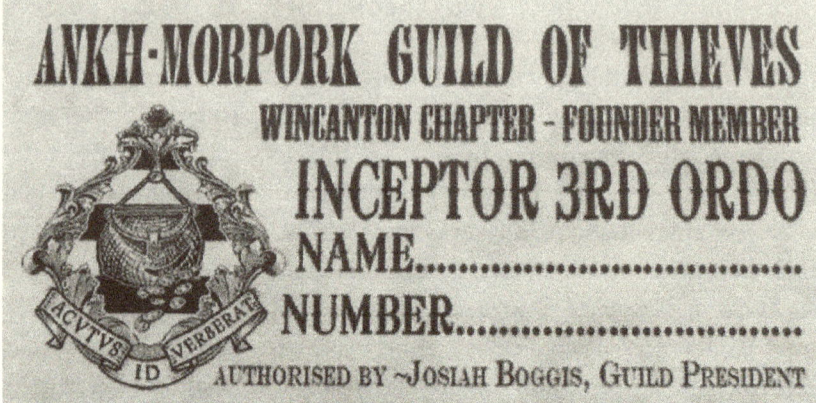

FIGURE 8.1. Guild of thieves' membership card, front, with the authorization of Guild president Josiah (Mr.) Boggis.

See all the new recruits (laughs Boggis)

They do not know what they've gotten themselves into gov', answers one of the villains

Right Boys! Show'em the ropes!

The two villains go through the rules of the thieves' guild. Special emphasis is placed on teaching the rule that all thieves in the guild are expected to leave a receipt for stolen goods. The EXTREMELY secret greeting, so that the members of the guild can recognize each other on the street, is displayed; once at normal speed and once in slow motion (for clarity). The greeting sequence comprises two hand gestures, of which one gesture contains an extended middle finger and the other gesture comprises an extended middle finger and index finger. After this, it's time to swear in the new recruits to the Wicanton chapter of Ankh-Morpork's thieves' guild. Pieces of paper are handed out and Mr. Boggis speaks first and the audience repeats. The oath is as follows:

I (INSERT NAME HERE) hereby pledge my loyalty to the Guild of Thieves. Do willingly give 15% of all my monies from my trade to support the Brotherhood of Larceny. Promise to abide by the articles of appropriation, smite the unlicensed and ALWAYS LEAVE A RECEIPT! Else my Figgins may be rent asunder over hot coals. (IF 2012, 4:1)

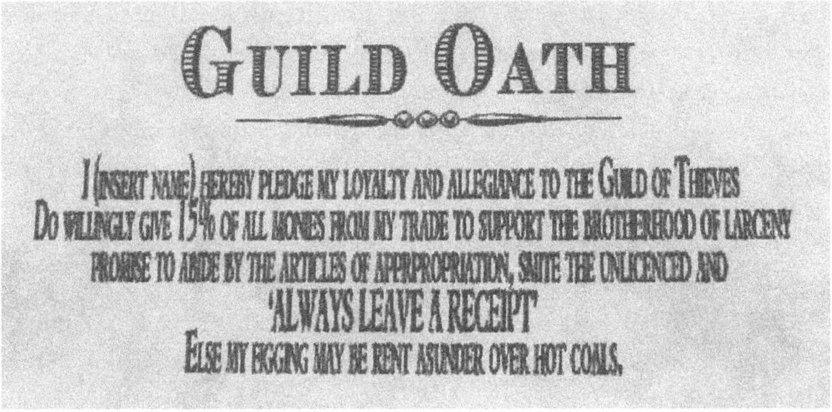

> # GUILD OATH
>
> I (INSERT NAME) HEREBY PLEDGE MY LOYALTY AND ALLEGIANCE TO THE GUILD OF THIEVES
> DO WILLINGLY GIVE 15% OF ALL MONIES FROM MY TRADE TO SUPPORT THE BROTHERHOOD OF LARCENY
> PROMISE TO ABIDE BY THE ARTICLES OF APPROPRIATION, SMITE THE UNLICENCED AND
> ## ALWAYS LEAVE A RECEIPT
> ELSE MY RIGGING MAY BE RENT ASUNDER OVER HOT COALS.

FIGURE 8.2. Guild of thieves' membership card, back: the guild oath.

The audience applauds, and all new participants in the Hogswatch celebration pick up a printout of the Mr. Boggis–signed membership certificate. It all takes about fifteen minutes. Then everyone returns to socializing and meeting new and old friends.

"FINLAND IS A LAND OF SEASONS": THE OPENING CEREMONY AT WORLDCON 75

WordCon is a much larger event than Hogswatch, and therefore the ceremony is larger in its execution. It includes several parts, such as songs, presentations of guests of honor at the convention, and thanking the organizers. The event is professionally produced: audiovisually framed with lighting, a PA system, and a video screen. The ceremony lasts about forty minutes, and in Helsinki it was witnessed by approximately 6,000 people.

The 2017 ceremony began with Barbadian author Karen Lord entering the stage and welcoming WorldCon number 75. Lord was the convention's "toastmistress" and the master of ceremonies during the various ceremonies. The theme of the ceremony was "Finland through the seasons of the year." Lord says "Finland is a land of seasons." The audience follow the Finnish seasons through performances of Finnish folklore and the Finnish ritual calendar, beginning with fall and ending with summer. The first performance is framed by the celebration of Kekri, a revived, traditional

East Finnish harvest festival (Simolin 2018) tied to the harvest in late summer. The performance consists of a dance that will emulate "magical" harvest celebrations, as well as a sketch. The central anthropomorphic personification of Kekri is the Kekri goat (Kekripukki in Finnish). In the ceremony at WorldCon, it is the convention's chair who is dressed as a goat. After a quick sketch, whose point is that Lord is frightened, the chair takes off his buck suit and officially opens WorldCon by hitting the chairperson's club against a Kekri gift he has received from Lord.

After autumn comes winter; after Kekri comes Christmas. Finnish Christmas songs are sung onstage. The songs are sung by a choir, all in a minor key and with lyrics about how dark and cold it is. After this, Santa enters the stage and hands out Christmas gifts; it is stated that no guests or participants in WorldCon have been particularly kind that year. Those who are called up to receive gifts are the authors who have been invited as the convention's guests of honor. They come onstage and introduce themselves. After this, it's time for spring and Easter. A group of children come disguised as witches and perform the Finnish version of the Easter witch tradition; they say a traditional rhyme and give Lord a decorated twig.

The summer consists of two numbers. First, a sextet sings two drinking songs: a Finnish translation of the French Renaissance drinking song "Tourdion" and "Song Number 17" from *Bacchi Temple* by Carl Michael Bellman—"Abandon all distress" (*Bort allt vad oro gör*), sung in Swedish. The second number is a dance that interprets midsummer magic—more specifically, the custom of putting seven different kinds of flowers under one's pillow. A group dances on the stage, carrying seven different kinds of flowers that are held up against a midsummer bonfire, which can be seen on the screen.

Following the Finnish seasons, the convention's president takes the stage and gives a speech about the work process and the pride in having the chance to host WorldCon in Helsinki. Recipients of awards for extraordinary efforts in the planning and volunteer work are announced. This is followed by Lord coming back onstage to conclude the opening ceremony with the words "I think you guys have a convention to attend, so go forth and enjoy yourselves to the fullest." The audience cheers. Then everyone pours out of the great hall, heading for the convention localities (WorldCon 75 opening ceremony).

FANDOM

Fandom has been discussed and defined according to different schools of thought, from psychoanalysis (Hills 2002) and social constructivism (Jenkins 2006a) to literary creationism (Hellekson and Busse 2014) and practice studies (Lamerichs 2014). Matt Hills (2002, 112) describes fandom in terms of *affective play*, involving fans' explorative and open-ended investment of emotion through activities that do not always have a predetermined limitation or set of cultural boundaries. Several researchers have described fandom through its various cultural practices. They include Karen Hellekson and Kristina Busse's work with fan fiction and literary practice (2014) and Nicolle Lamerichs's work with fans as producers and fan-affective practices (2014, 185). The practices Lamerichs describes include conventions, and it is further claimed that the skills and knowledge fans possess are learned in specific interpretive frameworks.

As a folklorist, I see fandom as constituting a *folk* who have and express their own *lore*. The *folk* element should be understood here as "at least two people who have something in common" (Dundes 1965, 2), and *lore* can be described as the various forms of aesthetic communication that give folklore its form and content (McNeill 2013, 178). Fandom has its own folklore, which includes fan fiction, conventions, folk art, and ceremonies (Löfgren 2018). The cultural expressions of fandom define the participants as fans, and the fans define which cultural expressions are useful within the fandom. Hogswatch is a celebration that expresses Pratchett-fandom; WorldCon is a more general celebration of fandom.

The difference between fan folklore and folklore in general is that the expression of a fandom takes inspiration from, and expresses feelings for, a specific writer, film, game, or other specific and recognizable categories of media content. Fandom is an intertextual practice. The intertextual relationship between the universe described in, for example, a book series and events in the "real world" is one of mutual transformation (Stewart 1979, 16–17). Such transformations may, for instance, be acted out through the arrangement of parties or the staging of ceremonies—displaying and forming communities based on the shared intertextual knowledge (Löfgren 2018).

Fan expressions are inspired by an *affective investment* (Grossberg 1992, 64), which differs from an investment of (mere) capital in that it is an investment of emotion, energy, and effort into practices (such as ceremonies) that gives sway over the creation of meaning and identity. It is a reciprocal form of investment: one invests passion and gains *the construction of possibility* (Grossberg 1992, 64), thereby increasing the signifying potential of the source media content. The affective investment gives and marks meaning and constructs *the feeling*, both in the reception of the source and in the performance of the fan-cultural expressions.

Fandom is easily recognized as an affective practice. The affective investment is the goal of the intertextual practices and expressions of fan folklore—which is affective investment put into practice. This practice conveys togetherness and common knowledge based on the investment, leading to continuity within the shared cultural expressions (cf. Hills 2002, 101) and creating an *affective alliance* (Grossberg 1992, 56): a community based on shared feelings for a franchise. The fact that you agree that you can have your beer stolen during Hogswatch if there is a receipt is an expression of belonging to the same affective alliance.

Within a fandom community, a social group shares an affective investment: you invest emotions in the same author or genre and transfer this into practices that allow you to take control over your relationship with the source texts (Grossberg 1992, 64–65). Henry Jenkins describes the community of fandom as *a participatory culture* (2006a, 41) and *a community of knowledge* (2006b, 259). Participating in leaving a receipt for stolen goods, dressing up, or participating in ceremonies are part of a process of self-definition and transfer of knowledge. To leave a receipt is to perform and communicate knowledge the participants possess—the knowledge that in the Pratchett universe, this may well happen—while showing that they are Pratchett fans.

All of the above-mentioned researchers agree that fandom, to some extent, is an expression of an identity. Lamerichs sees this identity expressed in creative practice (2014, 202), Lawrence Grossberg in the affective investment (1992, 57), and Jenkins in the involvement of a larger social context (2006a, 41). I claim that fandom identity is a *playful identity* (Lange et al. 2015): an identity that internalizes play in its basic structure.

THE PLAYING FANS

When Peter G. Stromberg discusses the concept of *play*, he includes it in his understanding of *entertainment*. Stromberg (2009, 7) sees entertainment as a special situation separated from everyday life: "Entertainment is playful activity undertaken for its own sake, in pursuit of pleasure that diverts the player from the day-to-day." Within the context of fandom, this diverting and playful activity—*for its own sake*—constitutes *fun*.

Play is separated from other activities in that it has different rules, places, perceptions of time, and equipment; further, it may encourage transgression and the creation of new, otherwise bizarre social contexts (Henricks 2008, 159). It is the performance of the specific rules that shows what group the play "belongs to" while at the same time defining and delimiting the perception, equipment, and transgressions that are viewed as appropriate within the group. Within fandom, the rules of playing are set within certain affective interpretations and with references to the franchise(s) one is a fan of. The references submit and contain that which makes the play activities meaningful, separating them from the everyday routine and creating the social context of fandom.

Play in fandom, Hills (2002, 112) states, is based in (1) the fans' affective investment and (2) the fans imaginatively creating their own set of boundaries within their own context. Play is a prerequisite for being part of and creating fandom. "Stealing" can be a game within fandom's own boundaries and context. Fandom assumes that one should play with references to a *mother text*. It is through play with references that the investment is expressed; stealing someone's beer and leaving a receipt is a game that expresses a reference to Pratchett's world while communicating a certain attitude and feeling. The performance of this kind of affective/intertextual connection is one of the reasons why people gather at fan events in the first place. In contrast, though, the connections set limits for the ceremonies. To be appropriate within the fandom, the connection to the secondary worlds of speculative fiction needs to be aptly displayed. Without references to Discworld, a ceremony at Hogswatch is not a Hogswatch-appropriate ceremony. References to literature and to prior experience with fandom events serve as targets for the play, creating and drawing on a common stock of knowledge (Stewart 1979). A gathering of fans needs these references to demonstrate how the play is affectively connected within their fandom. Within these intertextual boundaries of play, the variation of acts and expressions can be endless, as long as the shared affective investment is center stage.

Playing is a place- and time-bound aesthetic and communicative process (Saarikoski 2009, 36–37). Events like Hogswatch and WorldCon constitute a time and a place for maintaining a playful identity (Lange et al. 2015) and sharing intertextual knowledge. By playing with this knowledge, fans create identity and community and become members of the same affective alliance (Grossberg 1992). Through such playful activities, fans create their own culture by forming new traditions, or sets of biographical and historical resources that can be drawn on later. These are lasting structures (cf. Hills 2002, 118). Within such structures, new traditions—for instance, new ceremonies or ceremonial elements—can be conceived and nurtured, re-creating and evolving the fan events as specific cultural, recurring contexts for fan performance. According to Hills's (2002, 111) analysis, "Subcultural rituals arise in experiences of affective play rather than logically preceding these experiences." I find that the ceremonies of fandom are expressions that have sprung from playfulness rather than ones that precede playfulness. However, the ceremonies seem more like playful ceremonies than mock or pretend ceremonies.

THE RITUAL

A ritual never exists in splendid isolation; both form and content are always in dialogue with other expressions in the ritual life of a person or a community (Bell 1997). Like other forms of communication, a ritual is thus dependent on its context—historically, socially, and with regard to time and place (143). How one designs the words and deeds of a ritual is tied to one's social and cultural situation. The rituals and ceremonies dealt with here are bound to fandom, in both content and execution. Out of context, they may easily be perceived as nonsense (Stewart 1979). In fandom, ceremonies are based on intertextual knowledge, to the same extent as they are based on social context. While the topical foundation is sourced from the mother text, the form of the ceremony will often be inspired by ceremonies and rituals outside the fandom (Löfgren 2018).

Catherine Bell (1997, 414) states that rituals are held to be "particularly effective means of conveying tradition and change, that is, as a medium for integrating certain changes while maintaining a sense of cultural continuity." For cultural continuities to be created and maintained through ceremonial practices within the fandom, the ceremonies must be recognized as such, and they must be adapted to serve the context of the fandom. The ceremonies must be recurring, and they must feel ceremonial. In short, you can build ceremonies in fandom, because fans know what a ceremony should look and feel like.

This brings me to an important aspect: how rituals can be understood as publication channels for group-specific rationality. Michael Suk-Young Chwe (2013) has pointed out that the various textual components of a ritual—symbols, words, repetition of language—are formalized into a publishable whole, with the intention of conveying a level of common sense. The choice of using ritual and ceremony as a communication format is made because of the ritual's capacity to combine semiotic carriers like symbols, words, music, clothing, humor, and other components into a familiar, historically used, therefore recognizable whole. In this, the ritual conveys a specific rationality and communicates what is henceforth to be held as common knowledge (Chwe 2013). Historically, the form of the ceremony has been utilized for the publication of a new commonality in the aftermath of political revolutions, when a new set of symbols needs to be transmitted abruptly to a larger public (Chwe 2013; Hunt 1984). This occurs because a ritual "creates common" (Habermas 1984) and as such is a vehicle of coordination. Play also coordinates and presupposes common knowledge. But where the coordination of play has the potential to transport the player into an imaginary secondary world, the ceremony usually conveys what should be considered rational and real. Both play and ritual are actively coordinating common knowledge, but they may differ with regard to how the coordination is carried out and what kind of common knowledge is made public.

One way to coordinate is simply to communicate a message, such as "let's all participate." But because each person will participate only if others do, for the message to be successful, each person must not only know the message but must also know that every other person knows about it. In fact, each person must know that every other person knows that every other person knows about it, and so on; that is, the message must become "common knowledge" (Chwe 2013, 16–17). The knowledge of a ritual's content and form becomes shared only through participation. Through the involvement of participants, rituals and ceremonies become the publishing platforms of various layers of common, general, shared knowledge.

Coordination is a vital aspect of the ritual's communicative process (Chwe 2013, 111). Within fandom, there is already an anticipated shared knowledge in the intertextual references derived from reading the same books, watching the same type of fiction, anticipating playing with references, and understanding the contextual knowledge derived from participating in fandom events. This knowledge is used in fandom ceremonies to coordinate, consolidate, and evolve the common sense of fandom.

Ceremonies can be considered an eye-catching form of ritual, with a focus on pomp and circumstance and precise and flawless performance: "What is essential in the ceremony is the accurate and flawless execution, in accordance with rules, of many rituals and recitations" (Bell 1997, 128). The ceremonies dealt with here are created to be performed before an audience, much like the parades of European royal houses or the ceremonies at the Olympic Games. The fandom ceremonies are to be regarded as a public form of ritual that communicates a specific commonality. In this, the ceremony has an educational component. Within fandom, the various texts, symbols, and other ceremonial elements are chosen and elaborated on in an affective interpretive process that constitutes the use of reference in affective play (Hills 2002). This will remind participants of what constitutes their fandom and transmit a common sense of affective play, fandom, and intertextual knowledge through the form of ceremony. In this, fandom ceremonies function much like other ceremonies, in that they inform participants of the *master fiction* of the community (Geertz 1983). But they differ in the specific grounding of the intertextual common knowledge. The fandom ceremony should be regarded as the publication of a specific fandom commonality (Chwe 2013)—one of playfulness and affective investment. The affective investment, the knowledge of and ability to play with apt references, constitute a shared knowledge that is already there prior to the ceremony and that therefore can be played with in the ceremonial form.

INTERTEXTUAL CEREMONIAL FANDOM

The initiation into Ankh-Morpork's thieves' guild is based on the precept that the organizers of Hogswatch and the rest of the fans share an affection for Discworld. The ceremony is based on everyone knowing that everyone knows the references in the ceremony. It is no wonder that Mr. Boggis presides over the whole thing; if there is anyone who will preside, it is him. His and his subordinates' attire is as should be expected. The participants' promise to leave a receipt for theft or have their testicles roasted over glowing coals is reasonable. Every participant shares these references and thus has a presupposed intertextual common knowledge.

The Guild of Thieves operates in Discworld's largest city: Ankh-Morpork. In the books, Ankh-Morpork is a metropolis, with similarities to Victorian London. The city is ruled by a tyrant, Patrician Havelock Vetinari, who has decided that since there is crime in big cities, it might as well be organized crime. In the books about Discworld, the guild is thus described as part of the state apparatus—partly Mafia, partly to be regarded as a tax collector. The guild's task is to educate members in criminal activities and how to organize crime. This is done in the guild's school, where thieves are trained. Masters wear black-and-white–striped clothes, a badge with the guild's emblem on it, and a block for receipts. If you are robbed by a licensed thief, you have the right to see the badge and to receive a receipt. A licensed thief must be able to present receipts. The purpose of the receipt is so you can show that you have already been robbed by the guild and reclaim your property for appropriate renumeration. The guild's second task is to punish unlicensed robbers and burglars. If the guild gets hold of an unlicensed criminal, it has the right to hand out punishment; the unlicensed person may have their fingers or other body parts cut off or be killed (Pratchett et al. 2012, 46).

All of this is included in the common frame of reference, which Wincanton participants know everyone knows. The content of the ceremony, the attire of the master thieves, the existence and activities of Boggis and the thieves' guild constitute shared knowledge around which one can build a ceremony. The organizers base their choice of ceremonial elements on the knowledge that the participants know and are prepared to play with these references. In this, the ritual is rational in its design; an expression of common, general, shared knowledge (cf. Chwe 2013) in a playful form. The play with the form of the ceremony serves to enhance the common knowledge among fans of how playing with references is crucial to fandom.

WHAT YOU NEED TO KNOW ABOUT FINLAND

The most basic knowledge that is common and the knowledge about the knowledge that is common (cf. Chwe 2013) at an event like WorldCon is that all participants and organizers share an affective investment in speculative fiction. The members of WorldCon are there because they are fans of fantasy and sci-fi; everyone knows that. WorldCon travels; therefore, the organizers must ask themselves what a visiting fan needs to know about Finland.

An advantage of ceremony as a publication channel is how easily and comprehensively it conveys a baseline of common knowledge that serves as an orientation for further interaction: (1) everyone here likes speculative fiction, and (2) we who like speculative fiction are in Finland. Thus, WorldCon's opening ceremony is based on sketches about Finland. The fact that the ceremony includes intertextually linked sketches to (in this case) Finnish folklore has an educational purpose and adds a national distinctiveness to this international event.

The cultural expressions that are played and joked with in the ceremony are drawn from Finnish folklore and the Finnish ritual year. In addition, the expressions performed are linked to magic, anthropomorphic characters, and celebration. It is Kekripukki, Santa Claus, Easter witches, midsummer magic, and drinking songs that are in focus, not other markers that could represent the Finnish element. One could have imagined another master fiction (Geertz 1983) that could similarly mark the proceedings as Finnish: war, technology, Moomins, the Kalevala, and others. The organizers chose to represent Finland through folklore because those expressions (in addition to "being Finnish") convey a sense of magic and festivities. This is well in line with the knowledge of the audience's common interest in fantasy and sci-fi. The organizers aim to convey that this time the festival is held specifically in Finland by adding new pieces of common knowledge, ones about Finnish folklore. In this manner, the audience is also implicitly told that this WordCon is a specific and unique event, both similar to and different from the WorldCons they may have attended before.

FIGURE 8.3. Winners, presenters, and other participants in the Hugo Awards ceremony. *Courtesy*, Sanna Pudas, CC BY 4.0.

CEREMONY CONTENT AND THE CONSTRUCTION OF COMMUNITY

Constructing community is done at WorldCon and during Hogswatch through intertextual connections between the context you are in and the story world you have in common with the other participants: by the fact that you are in Finland to celebrate your relationship to speculative fiction, through intertextual connections to Pratchett's world, and through references to the guild.

In both cases, new common knowledge is also introduced. Pratchett has not described the initiation ceremony of the thieves' guild in any of the books; the oath that is sworn and the secret hand signals are something a fan can only experience in Wincanton. It will be a new common knowledge for all who celebrated Hogswatch there. The WorldCon ceremony works in the same fashion. You can only experience it if you were there. In this it can be said that both ceremonies are partly based on common knowledge and partly convey new common knowledge to those who participated onsite. Both ceremonies do this to situate the participant in a particular setting—as a fan of Discworld who is / has been in Wincanton or a fan of speculative fiction who is / has been in Finland / WorldCon 75.

For the intertextual common sense to be published and communicated, the communication format must also be part of the common knowledge. This is gained through experience with other ceremonies. Familiarity with the forms of initiation rites and opening ceremonies is acquired through everyday practices. This knowledge can be adapted to convey meaning, community, and feeling in the context of fandom. The knowledge of ceremonies is moved from one sphere of activity to another. The fandom ceremonies thus express both a more particular knowledge, about the story world of the mother text, and a more general knowledge, about the form and function of the ceremonies (figure 8.3).

GRANDEUR AND SECRET HANDSHAKES

WorldCon 75 is officially opened by the chairperson striking a gavel. The chair is onstage with an officially named toastmistress who guides the audiovisual show, with sketches and introductions of dignitaries. Hogswatch is opened with an initiation rite complete with secret handshakes and the participants being sworn into a guild.

For a form to be filled with content, you must know the form. WorldCon's opening ceremony has the same markers as, for example, an opening ceremony at the Olympics: country-specific elements that show which country you are in, a parade of important participants, and the awarding of medals. The site of the ceremony is the largest hall in the Helsinki Exhibition Centre, and it is filled to the brim.

An opening ceremony for a traveling grand event will be grand. It should include an audiovisual show and showcase the nation. The gavel will be struck to open an event of WorldCon's grandeur, and there will be an official master of ceremonies. In a similar way, the initiation into the thieves' guild is carried out according to commonly understood rules. A secret society uses secret hand gestures, and new members are sworn in with the promise of blood revenge against defectors. The ceremonies relate to rules and performances and include several ritual markers found in the collective knowledge of how such ceremonies should appear.

GRANDEUR? SECRET HANDSHAKES?

When you know what the rules are, you can reevaluate them. In his study of the early American Vaudeville scene, Albert F. McLean (2011) points out that it was in the ritualization of Vaudeville that symbols taken for granted could be reevaluated.

Similar reevaluations, through humour and play with established symbols, were carried out both at WorldCon and in Wincanton. At WorldCon, the form of an opening ceremony is played with. In Wincanton, the element of the secret hand gesture is laughed at. The gavel at WorldCon is struck, but this is done after the chairperson has stated that this is the way it must be done and tried to look for something to strike the gavel on. The form and rules of the ceremonies become a framework for jokes and play by reevaluating symbolic elements. The well-established form of a ceremony allows for play within it. By making informal comments such as "none of the guests at this year's WorldCon have been kind this year"; at the special moment of banging the gavel at a formal opening, looking for something to bang it on, and stating that it is "traditional"; or alluding to the secrecy of hand gestures, a sense of informality is communicated.

By playing with form and content so that rules and expectations of formality are turned upside down, the organizers communicate a new baseline for what everyone has in common: all participants are there to have fun. This message is conveyed through a combination of the rationality of the rite and the playful realignment of the social context (Henricks 2008, 159).

MEANINGFUL (AFFECTIVE) PLAYFUL CEREMONIES

Meaning created and published through ceremonies in fandom constitutes a framework for the ethos the events and organizers must maintain: playfulness and affection toward the source media content. The purpose of using ceremonies as a publication channel (Chwe 2013) is the same as that in any other ceremony: to create community. The content of the ceremonies is play based on the intertextual knowledge the fans share. The sketches are based on Finnish folklore, because WorldCon as an event should be perceived as a magical party. The initiation rite is designed so the participants together can state: I have never read / seen / experienced the thief's initiation ritual before, but of course it looks like this. This kind of co-creation is part of the fandom's knowledge community process (Jenkins 2006b, 259), where the transfer and analysis of knowledge are the basis for participation and for maintaining the identity of the fandom.

By using humor in connection with the intertextual references, the organizers informalize the ceremony and attract laughter. This reinforces the message that one wants to publish: we are here to play and have fun. Jokes are made with intertextual references to folklore and fiction, by alluding to the thieves' function in society and to the rules of the ceremony. Humor is a community-building component that works by alluding to shared knowledge. Fans know how to solemnly open a meeting with a club, so they can joke with that knowledge. In Wincanton, everyone knows you have to leave a receipt, so it's fun to swear an oath to do so.

Playing in ceremony creates a bounded and protected space for all the other play that is expected to follow; it frames and creates a playful space (Saarikoski 2009, 36) where one can express a playful identity. Furthermore, the ceremony demarcates the playful space you are in, as well as the event you are participating in. Both ceremonies are opening ceremonies for a specific event that is recurring. Both ceremonies therefore mark a tradition (cf. Bell 1997; Hills 2002). To mark the continuity of the events, ceremonies are in demand. To mark that the events are places for affective play and playful identity, one plays with common references in the ceremonies. This is not to say that the ceremonies themselves are less than ceremonial but rather that they fulfil the function of a ceremony by conveying common knowledge and coordinating people.

CONCLUDING REMARKS

Fandom ceremonies delimit and coordinate a time and space for play. By using ceremonies as a publication of shared knowledge (Chwe 2013), fandom's playful identity is maintained (Lange et al. 2015). Fandom ceremonies use intertextual references to fiction, magic, and a specific ambiance that are deliberately played with, showing an ongoing affective interpretation of one's own investment in the fandom. Intertextual knowledge and affective play are already shared knowledge among participants and can be used in ceremonies to confirm the fandom. The ceremonies are not "less ceremonial"; rather, they coordinate and publish an overall ethos of playfulness and affection for speculative fiction. Within this playfulness, it makes sense to play with the format of the ceremony itself. The format and the various intertextually derived jokes make a published whole, transmitting a thereafter common knowledge that intimates that "we are here to play."

REFERENCES

Unprinted and Archival Sources

Observation Protocol from Wincanton Hogswatch. Archived at: Kulturvetenskapliga arkivet Cultura, Abo Akademi, Abo, Finland. Archive signature: IF 2012, 4.

Worldcon.org. Accessed June 10, 2022. www.worldcon.org.
WorldCon 75 Opening Ceremony. Accessed June 10, 2022. https:// www.youtube .com /watch ?v = Y9onKot5PNo.

Literature

Bell, Catherine. 1997. *Ritual: Perspectives and Dimensions*. Oxford: Oxford University Press.
Butler, Andrew M. 2001. *Terry Pratchett*. London: Oldcastle Books.
Chwe, Michael Suk-Young. 2013. *Rational Ritual: Culture, Coordination, and Common Knowledge*. Princeton, NJ: Princeton University Press.
Dundes, Alan. 1965. *The Study of Folklore*. Englewood Cliffs, NJ: Prentice-Hall.
Geertz, Clifford. 1983. *Local Knowledge: Further Essays in Interpretive Anthropology*. New York: Fontana.
Grossberg, Lawrence. 1992. "Is There a Fan in the House? The Affective Sensibility of Fandom." In *The Adoring Audience: Fan Culture and Popular Media*, edited by Lisa A. Lewis, 50–69. London: Routledge.
Habermas, Jurgen. 1984. *The Theory of Communicative Action*, vol. 1: *Reason and the Rationalization of Society*. Boston: Beacon.
Hellekson, Karen, and Kristina Busse. 2014. *The Fan Fiction Studies Reader*. Iowa City: University of Iowa Press.
Henricks, Thomas. 2008. "The Nature of Play: An Overview." *American Journal of Play* 1 (2): 158–80.
Hills, Matt. 2002. *Fan Culture*. London: Routledge.
Hunt, Lynn Avery. 1984. *Politics, Culture, and Class in the French Revolution*. Berkeley: University of California Press.

Jenkins, Henry. 2006a. *Convergence Culture: Where Old and New Media Collide.* New York: New York University Press.

Jenkins, Henry. 2006b. *Fans, Bloggers, and Gamers: Exploring Participatory Culture.* New York: New York University Press.

Lamerichs, Nicolle. 2014. *Productive Fandom: Intermediality and Affective Reception in Fan Cultures.* Maastricht, The Netherlands: Maastricht University Press.

Lange, Michiel, Joost Raessens, Jos Mul, Sybille Lammes, and Valerie Frissen. 2015. *Playful Identities: The Ludification of Digital Media Cultures.* Amsterdam: Amsterdam University Press.

Löfgren, Jakob. 2018. . . . *And Death Proclaimed "HAPPY HOGSWATCH TO ALL, AND TO ALL A GOOD NIGHT"—Intertext and Folklore in Discworld-Fandom.* Åbo, Finland: Åbo Akademi University Press.

McLean, Albert F. 2011. *American Vaudeville as Ritual.* Lexington: University of Kentucky Press.

McNeill, Lynne S. 2013. "And the Greatest of These Is Tradition: The Folklorist's Toolbox in the Twenty-First Century." In *Tradition in the Twenty-First Century*, edited by Trevor J. Blank and Robert Howard, 174–85. Boulder: University Press of Colorado.

Pratchett, Terry. 1997. *The Hogfather.* London: Victor Gollancz.

Pratchett, Terry, Ian Mitchell, Reb Voyce, Bernard Pearson, and Isobel Pearson. 2012. *The Compleat Ankh-Morpork.* London: Random House.

Saarikoski, Helena. 2009. *Nuoren naisellisuuden koreografioita, Spice Girlsin fanit tyttöyden tekijöinä.* Helsinki: Suomen Kirjalisuuden Seura.

Simolin, Oona. 2018. "Kekri, halloween, pyhäinpäivä—mikä kumma?" Päivystävä folkloristi-blogi. Accessed June 10, 2022. https://blogs.helsinki.fi/folkloristi/kekri-halloween-pyhainpaiva-mika-kumma/.

Stewart, Susan. 1979. *Nonsense: Aspects of Intertextuality in Folklore and Literature.* Baltimore: John Hopkins University Press.

Stromberg, Peter G. 2009. *Caught in Play: How Entertainment Works on You.* Stanford: Stanford University Press.

9

Lutfisk—Nothing to Sniff At

Migration Heritages and Ritualized Play in Scandinavian America

LIZETTE GRADÉN

November 15, 2020, was a cold day, with biting wind. In the parking lot of the American Swedish Institute (ASI) in Minneapolis, Minnesota, a line of cars creeps forward. Museum staff and volunteers hasten between the parked cars and the museum. Wearing winter jackets, boots, snow pants, knit scarves, and hats, they carry white paper bags. Several of the cars waiting in the parking lot have bumper stickers with Swedish flags and messages that variously communicate Scandinavian identification in an American context: "Proud to be Swedish American," "Honk if You're Swedish," "Norwegian by Marriage," and the Norwegian-sounding "Uff Da." A rickety blue Volvo catches the eye. The reggae song "Legalize It" by Peter Tosh plays from the car's rolled-down window. While younger people onsite associate the song with the legalization of cannabis in several US states, in its Scandinavian American context the song has other associations, including jokes about lutfisk (dried ling or cod soaked in potassium carbonate or sodium carbonate and slaked lime), the Scandinavian dish notorious in America for its smell and texture—qualities more related to how the fish is prepared than to the fish itself.[1]

---

[1] For parodying of lutfisk in a Norwegian American context, see Leary 1996, 59–60.

https://doi.org/10.7330/9781646426751.c009

The masks, face shields, and gloves worn by museum staff and volunteers elicit giggles from many of those present. For a little while, pandemic anxiety and fear fade into understanding, fellowship, and hope—a little lutfisk can go a long way, according to one server who identifies as Swedish American. The act itself alludes both to Scandinavian America's oft-expressed love-hate relationship with lutfisk and to the four Gospels (e.g., Mark 6:35–44), which tell of Jesus feeding thousands of people with five fish. In both cases, the act transforms the ASI into a benefactor of the people in a time of existential crisis.

ASI's drive-through lutfisk dinner was a consequence of the Covid-19 pandemic. In this chapter, the dinner becomes a prelude to a broader analysis of the role of lutfisk in ritual and play connecting Scandinavian American cultural heritage and popular culture. I will examine and discuss the ways institutions, groups, and individuals both relate to and represent lutfisk as part of what I call *migration heritages*: cultural heritages shaped *through* and *with* the transformative experience of displacement (forced and voluntary) from one place to another. In doing so, I will introduce the concept *ritualized play* in addressing and providing comfort during perceived threats and crises, both within and outside established cultural institutions engaged in such heritage making. First, a few words on lutfisk as it can be understood in a Scandinavian context.

PISCIS LIXIVIO MACERATUS = LUTFISK

Preparing and eating lutfisk at Christmas is a tradition that dates to the Middle Ages in Sweden, Norway, and Finland, whereas the concept of Christmas food dates to the mid-twentieth century.[2] The food served at Christmas was the best permitted by conditions such as class and geography. In the Scandinavian countries, preparation of lutfisk by soaking dried fish at home beginning on December 9 has given way to the vacuum-packed version, ready to stick in the oven. But even sales of pre-soaked fish have declined in the past decade, and at my local grocery store marked-down packages linger in the refrigerator until removed in mid-March. Shopkeepers say lutfisk consumption at home during Christmas is

---

2   I use the Swedish spelling lutfisk, also known as lutefisk in Norwegian. After the Reformation, the tradition of eating lean fish moved from the fast before Christmas to the celebration itself.

fading with generational shifts.³ One may ask, what is happening to this tradition? Folklorist Barbara Kirshenblatt-Gimblett (2004a, xi–xiv) discusses heritage foods, dishes that are given high symbolic value and considered important to preserve for the future. I would argue that lutfisk is morphing into a heritage food. Having declined both at home and on the commercial *julbord*, introduced in the mid-twentieth century, efforts are made to save it from oblivion. In 1991, the head chef at Edsbacka restaurant, outside of Stockholm, formed the network Friends of Lutfisk, which later developed Lutfisk Day, held in November.⁴ These chefs used their cultural capital to create a following and perform new variations of lutfisk in fine dining establishments across Sweden, re-packaging it to fit the edible heritage and feeding ideas of national foodways.

Lutfisk can be understood as meta-cultural production, something that is transferred from one environment to another and framed in novel ways (Kirshenblatt-Gimblett 2004b). During the twentieth century, lutfisk was symbolically charged and re-packaged for a second life in museums. A recent phenomenon is the Museum of Lutfisk (Lutfiskens museum) in Mollösund, Sweden. At this museum, the past progressive tense is used to describe the way fresh ling were stretched on spindles and dried before being sold and processed into lutfisk in Scandinavia. The museum uses lutfisk to tell the story of how modernization and the introduction of fishing quotas changed conditions for fisherfolk in the twentieth century. As a symbol, lutfisk serves as a touchstone for self-identification and identification of the other, whether a professional group or a nation. As such, lutfisk as symbol concretizes and articulates that heritage belongs to what Rodney Harrison calls future-making practices (2021; cf. Kirshenblatt-Gimblett 1999) that serve political, economic, and ideological goals. As such, heritage making raises questions about power relations and calls for closer scrutiny of situated practices where such heritage is made. I will show how lutfisk manages to articulate migration heritage, connect people, and invoke existential issues—summoned as deeply felt cultural connectivity with life as well as threat of demise. These challenges emerge not least when heritage making takes on a humorous twist.

---

3   Field notes and conversations with staff of ICA Brommaplan, 2017, and ICA Tuna, Lund 2018–21.
4   Lutfiskens vänner, www.lutfisk.nu, accessed December 20, 2020.

ANGLING FOR LUTFISK DURING COVID

Swedish American lutfisk jokes are in flux. The butt of the jokes varies, as does the choice of media. As a response to restrictions to gather in groups, prompted by Covid-19, lutfisk practices began to move online in 2020. They included analog productions recorded and shared as film clips through social media and email. Among them were recorded lutfisk dances, ring dancing in which people had replaced *folkdräkt* (traditional dress) with fish costumes. There were also memes, created digitally for digital use. One meme was pandemic-safe canned lutfisk, packaged to resemble Spam, the pressed ham launched in 1937 as a meat alternative and which later entered international popular culture through Monty Python's sketch "Spam," in which the name of the dish is repeated to such an extent that it has given rise to the internet phenomenon of spam, or junk email. Another was "Liquidized Lutfisk," spread over the internet as a "vaccine" against Covid-19. The physical staging of lutfisk jokes shared over the internet demonstrates how analog and digital cultures merge and how the expressions flow back and forth and influence and impact one another. The sharing of jokes through social media and email chains confirms the value of rituals to foster and sustain groups. For the jokes to solicit laughter, the people receiving them must be able to relate to the customs and rituals being played with.

At a time when I was unable to travel to the US for fieldwork, this transatlantic play provided insights and generated a dialogical method in which participants with different cultural competencies and roles formed a base material. In addition to the digital material, I have recycled lutfisk material and representations I worked with in previous projects. My academic interest in heritage making and popular expressions has given me a place as a recipient, an audience, and a co-performer. As Christmas approaches, friends, family, and colleagues in the US have offered new ways to use lutfisk. Taken together, these materials offer comparisons over time and show how the nimble use of ritualized play sustains Scandinavian traditions in America while reinforcing transatlantic dialogue and networks (figure 9.1).

FIGURE 9.1. Coffee mug "McOlson's Lutfisk Burgers—1 sold," a playful reference to the preparation process of lutfisk and exaggerated antagonism toward American fast-food culture, all the while serving the idea of Scandinavian coffee consumption. Author photo.

FROM RITUAL AND PLAY TO RITUALIZED PLAY: THE DYNAMICS OF MIGRATION HERITAGES

The term *ritual* has different meanings in different contexts. As Barbro Klein (1995, 19) points out, the concept's polyvalence makes ritual interesting in the research on public events: a festival, a parade, or a lutfisk drive-through dinner. Rituals can be understood as actions that are repeated according to a pattern, often with sacred overtones. In such a sense, rituals have transformative and rejuvenating power for individual participants, groups, and entire communities (19–41; cf. van Gennep 1960 [1909]). As Edith Turner (2012) has argued, the transformative power in ritual may enable participants to establish *communitas*, here understood as togetherness with each other and with other worlds, real and imagined, outside the event itself. Since the 1970s, the concept of ritual has also been used to study secular rituals, cyclical and patterned contexts capable of creating a sense of belonging among people (Moore and Myerhoff 1977). As several ethnologists have shown, secular rituals also have a renewing effect on participants—for example, a May Day procession (Engman 1999), the celebration of Norwegian Constitution Day (Blehr 1995, 2000), or a soccer game (cf. Hellspong 1991; cf. Herd, chapter 6, this volume). Contributing to the complex Scandinavian heritage in America, the malleable lutfisk demonstrates a particular ability to bind secular and religious realms together. Although lutfisk is most evident as part of the Christmas ritual, in the United States, it reverberates and resurfaces in public events, rituals, and festival complexes throughout the year (Gradén 2003, 195–204; 2017). Let's take a closer look at what is at play.

When someone signals play and establishes a play frame within a ritual, play comments on the ritual itself (Bronner 2010; Drewal 1992, 17, 75; Mechling 2005; cf. Bateson 1956). The play element has the capacity to articulate what is considered important by whom and at a particular moment in time (Huizinga 2016). The dynamic references and boundaries of the play element reflect people's various perspectives and the fact that different perspectives can be accommodated within the same ritual process (Handelman 1980, 2004; cf. 1998). The crafting and performance of play elements are potentially powerful regulating elements within larger ritual structures. The introduction of a play frame within a larger public event may identify boundaries and express what is central and what appears peripheral within a performative act that requires both focus and flexibility. In a Scandinavian American context, I see lutfisk as a symbol with the capacity to articulate temporalities as well as religion's place in secular life. As a symbol, lutfisk holds and balances ritual and play, creating cyclical movement in people's lives. I argue that in such *ritualized play*, the multivalent play element ingrained in ritual serves as a kaleidoscopic window to streams of struggle that takes place in society. Ritualized play thus becomes particularly important to understanding *migration heritages*, which are shaped *through* and *with* displacement—here, a transatlantic move. It also becomes an entry point to analyze competing communities and people's quest for an existentially sustainable future.

LUTFISK ON PARADE AND OTHER LUTFISK PLAY OUTSIDE THE CHRISTMAS HOLIDAY

Lutfisk is part of a performative context and appears year-round. In the parades that are part of festivals and public events, entire floats are often dedicated to lutfisk. One such parade, where lutfisk floats have become an art form and a ritual in themselves, takes place as part of Svensk Hyllningsfest—held every other year in Lindsborg, Kansas, a town of 3,000 people founded by emigrants from Sweden. For many, the parade is considered the highlight of the festival, and people travel from distant places in the United States to see and be a part of it. The parade attracts Lindsborg residents, former residents, college alumni, visitors from overseas, business and embassy representatives, family and friends, and other people with connections to the community. The event resembles a giant family reunion.

In 1997, the Tomte Smörgåsbord float generated resounding applause. The float consisted of people dressed in gray wool capes, red hoods, and white beards. All the Santa figures wore antique oxygen masks, taken from a disaster-response stockpile. On the float they stood crowded around a cauldron labeled "lutfisk." From the pot stuck three-foot-long gray fish fins made of cardboard (figure 9.2). Dry ice created the impression that the cauldron's contents were steaming. As the float passed the two blocks of the downtown, polyphonic laughter erupted. Some wolf-whistled. A family of four standing beside me held their noses. In a dramatized gesture and a theatrical voice, the teenage boy shouted "oh no, it's lutfisk," whereupon his parents let go of their noses and let out a resounding laugh (see also Mechling 1999, 283, for the role of meals as institutional ceremonies for children). There's no doubt that in Swedish America—when it smells like lutfisk, in real life or in the imagination—laughter soon arises. The Swedish aspect is usually (but not always) a recessive identity, demonstrating the importance of cultural heritage in expressing what it means to be American. It is never either/or but rather both/and.

In September 1997, I visited the man who designed the Tomte Smörgåsbord float. Scattered among stacks of papers that covered his desk were half a dozen lutfisk fins. He had been creating floats for the Svensk Hyllningsfest parade since 1948, and for each one of them he had created lutfisk fins identical to those now on his desk. He described to me how year after year he strived for perfection, to make the fins "a little prettier" than last year. "How do you make them," I asked. "Let me show you," he said. The man pulled out a large piece of cardboard from a pile in the depths of his office and demonstrated the process to me. He drew a sketch of a three-foot fin on the piece of cardboard and cut out the figure with a scalpel. When cut, he gently stroked the edges with an oilcloth to smooth

FIGURE 9.2. Cardboard fins for the lutfisk float at the Svensk Hyllningsfest parade, 1997. Author photo.

them. Then he applied a base layer of light gray oil paint to the cardboard fin. He added paint in a darker shade. "The two shades are important. It gives life to the lutfisk," he chuckled. Every step of the work was done with care and attention to detail. At the time of my fieldwork, his lutfisk fins had adorned many parade floats. He summarized: "I've lost count of how many times I've made them and how many I've made." His delight at the recurring ritual of making lutfisk fins and using them as props to tackle topical political issues was unmistakable. For him, the preparation of fins, the making of floats, the parade itself, and the discussion afterward constituted a never-ending creative play. Strung together, they formed a continuum—the continuing story about the place of Lindsborg's Swedish Americans in relation to the world at large.

Lutfisk has often been used in the parade to comment on global challenges and international relations. In 1979, the float "The Swedish Alternative to Arab Oil" was created. On the bed of an old Ford pickup, the float makers had placed a giant pot of cardboard lutfisk fins. A sign announced

"Lutfisk" to assure the audience of the pot's contents. Placed just behind the pot was a large barrel with a sign "Fisk-ahol." Lutfisk fins were spun in a circular motion and ground down to a coarse liquid, which was then strained. The liquid was drained through a hose, resulting in distilled "fisk-ahol." A man wearing a white coat and glasses—a cartoon scientist, the float maker pointed out—was diverting fisk-ahol from the hose into a tiny cup. A sign on the door of the truck that towed the scene announced "running on fisk-ahol." The truck moving down Main Street demonstrated to the parade's audience that the fisk-ahol really worked to fuel a vehicle.

The construction of the floats contained elements of ritualized play. The float-making groups met in September and October, to plan, design, and build. During construction, the experienced float makers passed around the rules of play. Newspaper clippings and photos from 1979 became part of the presentation when a float maker recounted: "This was one of the floats that I chaired, and I put in a lot of work. I stayed up late at night to rig this with a handle that could be cranked around." He burst out laughing at his invention and explained, "The point is that you can crank it and make the lutfisk fins go around and around and around; [it] never ends, like a mill wheel" (field notes 1997; interview 1998). When the float maker summarized how his cardboard lutfisk fins moved around and around in a circular manner, he emphasized a symbolic circular act without beginning or end. The analogy to a mill wheel shows how the lutfisk fins channel power and amplify dynamics—a prerequisite for a driving force to be sustainable.

The joke becomes clear when we shift our gaze from the scene played out on the truck bed to its physical and metaphorical framing. Around the truck walk a handful of people in black, foot-side attire, white headscarves, beards, and dark sunglasses. They carry placards reading "We're out of gas" and "Unfair to OPEC!" The float commented on the oil crisis of the 1970s and suggested within the play frame how the Swedes might offer a more sustainable alternative. The term *fisk-ahol* alluded to the then-controversial gasohol, a product that was 90 percent gasoline blended with 10 percent ethanol, the latter produced by fermenting grain waste. The Swedish American version also implied internationally significant power struggles: conflict between the US and the Middle East and the tug-of-war between those who advocated gasohol as a more environmentally friendly alternative and those who perpetuated the continued use of gasoline. By playing with lutfisk, the float suggested superiority: with

Swedish American innovation, it is possible to defeat the Middle East, the Organization of Petroleum Exporting Countries (OPEC), and fossil fuel addiction. The float also had deeper roots as a commentary on behalf of Kansas grain farmers. In 1977–78, the American Agricultural Movement advocated the further development of gasohol, to reduce carbon dioxide emissions, and the reuse of agricultural waste while also providing the agricultural industry with an additional revenue source.

Common to performances that include lutfisk is a playful engagement with perceived threats to human existence and symbolic resistance to them (Gradén 2003, 195–208). The kind of Rabelaisian laughter (Bakhtin 1984 [1946/1965], 94) such ritualized play implies may have its specific place within a ritual tradition. A float from 1961, one year after the testing of Tsar Bomba (Ivan) and one year before the Cuban Missile Crisis, displayed an image of Soviet prime minister Nikita Khrushchev. This float was re-staged verbally in interviews and conversations with Lindsborg residents in the 1990s and 2000s and was highlighted as one of the funniest ever. In an interview, the float maker explained to me that "at the time it was a serious matter about the fallout shelters because of the threat from Russia and Nikita Khrushchev. The Kansas governor was advising people to make fallout shelters in preparation for the nuclear attack . . . It was 'the thing' to build, an underground shelter, and prep it with food. And a lot of people, *thousands of people*, did." The float maker recounted how his committee had placed among a Swedish family of five a kettle filled with his cardboard lutfisk tails. As with previous floats, they had put dry ice in the pot to make it smoke. On top of the shelter, they had situated "a giant paper cut-out that portrayed Nikita Khrushchev, holding a flag of surrender, and disgusted by the smell, holding his nose as well."

Utterly pleased with his creation (and with narrating the story), the float maker concluded "lutfisk, that's what eventually ended the Cold War, I guess, ha, ha, ha." As the floats and the re-counting of them show, the float makers turned to play to handle serious matters. The greater the threat, the more powerful the lutfisk joke. These floats mobilized lutfisk and engaged difficult topics, including the 1970s oil crisis, the Cold War, and the terrorist attack on the Twin Towers on September 11, 2001 (see Gradén 2003). The kind of liberating laughter these playful displays generated (Bakhtin 1984 [1946/1965], 94) enabled the people involved to deal with an anxiety-causing experience.

At large, the Svensk Hyllningsfest is a serious ritual that begins and ends with a service in Bethany Church. The general mood of the parade is also serious, with dignitaries, military, and strict curation. The lutfisk performances add playfulness and the element of laughter. Dispersed evenly across the parade, they deploy the *mot juste* to prompt laughter and recognition among those who know Lindsborg and who follow national and international news. The lutfisk installations are locally long-awaited features, worth waiting in line for. They provide individuals with the opportunity to participate—as actors and audience—in a repeated collective act of meaning making (Drewal 1992; Turner and Turner 1995). These jokes are done tastefully and for the benefit of the local audience, not intended to oppress or ridicule but to articulate a shared experience, to reflect on it but also to look at current events with a critical eye—a satire with a political edge. In this way, the play elements provided by the parade floats have an empowering effect. Through the stories of the floats and their creation, play is perpetuated, even ritualized, as a symbolic refuge in times of difficulty and crisis. Each new parade has its place in a series of parades, and its survival requires meaningful content and aesthetic articulation: serious play with current events as well as probing the future.

WALK BY FAITH, NOT BY SMELL: LUTFISK CHURCH DINNERS

Among Swedish and Norwegian communities in the United States, the lutfisk dinner is a perennial subject of both ritual and play. At a time when few people prepare lutfisk by rinsing it and soaking it in lye at home, lutfisk can be purchased vacuum-packed or as a frozen TV dinner. But mainly, lutfisk is cooked to be eaten with others. Beginning in October each year, many Americans of Swedish and Norwegian descent and their friends travel to churches for lutfisk dinners. Such journeys are often several hours long and take the form of a pilgrimage, a ritual of religious devotion and spiritual renewal undertaken once or repeatedly (Turner and Turner 1995). In the ecclesial context, these dinners become acts of communion, in the religious sense of sharing a meal. Eating lutfisk together in church with family, parishioners, and friends is a religious ritual that in American Scandinavian communities dates back at least to the 1860s. Around 1865, church lutfisk dinners began to be advertised in Swedish-language newspapers in the Midwest.

In the 1950s, the Swedish and Norwegian churches discovered that lutfisk meals could generate income.[5] Today, many Lutheran churches in the Upper Midwest coordinate with one another to avoid having dinners the same weekend (Gilmore 1997, 39–40). This weaving of lutefisk/lutfisk dinners requires driving and queuing, a different kind of pilgrimage experience that creates careful orchestration and competition. In some small midwestern churches, the lutfisk dinner has declined due to a lack of volunteers and revenue. In 2018 the pastor of Forest Lake's Faith Lutheran Church in Minnesota wrote in the *Forest Lake Times* obituary section that "the lutefisk dinner has peacefully died at the age of 70" (1947–2017), explaining that even after outsourcing the preparation to the company that sold the fish, there were not enough volunteers to justify the work.[6] In other, more urban areas, dinners have grown into their own ritual complex, an occasion for congregations to gather around a special meal and invite guests. At Elim Lutheran Church in Minneapolis, the lutfisk dinner attracts 600 paying attendees annually.[7] The lutfisk dinner as a Scandinavian American ritual sustains and reinforces both the Scandinavian church community and the notion of ethnic belonging, as identifying with one or more ethnic groups is viewed as part of the American national identity (cf. Gilmore 1997; cf. Nikielska-Sekula 2019). As lutfisk meals have moved from private homes into churches and even to museum organizations, they provide both fellowship for participants and financial security for the organizers. Hence, food and foodways such as the lutfisk dinner may be understood as the bread and butter of migration heritage making.

In 2020, when eating lutfisk together in the church was impossible due to the pandemic, a window of opportunity opened for the ASI, which identifies as a museum, historic house, and cultural education center with a mission to be a "gathering place for all people to explore diverse experiences of migration, identity, belonging and the environment through arts and culture, informed by the enduring links to Sweden."[8] Having had to close on March 14, 2020, because of the pandemic, ASI pursued multiple ways of making itself relevant to the community while seeking new sources

---

5   Their development follows the same trajectory as that of the ethnic heritage festivals, created in the wake of the civil rights movement.
6   Anne Ewbank, "RIP Faith Lutheran Church Scandinavian Dinner, 1947–2017," *Atlasobscura*, December 6, 2018.
7   Retrieved from the Elim Lutheran Church website, https://www.elimlutheran.net/, 2019.
8   https://asimn.org/ accessed in 2020.

of income. As president and CEO Bruce Karstadt stated, "The times are tough, not least financially" (Zoom interview, January 27, 2021). As the state public health authority had called for the closure of all museums, the museum's management decided to implement a drive-through–style lutfisk dinner, delivering food directly to guests' cars, like McDonald's does. Thus, the tradition of slowly preparing dried ling or cod was transformed into a fast-food phenomenon.

The ASI's decision to host a drive-through lutfisk dinner was based on an understanding of the social communities as well as institutional economic needs. Lutfisk is both loved and despised for its strong smell and gelatinous texture, but it's a culinary experience that "everyone should have at least once," insisted Karstadt, using vocabulary reminiscent of pilgrimages, when we spoke via Zoom after the event. He stressed that one of ASI's members had contacted him and thanked him. "She called our lutfisk dinner the Happy Meal of the year and of Christmas. We made a difference in her life," he emphasized (Zoom interview, January 27, 2021).

The drive-through lutfisk dinner thus renews old performances and introduces new ones (figure 9.3). The ritual incorporates the existing notion of fast food as incompatible with the perceived care required in Scandinavian cooking in general. When the drive-through lutfisk dinner is described as the year's Happy Meal, a connection is made between Christmas's religious significance and fast food and commercial culture. To make sense of this connection, one needs to have knowledge of both practices. Most important, the ASI situated the ritualized Swedish American lutfisk within the twenty-first–century Covid-19 pandemic.

DRIVE-THROUGH LUTFISK DINNER AT THE AMERICAN SWEDISH INSTITUTE

As in Sweden and Norway, the preparation of lutfisk varies slightly from place to place, but the meal often includes boiled potatoes, béchamel sauce, and allspice. ASI combines in its lutfisk dinner several dishes that are in demand for Christmas among Minnesotans of Swedish and Norwegian heritage.

The ASI menu, posted on the website as part of advertising the event, was described as follows:

FIGURE 9.3. The lutfisk dinner is packed in boxes in the ASI kitchen and stacked, waiting to be delivered to guests in their cars. Each part of the meal is delivered in a separate small paper container, all of which are placed on a plastic plate together with cutlery and a napkin. The meal is delivered ready to eat even in the car. *Courtesy*, Curt Pederson.

> Oven-baked lutfisk
> Swedish meatballs
> Red potatoes
> Cucumber salad (*note*: refrigerator pickles with parsley)
> Lefse, a traditional Norwegian flatbread
> Clarified butter and béchamel sauce
> Dessert: rice pudding with lingonberry sauce and gingerbread
> BYOS—bring your own spices
> Price: $40 per person for ASI members / $45 per person for non-members

According to the magazine *ASI Posten*, the organization has been serving a lutfisk dinner to its members for more than forty years. In 2020, the situation was different: no dinners were served in the churches, and the museum was closed to visitors. As an organization, ASI wanted to create an impact among members of society and make itself visible: "To remain relevant in our community and do what we do best, we must adapt and innovate. Lutfisk in itself is a strong Swedish American tradition. Combining this with a drive-thru gives it a fun, unique, and playful twist. It's also a way of serving food that's completely COVID-safe" (*Star Tribune*, October 21, 2020). This is how Bruce Karstadt presented the lutfisk dinner when the *Star Tribune* asked why the museum chose to host a drive-through dinner. According to Karstadt, the museum's management and staff never doubted that a lutfisk dinner would be held in 2020, but the staff thought long and hard about how to make it happen. They arrived at the solution in which Fika restaurant prepared and dished up the food in ASI campus's commercial kitchens; ASI staff acted as servers.

MASKS AND PPE: PLANNING AND IMPLEMENTATION

The ASI's decision to serve a drive-through lutfisk dinner in a Covid-safe manner required extensive planning that went beyond the ritual performed in other years, when the museum restaurant prepared and served the food. Staff members from the museum's experience department were tasked with organizing the event. As with many other rituals, preparation took much longer than its staging. At ASI, the run-up began in September.[9] In October, notice of the "lutfisk takeout" was sent to ASI members and advertised on the museum's website: "November 15th. RSVP by November 8th. From 2 p.m. to 6 p.m., with pick-ups every half hour." By November 8, tickets had sold out, and museum staff expected to serve more than 200 guests in a parking lot that fits 123 cars. The following memo with instructions was sent to the staff: "If you work at ASI during the day and park in your usual spot, please move your car by 3:45 p.m. The entire parking lot along Oakland Ave. will be earmarked for cars waiting to be served, and also for guests who wish to eat on-site in their car. We require as much social distancing as possible. No staff are allowed to park there! The entire side towards Park Avenue will be reserved for customer food pickup." On November 14, the day before the event took place, a timetable and the following instructions were distributed: "According to the weather report, the weather will be overcast and cold. Dress accordingly. As they say in Swedish, 'there's no bad weather, only bad clothes.' Wear a jacket, long johns, boots, and gloves! And remember, *wear your facemask at all times* (original emphasis)!"

---

9   In September, I received a draft description of plans from the curator with a note saying "guess what's cooking at ASI. I think you'd enjoy this!"

The request to wear warm clothes does not precipitate comment among Minnesotans. But staff members of Swedish descent giggled at the stern order to wear a mask. They know their lutfisk jokes, and the curator who knows his *Lutfisk Digest*—a joke book that satirizes dinners where participants forgather wearing nose plugs or oxygen masks—found it hard to contain his laughter. Gloves, in the context of the museum, also attract little notice. Both cotton and latex gloves are used for handling artifacts. But face masks in a museum context are only used to remove mold or vermin, and it is here that several contexts, both parodic and serious, combine to make new lutfisk jokes. The combination of the lutfisk with masks and personal protective equipment (PPE) reinforces belonging among the already initiated. It forms a symbolic bond among those with Swedish American cultural competence.

Traveling to a far-flung church or waiting in line for lutfisk is a ritual, a pilgrimage that creates a context, which is the phenomenon ASI deliberately sought to capture with its drive-through event. The approach combined such phenomena as the lutfisk dinners, the pilgrimage to the dinners, and the shoppers lined up outside Scandinavian specialty stores. Drive-through lutfisk connected the present with the past, the pandemic with the time before and the time to come. Drive-through lutfisk combined the cultural heritage of museums with ecclesiastical heritage, secular life, and Christian tradition. Elements of play notoriously allow for both paradox and ambivalence, and the lutfisk jokes allow people of Scandinavian immigrant descent to honor, but at the same time mark a distance from, the traditions of the old homeland. Swedish Americans' love-hate relationship with Lutfisk is evident. As one friend explained: "I see lutfisk as part of our heritage . . . We eat the lutfisk to honor those brave souls who had the daring and courage to leave their ancestral homes, travel across the ocean, and make their way to this bleak and dark prairie . . . So instead of that fine wine, take a spoonful of lutfisk and toast the Swedish pioneers who once brought us here."

Even if people appreciate the jokes about this presumably stinky and jelly-like fish, they may also think the lutfisk meal is a tradition that should continue, even if only once a year, at Christmas. Turning up one's nose at lutfisk is, to people who cherish the tradition, disrespecting to those who deserve the utmost respect: the ancestors and their migration heritage.

However, today, Lutfisk is marketed based on ethnic stereotypes and even racialized differences, in the same way as Chinese sweet-and-sour dishes and Uncle Ben's–brand rice and products such as Swedish *köttbullar*, Norwegian *lefse*, Danish *aebleskiver*, and Icelandic fermented shark, *hákarl* (Comaroff and Comaroff 2009; Klein 2000). These foods carve a space for inclusion and exclusion, nearness and distance, equality and hierarchy. While cooking, serving, and consuming Lutfisk is a tradition that immigrants from Scandinavian countries brought to America in the nineteenth century, its role in ritualized play is receiving much more attention in its transatlantic context than in the countries where it is said to originate.

CONCLUSIONS

The analysis in this chapter has shown how Lutfisk enables people to symbolically address a variety of experiences in life, both past and present. At a time when few people prepare lutfisk by rinsing it and soaking it in lye, lutfisk and its rituals have found new life in other formats. It has become a frame and a meta-communicative sign that at once unites and deepens, excludes, and creates distance. But it can also serve as an integrator into Scandinavian American culture and community. Although lutfisk's ritual significance is most evident as a prelude to and part of December's Christmas celebrations, lutfisk representations are a vital part of public events throughout the year. As a component of secular rituals, those representations also comment on religious ones. Secular rituals offer the possibility of combining religious ritual and play, which provides an existential sustainability that is flexible and sensitive.

After the secular versions of the rituals and the creative play have ended, lutfisk and its multipurpose substance live on in stories. One of many examples is the float maker and creator of the lutfisk fins in Lindsborg, whose creative play served as a substitute for the annual lutfisk-soaking ritual that took place in his childhood at his grandmother's home. Through creating, using, and discarding the lutfisk fins, they became part of a ritual that marks the changing seasons and the year's progress. In his own way, he maintains his *individual part* of the collective ritual process (cf. Drewal 1992; Mechling 1991; Turner 2012) to keep the creative play going. Satisfaction arises when he can surprise the audience and surpass his previous creations.

Staged as a smelly, jelly-like mythical substance, lutfisk breaks out in a seemingly spontaneous performance, in which aversion to it is demonstrated with grimaces, nose clips, oxygen masks, and masks covering the mouth and nose. Its smell and texture are used to express ambivalence, disapproval, and distance. Tests of strength, often with exaggerated agonism—for instance, in the form of eating disgusting foods—play an important role in the processes when collectives playfully define themselves and each other in a multifaceted society (cf. Drewal 1992; Turner 2012). Exposing groups, companies, or individuals who hold power to the smell of lutfisk is both affirmative and subversive. In play, one is permitted to simultaneously like and dislike lutfisk and what it may symbolize. Within the elements of play, high can become low, which is to the advantage of Swedish Americans and Norwegian Americans in this case, since it permits poking fun at one's own group and representing the multivarious layers and versions of Scandinavian American life.

The re-creation of lutfisk play articulates the importance of the creative process in people's lives and the importance of fellowship in shaping sustainable social communities. While very few may watch a lutfisk-themed parade float pass by, or participate in a lutfisk-eating contest, or line up for the lutfisk drive-through at the American Swedish Institute, the message spreads through the surrounding networks, including social media. Those in the know recognize that playing with lutfisk and the multifaceted jokes about its smell and texture are acts of resistance to real or imagined threats. Energy crisis, war, and pandemic—anything can be articulated using lutfisk. While the threats to be met and overcome are very serious, the means of engaging them are marked by acts that incite laughter. At the same time, the fact that a vast number of people are familiar with lutfisk as a comic marker and a meta-communicative signal helps maintain the importance of serving and eating lutfisk as a serious and religious act and a dominant symbol (Turner 2012; Turner and Turner 1995, 245) in Scandinavian America.

Playing with lutfisk in a ritual context has not diminished with time. It has instead persisted and reappeared in renewed forms. Many of the religious rituals have been secularized, and the festivals and artistic expressions of floats have been joined by jocular materializations—including mass-produced stickers, coffee mugs, and, more recently, digital variants such as recorded lutfisk dances and drive-through dinners. These expressions have renewed the old performative genre while introducing new ones. In my analysis of lutfisk's roles, I have shown that ritual and play share a great deal. Secularized rituals can accommodate religious ritual as well as play. They provide ways to remain secular and at play while connecting with the religious world.

ACKNOWLEDGMENTS. Thanks to friends and relatives in the US for having shared lutfisk experiences in different shapes and helping me appreciate and understand the ritual context of playing with lutfisk. Many thanks to the late Curt Pederson and his team and to Bruce Karstadt. Thanks to Jim Leary, Janet Gilmore, and Tom O'Dell, who made valuable suggestions. Thanks to the Riksbankens Jubileumsfond for funding the project "When the Budget Is Tight, Whose Heritage Counts the Most," which enabled me to write this text.

REFERENCES

Unprinted Sources

The chapter is based on fieldwork and digital collaboration fieldwork, including Facetime, conversations, interviews, email correspondence, and photos. The materials are kept in the author's collection.

Literature

Bakhtin, Mikhail. 1984 [1946/1965]. *Rabelais and His World*. Bloomington: Indiana University Press.
Bateson, Gregory. 1956. "The Message 'This Is Play.'" In *Group Processes*, edited by Bertram Schaffner, 145–242. New York: Josiah Macy Foundation.
Blehr, Barbro. 1995. "'Og føler intenst et eller annet' 17 maj i Stockholm ur en deltagares perspektiv." In *Gatan är vår: Ritualer på offentliga platser*, edited by Barbro Klein, 107–33. Stockholm: Carlssons.
Blehr, Barbro. 2000. *En norsk besvärjelse: 17 maj-firande vid 1900-talets slut*. Nora, Sweden: Nya Doxa.
Bronner, Simon J. 2010. "Framing Folklore: An Introduction." *Western Folklore* 69 (3–4): 275–97.
Comaroff, John L., and Jean Comaroff. 2009. *Ethnicity, Inc*. Chicago: University of Chicago Press.

Drewal, Margaret Thompson. 1992. *Yoruba Ritual: Performers, Play, Agency*. Bloomington: Indiana University Press.

Engman, Jonas. 1999. "Rituell process, tradition och media: Socialdemokratisk första maj i Stockholm." PhD dissertation, Stockholms Universitet, Stockholm.

van Gennep, Arnold. 1960 [1909]. *The Rites of Passage*. Chicago: University of Chicago Press.

Gilmore, Janet C. 1997. "Making Time, Honoring Connections, Recording Meaning." In *Wisconsin Folk Art*, edited by Robert Teske, 29–47. Cederburg, WI: Cederburg Cultural Center.

Gradén, Lizette. 2003. "On Parade: Making Heritage in Lindsborg, Kansas." Acta Universitatis Upsaliensis Studia Multiethnica 15. PhD dissertation, Uppsala Universitet, Uppsala.

Gradén, Lizette. 2017. "Selected Stops along the Norwegian Highway: Norwegian-American Heritage Practice in Seattle after 1945." In *Norwegian-American Essays: Freedom and Migration in a Norwegian-American Context*, edited by Terje Mikael Hasle Joranger, 225–55. Oslo: Novus.

Handelman, Don. 1980. "Play and Ritual: Complementary Frames of Meta-Communication." In *It's a Funny Thing, Humor*, edited by Anthony J. Chapman and Hugh C. Foot, 185–92. Oxford: Permamon.

Handelman, Don. 1998. *Models and Mirrors: Towards an Anthropology of Public Events*. New York: Berghahn.

Handelman, Don. 2004. "Why Ritual in Its Own Right: How So?" *Social Analysis* 48 (2): 1–32.

Harrison, Rodney. 2021. "Heritage Practices as Future Making Practices." In *Cultural Heritage and the Future*, edited by Cornelius Holtorf and Anders Högberg, 29–45. London: Routledge.

Hellspong, Mats. 1991. *Korset, fanan och fotbollen*. Stockholm: Carlssons.

Huizinga, Johan. 2016. *Homo Ludens: A Study of the Play-Element in Culture*. Kettering, OH: Angelico.

Kirshenblatt-Gimblett, Barbara. 1999: "Playing to the Senses: Food as a Performance Medium." *Performance Research* 4 (1): 1–30.

Kirshenblatt-Gimblett, Barbara. 2004a. "Foreword." In *Culinary Tourism: Material Worlds*, edited by Lucy Long, xi–xiv. Lexington: University of Kentucky Press.

Kirshenblatt-Gimblett, Barbara. 2004b. "Intangible Heritage as Metacultural Production." *Museum International* 56 (1–2): 52–65.

Klein, Barbro, ed. 1995. *Gatan är vår: Ritualer på offentliga platser*. Stockholm: Carlssons.

Klein, Barbro. 2000. "Folklore, Heritage Politics, and Ethnic Diversity: Thinking about the Past and the Future." In *Folklore, Heritage Politics, and Ethnic*

Diversity, edited by Pertti Anttonen, 23–36. Botkyrka, Sweden: Multicultural Centre.

Leary, James P. 1996. "Ole in Dairyland: Scandinavian Ethnic Humor." In *Down Home in the Dairyland: A Listener's Guide*, edited by James P. Leary and Richard March, 59–62. Madison: University of Wisconsin–Extension.

Mechling, Jay. 1991. "Homo Ludens Subsp. Scientificus." *Play and Culture* 4: 258–71.

Mechling, Jay. 1999. "Children's Folklore in Residential Institutions." In *Children's Folklore: A Source Book*, 2nd ed., edited by Brian Sutton-Smith, Jay Mechling, Thomas W. Johnson, and Felicia R. McMahon, 273–92. Logan: Utah State University Press.

Mechling, Jay. 2005. "Boy Scouts and the Manly Art of Cooking." *Food and Foodways* 13: 67–89.

Moore, Sally F., and Barbara G. Myerhoff, eds. 1977. *Secular Ritual*. Assen, The Netherlands: Van Gorcum.

Nikielska-Sekula, Karolina. 2019. "Migrating Heritage? Recreating Ancestral and New Homeland Heritage in the Practices of Immigrant Minorities." *International Journal of Heritage Studies* 25 (11): 1113–27.

Turner, Edith. 2012. *Communitas: The Anthropology of Collective Joy*. Basingstoke: Palgrave Macmillan.

Turner, Victor, and Edith Turner. 1995. *Image and Pilgrimage in Christian Culture: Anthropological Perspectives*. New York: Columbia University Press.

10

Playing for Keeps

Tradition, Transformation, and Anti-Racist Protest in an American Capital

SALLIE ANNA PISERA

In protest, we grapple physically and emotionally with space, identity, and relationships as we perform communicative acts of re-inscription that subvert hegemonic narratives (Brogden and Harper 2021, 38). Protestors practice serious play, "operat[ing] as guerrillas in the cultural terrain in which they live, achieving surprise through a combination of transgression and prefiguration," and engaging in "play and ritual that help to resolve societal conflict" (Bogad 2016, 5). In the case of Madison, Wisconsin–based actions responding to the murder of George Floyd, protestors practiced serious play by calling on participants to reclaim space and narratives and to witness, memorialize, and place themselves within the perspectives of Black people murdered by police. Protest organizers in Madison during summer 2020 furthermore called on participants to imagine and create a world where "we protect us" by performing solidarity and grassroots community-care at actions and by learning and passing on the knowledge and traditions of the abolitionist Black movement through anti-racist and anti-capitalist actions.

During summer 2020, I turned out in the streets of Madison along with thousands of others to grapple with and lift up a regional tragedy that became an international rallying point for people opposing police

https://doi.org/10.7330/9781646426751.c010

violence. In the interviews I conducted following that summer, place and memorializing again returned as significant themes in protest. Activists in Madison during summer 2020 created opportunities for collective transformation through expressive genres like chanting, occupying space, learning and teaching activist traditions, and celebrating marginalized heritages and knowledge systems to enact personal and social transformation. This chapter studies the use of play elements in producing and communicating political messages and shaping a political movement. I participated in the protests that are described, and in this text, my own perspectives blend with those of the organizers I interviewed.

WHY NOW?

In the days leading up to Saturday, May 30, 2020, I could feel the heat build. It was on Monday, May 25, that George Floyd was crushed to death under the knee of Minneapolis police officer Derek Chauvin. Within just a day or two later, we had all seen and heard at least snippets from the video showing what happened: George's crying and pleading; Chauvin's smugness as he choked the life out of this man. For Black and Brown people in the US and for allies who have been supporting the Black Lives Matter movement for nearly a decade, none of these details or their outcomes were new. What was different was the massive wave of regional, national, and international support George Floyd's case received.

The context surrounding George Floyd's murder and its response is complex, and there is arguably no single reason why the circumstances aligned in that final week of May 2020 to spark such a massive movement. Perhaps it was the predictable result of four years of festering anger over the Donald Trump presidency. Perhaps it was influenced by the Covid-19 pandemic and the lockdowns ongoing in many places, the restlessness that pervaded society. Perhaps it had to do with the eyewitness video documenting Floyd's killing—its clarity and brutality and the amazing speed at which it spread around the world (Allen 2022). Perhaps George Floyd's murder came at a particularly opportune time for anti-racist activists in many places: a time when they were ready to organize and to draw connections between Floyd's murder and issues ongoing in their own communities; a time when they were ready to speak on local, national, and international levels about the intersectionality of oppressions and the interconnectivity of struggles through a human rights lens (Rameau, Adams, and Robinson 2014). Regardless of the reasons, in Madison and around the nation and the world, we witnessed a coalescing of people, transformed from individuals representing different walks of life and different worldviews into a collective oppositional body chanting "Whose streets? Our streets."

NO SINGLE REASON, NO SINGLE RESPONSE

Researchers observing and describing African diaspora folklore have commented on the polyphonic and polyrhythmic nature of its layered materials, movements, and sounds (Barkley Brown 1989, 1991; Sithole 1972; Steiner 2019; Thompson 1984, xiii, 207–23). Civil rights organizing in the United States and elsewhere is infused with the polyrhythms and polyphonics of Black folklore, and I experienced many performative, Afrocentric modes of inquiry and opposition in Madison protests responding to the murder of George Floyd. Chanting blended with dancing blended with sign waving blended with music; volunteers served food; artists responded through visual media; and the crowd moved toward centers of action as they were drawn to the irresistible,[1] healing *communitas* of speeches and music and—eventually—as they were pushed and pulled in chaotic standoffs and pursuits with armored riot police kettling protestors and firing tear gas.

A polyphony of elements thus combined to create a layered response that played toward a common goal of liberation whose symmetry and sense of collective action was borne out through the diversity of participants' actions, utterances, movements, and creations in Madison during that last week of May 2020. This symmetry borne out through diversity resonates with pianist Ojeda Penn's description of jazz music as "an expression of true democracy, for each person is allowed, in fact required, to be an individual, to go his/her own way, and yet to do so in concert with the group—to be an individual in the context of the community" (Penn 1986, quoted in Barkley Brown 1989, 924). The ensemble of different modes in protest offers "different potential for making meaning" in this emergent, playful, and ever-changing context (Kress 2010, 79).

---

1 Local activist Mahnker Dahnweih (interview 2021) described to me how she plans for protest actions by posing the rhetorical question: "How am I making this movement irresistible?"

Likewise, the ability of participants and onlookers in the spectacle of the Madison protest actions to shift roles and perspectives and to "move in and out of the action" mirrors features of Yoruba ritual performance and play in that West African context, where "the relationships between spectator and spectacle are unstable, one always collapsing into the other. Participatory spectacle does not set up fixed unequal power relationships between the gazer and the object of the gaze; rather the participatory nature of Yoruba spectacle itself means that subject and object positions are continually in flux during performance" (Drewal 1992, 15).

Playful, shifting positionalities were manifested in the Madison protests responding to the death of George Floyd through elements such as chants that implored participants to witness in the call-and-response style of African American oral tradition. In Yoruba ritual, furthermore, play elements are introduced to open up possibilities for changing locked situations (Drewal 1992, 12–28). In Madison, protestors used their bodies and their creativity to march, dance, hold signs, make art, feed and care for one another, and generally occupy—unlocking spaces of state and capitalist power to introduce narratives of divestment from police infrastructure and investment in grassroots community.

In several of her publications, Black feminist scholar Elsa Barkley Brown underscores the significance of such modes of layering and polyrhythmic interaction in Black culture by referring to a story told by African American spiritual teacher Yeye Luisah Teish (1985). In the story, Yeye Teish describes returning to visit her family in New Orleans and immediately being met with a wellspring of overlapping conversation, which Yeye Teish calls "gumbo ya ya"—creole for "everyone talks at once": "It is through gumbo ya ya that Yeye learns everything that has happened in her family and community and she conveys the essential information about herself to the group. That is, it is through gumbo ya ya that Yeye tells the history of her sojourn to her family and they tell theirs to her. They do this simultaneously because, in fact, their histories are joined—occurring simultaneously, in connection, in dialogue with each other. To relate their tales separately would be to obliterate their connection" (Barkley Brown 1991, 85).

The powers of community interconnectedness and of storytelling are deeply embedded in Black traditions and cultural expressions. This "solidarity of community" is present in the warm embrace of family, as described by Yeye Teish (1985), and has simultaneously been a force of survival in the darker contexts of slavery and continuing oppressions (Starhawk 1985, xvii). This cultural approach to speaking and acting in concert and in relationship with others has likewise become an important mode of power building in the Black Lives Matter movement. Launched in 2013 by Alicia Garza, Patrisse Khan-Cullors, and Opal Tometi in response to the shooting death of seventeen-year-old Trayvon Martin and the subsequent acquittal of his killer, George Zimmerman, #BlackLivesMatter sought to connect the many cases of Black people murdered by supremacist actors—both those acting directly on behalf of the state, like police, and private citizens enabled by the state, like neighborhood vigilante Zimmerman. Garza, Khan-Cullors, Tometi, and the people they inspire furthermore "take an expansive view of 'state violence'" as defined not only by "police shootings of unarmed black men, women, and children" but also consisting of "slower but no less pernicious forms of violence such as environmental racism and systemic neglect by the medical industry" (Austin et al. 2020, 15–16).

This intersectional truth-telling mirrors Barkley Brown's (1991, 85) observation that "history is also everyone talking at once, multiple rhythms being played simultaneously." In discussing the different lives lived by women of different races and classes in the United States, Barkley Brown calls on other scholars to "recognize not only differences but also the relational nature of those differences." She elaborates: "Middle-class white women's lives are not just different from working-class white, black, and Latina women's lives; it is important to recognize that middle-class women live the lives they do precisely because working-class women live the lives they do. White women and women of colour not only live different lives but white women live the lives they do in large part because women of colour live the ones they do" (86).

This same desire to draw connections dismissed and obscured by the American Police State catalyzed protest leaders and participants who turned out in Madison streets in response to the murder of George Floyd. The polyphonic forms of protest they played out flipped hegemonic scripts and sought to transform society in the image of protestors' anti-racist and anti-capitalist aspirations.

HOLDING SPACE IN THE DOWNTOWN LANDSCAPE

Madison is a state capital that for decades has been known as a potent space of activism and lively protests. The layout of downtown Madison's Capitol Square makes it a unique space for engaging in public performances of political discourse and opposition: the publicly accessible but persistently white space of the capitol building centers Madison's Isthmus, opening out onto a square of one-lane avenues that, in turn, fan out into mixed-use streets. Urban planning scholar Tali Hatuka (2018, 34) points out that "city squares have particular power as symbolic meeting places, serving as a pause within the city network." When employed as the setting for protest actions, Hatuka points out that the enclosed nature of a square (1) increases the action's sense of ritual and solidarity, (2) challenges social distances among participants, and (3) prompts marked engagement with and display of symbols in the space in which the congregation of protestors gathers. In the hybrid square/street space of downtown Madison (figure 10.1), the features of protest commonly observed in squares bleed over into those Hatuka observes in street spaces, where protestors engage in dynamic marching; where they can amplify the message and often physically grow the group through interactions with passers-by and bystanders; and where protestors in an action can more effectively call attention to their presence by impeding traffic and paralyzing the city's network (34).

Madison's Capitol Square is also potent as a site for protest because it is home to many overlapping city, county, state, federal, and commercial properties. This fact also makes it a heavily policed area, with fifteen city, county, capitol, state, federal, and university law enforcement agencies all operating within the city limits (Redman 2020). Buildings associated with these law enforcement agencies likewise dominate the Madison skyline. The Wisconsin capitol building rises highest in the center of the Isthmus and is surrounded by numerous government buildings, particularly concentrated along the southern end of the Capitol Square overlooking Lake Monona and the major lakeside highway John Nolen Drive, which was the site of several traffic blockades by protestors responding to the murder of George Floyd during summer 2020. The contentious identity of Madison's Capitol Square as a public space under heavy oversight by the state and with a significant capitalist presence also makes it a location where the

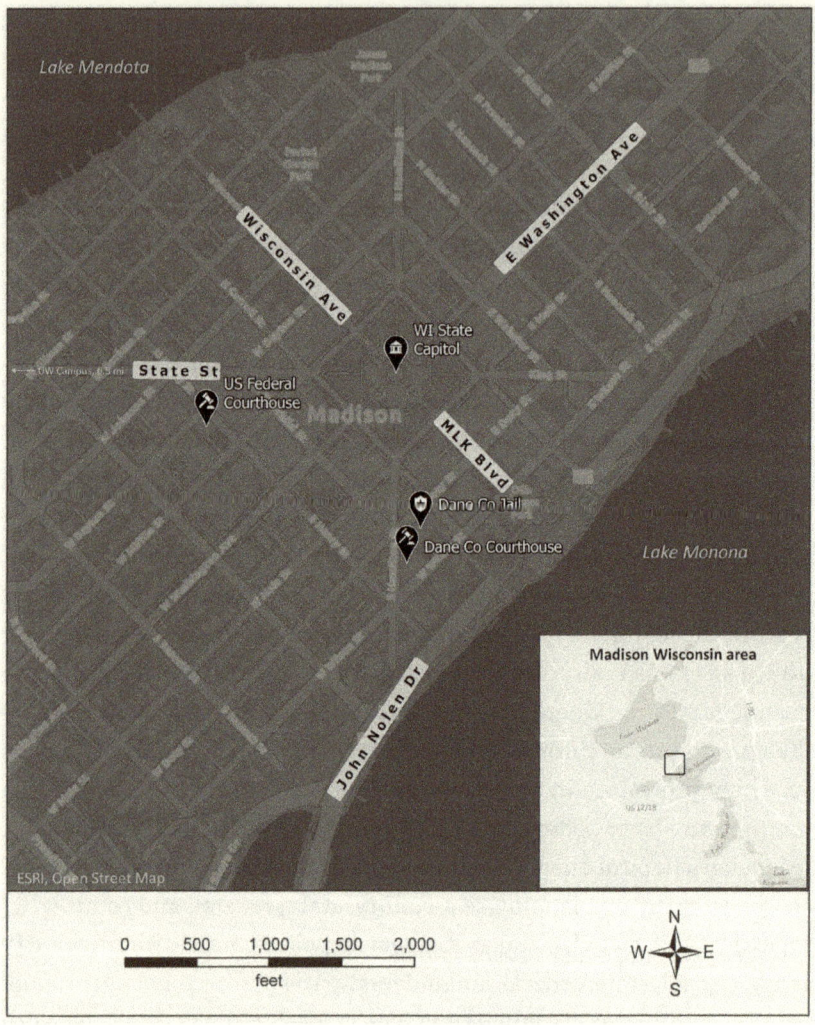

FIGURE 10.1. Map of downtown Madison. *Courtesy*, Kerry Wilcox.

subversive play and rule-breaking behavior inherent in protest can quickly become particularly charged and fraught.

Activist groups operating in downtown Madison are acutely aware of the heavy presence of state control. The area's architectural geography further informs how activists perform their actions. I had the opportunity to speak at length with Mahnker Dahnweih, co-executive director of Freedom, Inc., a Black- and Southeast Asian–led nonprofit founded in Madison in the early 2000s that "engages low- to no-income communities of color" in

Dane County and whose "mission is to achieve social justice through coupling direct services with leadership development and community organizing" (Freedom, Inc. 2017). Freedom, Inc., focuses on building community power not only through protest actions but also through community engagement by hosting dance groups, meal programs, reading groups, and other solidarity groups and community events geared primarily toward Hmong, Khmer, and Black women, children, queer people, and elders.

I have attended a number of Freedom, Inc.–led anti-racist actions in Madison since moving to the city in 2013. The group was particularly visible and involved in the summer 2020 actions responding to George Floyd's murder. Raised in Chicago in a Liberian refugee family, Mahnker has likewise taken part in many anti-racist actions since moving to Madison in 2016 and becoming involved with activist work in the city. She was a key organizer of the march on May 30, 2020, that brought more than 3,000 people to Capitol Square in defense of Black life. Mahnker commented in our interview on how her activist work has shifted the lens through which she views the downtown landscape:

> When I first moved to Madison, when I would go on John Nolen and see the whole city view and everything like that, I was like, "Wow, all the pretty buildings, oh my gosh, that's great." Now, I see the jail. Now I see the courthouse, the federal courthouse. Now I see all these places that I know people got arrested or murdered at. I see places and sites of exclusion for my people, like, that I know that someone that's in my programming wouldn't be able to access that, right? I see the surveillance of the police and things like that. I see different things now that I've had to go to a meeting at the courthouse with one of my clients where I just feel how oppressive it feels, right? Or I've had to go to the jail or I've had to—so, it's just allowing people to understand the landscape or even how these buildings look and how they play a part in making us feel smothered or oppressed. And just wanting other people to understand that these people sit right here and these buildings look really beautiful, but they sit right here and they ruin people's lives literally with the stroke of a pen. (interview with Dahnweih 2021)

Mahnker describes leading call-and-response dialogues during actions to bring awareness to the deeper meanings of places and landscapes and to educate people about where they need to go to get a seat at the table to demand real change: "Everything that I do—or the people who are leading the actions—it's not that I need to know that we're marching past the city council hall, where the mayor is at, that I say 'hey' and people say 'hey.' And I say, 'Y'all know where we're at? This is where the mayor . . . [trails off]'" Callouts deeply situated in the context of place are a major part of the physical play of subversion and opposition at Freedom, Inc., actions held in downtown Madison, the goal of which is to transform participants' awareness through the power of naming and storytelling from a Black, queer, feminist perspective (figure 10.2). This technique is grounded in older African American cultural traditions around calling out and calling in through give-and-take verbal interaction between speakers and audiences (Williams 1972).

In addition to their uses in the reclamation of space and memory, call-and-response chants have the purpose of fostering group engagement and direct democracy decision-making at actions. Mahnker gave examples in our interview of how she lets the groups that join her at an action lead by using call-and-response chants to solicit responses to questions such as whether to stay or go from a particular place. She also talked about leading groups in chanted choruses of "drink water" and "turn the group" as means of giving direction and of practicing techniques like "human shield," which can be employed to guard the group in dangerous encounters with adversaries wielding guns or cars. In this way, chanting becomes a pragmatic means of practicing safety and caring for the group in a mass action. When activists play with non-hierarchical approaches to collective care, they break down boundaries between leader and follower, "open[ing] up the opportunity for a richer, more genuine, and more pluralistic account of equality and democratic life" (Tronto 1996, 149). A space emerges in that playful opening for building collective strength and developing activist leadership—key parts of how Mahnker characterizes a successful action: "To me, [a successful action is] when someone takes on a new role they haven't taken on before, when someone acts as an ambassador for the cause. Even the act of asking five people to come with you to the action is leadership development, right" (interview with Dahnweih 2021).

Voice and presence are powerful concepts in protest. Whether understood literally or metaphorically, voice and presence define the physical subversive play of protest actions. As Hatuka (2018, 105–6) writes:

Playing for Keeps 193

FIGURE 10.2. Collage of photos from the May 30, 2020, march, led in large part by Freedom, Inc. This collage was pasted to plywood that covered the front door of Overture Center for the Arts on State Street during the uprisings that followed the murder of George Floyd. Mahnker Dahnweih appears holding a megaphone in a photo on the bottom left-hand side of the image. Author photo.

To be sure, all protests start with the body. During protests bodies are used for various roles, tasks, and strategies in different places . . . In addition, although often taken for granted as something that needs no explanation, the body is the anchor of a physical protest, becoming a "turbulent performative occasion." Public gatherings enable and enact a performativity of embodied agency, in which we own our bodies and struggle for the right to claim our bodies as "ours." This position implies that both bodies and spaces are performative, with no ontological status or fixed characteristics. Therefore, instead of thinking about spaces and places as preexisting sites in which bodily performances occur, we need to examine bodily performances themselves as constituting or reproducing distance, places, and events. In this respect, the body cannot be separated from the event, and it has the crucial power to adjust and modify the setting of a place—as such, the spatial setting and the body should be regarded as mutually constitutive, creating the event's spatial choreography.

Hatuka points to four key interrelated concepts involved in the study of protest through the lens of spatial choreography: design, bodies, hierarchy, and vulnerability. The interplay of these concepts was particularly salient in instances where Madison protestors who were responding to the murder of George Floyd asserted control over space. Taking over locations by holding and transforming space were some of the most direct ways protestors subverted hegemonic scripts. Mahnker framed occupying space in terms of creating direct, material shifts for people of color in the Madison landscape and social-scape:

> Places where people are afraid to be or were being pushed out of before, we intentionally take up those spaces . . . When you see another Black person murdered on TV or when you hear a siren—there's so many triggers throughout the day, just being Black or being queer or being a woman, and if the action we've done has created a space where folks feel safe and feel validated, that's also a material shift. Like, someone has breathed today and let their shoulders down and had time to think about themselves in a different way than just, like, a survival mode, right? (interview with Dahnweih 2021)

Creating material shifts through the radical Black movement is also about abolition—about taking back and asserting agency over aspects of American society that are built on the legacy of slavery. For Jessica Williams, gender justice director at Freedom, Inc., involvement in radical Black activism did not begin until adulthood, when she started connecting with people in Madison's cooperative housing movement. However, realizations about the toxic relationship between Black people and the US government dawned on her at an early age:

> I think that just based on identity, like, that radical feminist lens, it started before I was politicized in the ways that I am now. Right? Like, I think that being a Black kid—a Black girl—and seeing the ways that my own communities were treated, seeing the things that my mom had to struggle through, seeing the things that other Black women struggled through, and seeing how we were looked at or responded to by other people, right? And just knowing the history of Black people in this country—like, I definitely remember being in the third or fourth grade and being, like, very blatantly, like, f— this country. This is not my country. This country does not love me. No, I will not stand up to say

"pledge allegiance to the flag," I just will not do it. I'm gonna completely ignore it. Right? And no one—like, my family isn't a political family, we didn't have conversations about those things. I believe it was just from my own worldview and my own experience at the age of, like, 10, 11, 12 that I was just like, "I'm not participating in this." Right? I would go to school and I was, like, "I refuse to stand up for the flag, I refuse to say the Allegiance," and my teachers would get so angry, but I felt like I was doing the right thing and I felt very validated, even if no one else was talking with me about that or sharing that belief with me. So yeah, I definitely think about being in that space at such a young age but without people having to tell me, and I think if we look at a lot of Black children and children who are marginalized in other ways, I feel like there's definitely some of that that lives in them. Right? That they see, that they learn, that they just picked up from a really early age. (interview with Williams 2022)

Jessica's first encounter with liberation organizing occurred following the murder of Tony Robinson, a nineteen-year old unarmed Black man, by City of Madison police officer Matt Kenny during a check-person call on March 6, 2015. Jessica told the story of how she had attended a concert by the politically conscious Latino rapper Olmeca that night. During the concert, Olmeca learned about Robinson's shooting death and invited the audience to march to the scene with him to witness. Jessica said this was her first experience with direct action. Watching the events of that night and the protests and actions that occurred in the months that followed in an effort to get justice for the Robinson family had a profound impact on her political journey. She saw the power of showing up in a movement: "It just became this really huge and powerful moment, and I think that is what really shifted something in me. Like, seeing that without this protest and without people in the street, this family would have had so little support. It maybe would have hit the newspapers and would have been just, like, a small blurb in the newspaper. But because so many people showed up and took to the streets that night and did that immediately, Tony Robinson became a name that we know really widely around the city and around the state" (interview with Williams 2022).

In her work at Freedom, Inc., Jessica is an advocate for Black girls and women who experience gender-based violence—violence that in many ways is rooted in the racist, capitalist systems of American settler-colonial society and the legacy of slavery. Thus, occupying spaces in protest is for Jessica an abolitionist act, as the ripples of slavery still structure and inform American social, economic, and government systems. Jessica pinpoints the way chanting at protest marches is integrated with her overreaching political ideology:

> I own everything that this country has. Any good that has come from this country, it is because of my ancestors, it's because of me, it's because it's built up off the backs of people who look like me. You know the chant "Whose streets? Our streets." Really, it is our streets. There's so much that's owed to us that's not acknowledged. There's so much that we've given that's not acknowledged. So in taking those things, I feel like—like, when we occupy streets or when we take over or shut down business as usual, I think a lot of that is about reminding people that these things, they don't exist out of nowhere. They don't exist outside of us. They exist in spite of us and off of the backs of us. (interview with Williams 2022)

Transforming society begins with the body. Challenging white supremacy and capitalist hegemony in the ways protestors responding to the murder of George Floyd did by occupying and disrupting the downtown Madison landscape is contentious and sometimes dangerous—but it can also bring pleasure and transformation through bodily performance. As Mahnker recalled Freedom, Inc.'s summer 2020 occupation of John Nolen Drive, she reminisced about a moment when the crowd sat silently on the highway together in quiet relaxation—hundreds of people gathered, enjoying the breeze from the lake amid what was normally a busy automobile thoroughfare. Pleasure, Mahnker said, is a key aspect of queer, Black, radical feminism because pleasure is the opposite of violence and fear. Pleasure motivates people and is part of world making. Mahnker gave the example of dance at protests as not just about fun but also about participants connecting with their bodies in a serious way—in a way that undoes the harmful dissociation between self, and self and other, caused by capitalism. She asserted that having fun at actions also contributes to the movement, that it is also an act of rebellion and resilience and also represents a material shift. Bodily performance and play by oppressed people reconnecting with their selves and their landscapes is decolonization (Umangay 2016).

PROTEST IS A DOCUMENTARY ACT: AN ETHNOGRAPHIC INTERLUDE

It was late afternoon on Saturday, May 30, 2020. The powerful march I took part in that morning, organized by Freedom, Inc., had hours since finished its winding way from the Dane County Jail, around the Capitol Square, and down East Washington Avenue. The way we had taken over East Washington that morning was like water takes to a dry streambed—I set out with thousands of others down the drive leading out from the capitol building, and it became an unstoppable flood of people pouring over all parts of the avenue as we began our hopeful descent down the hill from the Capitol Square.

Chants sprouted up here and there as signs and people waved and fanned about. We were led by a line of marchers holding a massive banner that read "COMMUNITY CONTROL OF THE POLICE". When we reached the bottom of the hill, organizers paused the march and speeches began. At this point I was near the front of the group, and I looked up to see a police drone hovering just above my head, surveilling the crowd. The atmosphere was like electric hope, and the presence of state surveillance would not deter this sense of possibility. I waved at the drone. I looked up at the crowd of people still descending from the square. We felt big, I thought; we felt joyous.

Now it was several hours later, and that joyous mood had turned into more aggressive indignation. At first, I avoided the crowd, which had assembled on State Street following the morning's actions with more destructive intent. I returned to my apartment a few blocks from the Capitol Square and watched the livestreams from State Street in an anxious mood.

As I followed social media updates, I learned that the crowd had attacked and destroyed the Under Armour store on State Street. Under Armour contracts with police and the military to provide gear and uniforms. This told me that the collective mind behind the crowd on State Street was intelligent, even if I wanted to avoid their aggression—they knew what they were doing. But still, I stayed home.

Then I began to hear on the livestreams that police had assembled and were firing tear gas. I felt a pang in my heart and so I had to go out, pulled by some feeling of needing to pick a side in this battle going on just a few blocks away. I arrived at the top of State Street holding my favorite sign, a well-worn broadside I had picked up at an anti–Donald Trump rally a few years before that read "FREE HEALTHCARE AND UNION JOBS, NOT RACIST HATE." In my purse I carried a jug of milk, taken hastily from my fridge, to pour into the eyes of people who were gassed. A home remedy of resistance.

When I arrived on the scene, the police had separated the large group of protestors into two units, one at the top of State Street and one a few blocks down. The smell of tear gas—a particular kind of smoky smell, like burnt chili peppers tainted with chemicals—lingered in the air, as did a grayish-purple fog left over from the gas.

Some protestors at the scene were very agitated, yelling in the faces of the riot cops. Others stood slightly back, mostly observing, with signs raised here and there. An air of uncertainty and anxious anticipation was alive in the space. I looked around and only serious, mostly silent faces looked back at me. I saw crossed arms, frowns, and furrowed brows. A few angry shouts erupted here and there. Occasionally, a water bottle would launch from amid the assembled crowd and pelt the police line before us. I looked up at the rooftops above us and saw police scouts looking down.

The line of police before us stood firmly shoulder to shoulder, serious and mostly silent. One of the cops—a big white guy—kept shaking his head from ear to ear, cracking his neck as if preparing for a fight in a ring. Another cop—a smaller Black man—made eye contact with me and glanced at my sign, giving me a barely perceptible nod—of agreement? I felt a rush of dismay, uncertain about what to do with this man's approval, sent out across the invisible but firm demarcation line between us.

Occasionally, a loudspeaker would ignite and a stern, cold voice would blare out the category of trespass violation we were collectively breaking, warning us that a gassing was imminent. No one cared. The canister would be launched and everyone would bolt momentarily, moving in closer again when the gray, shimmery fog started to settle. As we became more accustomed to the game, some stayed behind when canisters launched. Those protestors who chose to take the police up on their game of chess gathered big orange traffic cones from a nearby construction site and used them to cover unexploded canisters, imitating a technique we had learned from pro-democracy activists in Hong Kong the previous year. The cone wielders hopped from canister to canister, neutralizing the gas.

Here and there, I pulled the jug of milk from my purse to assist people with red eyes and tears streaming down their faces. I particularly recall administering the liquid into the eyes of a young white man wearing an Industrial Workers of the World patch on his hat. I thought about the various symbols and groups that intersected in this space, all seeking liberation from the American Police State.

A group of protestors had the idea to address the root of our problem by taking a fence from the nearby construction site and wrapping it around the line of police, caging *them* in. For a moment, it was like we had won. Having separated ourselves from the police with this fence, people began to cheer in victory. I saw smiles erupting once again as arms raised over people's heads in happy defiance.

But the police resisted the walling in, and reinforcements soon arrived—entering the field from behind, near Wisconsin Avenue. They ran along the edge of the buildings lining the square, covering themselves with riot shields held Roman-style as water bottles and shouts of indignation lashed them. A few brave protestors gave chase, but soon the police reinforcement made it behind the fence line—which was torn down brusquely—and the tear gas launcher sprang to life once more. This time I stood close and in the center of the group, holding my sign high. The canister whooshed into the air and landed at my feet. A flash of red filled my entire field of view as it exploded, and I turned and ran.

Later, in the night, after the National Guard had been called to the Capitol Square to enforce a curfew, I was joined by friends and we flung the windows wide open, playing political breakbeat loud for the passing armored vehicles to hear:

Run, citizen, run
The policeman has got a gun.
(Vader 2001)

SAY THEIR NAMES

Supremacist systems are adept at maintaining their own institutional memory and at systematically stripping institutional memory and the means to create it from the people they oppress. Alternative means of knowledge keeping and sharing, such as folklore, stories, archives, and "evolving repertoires of resistance" (Bogad 2016, 3), thus become particularly important in the context of tactical performance. Passing on tradition within the radical Black movement is an important part of keeping the cause alive in a context where the message is sustained largely through subaltern expressive communication. Protest actions therefore function as sites of teaching and learning—a practice and praxis of serious play. As Mahnker Dahnweih said in our interview, "It's not like people are going to get this kind of popular education or political education anywhere else" (interview with Dahnweih 2021).

Protest is therefore a documentary act: by protesting, we witness, remember, and memorialize through modes of expressive communication that bring people and moments from the past and present forward into the future. In chants like "Say Their Names," the activists who showed up in Madison in summer 2020 brought forth—consciously and not—ancient African traditions of speaking powerfully and simultaneously to enact change within the context of community. This simple, flexible chant goes, for example, "Say his name. George Floyd." or "Say her name. Breonna Taylor." It can be easily repurposed to name and memorialize the many victims of police violence. A more complex riff on this basic chant, heard often in Madison, goes "What's his name? Tony Robinson. Who did they kill? Tony Robinson. Who did they murder? Tony Robinson."

Writing about elegiac poetry that emerged through the Black Lives Matter movement, scholars Tiffany Austin, Sequoia Maner, Emily Ruth Rutter, and darlene anita scott (2020, 14) note that "the elegy has proven to be a vital vehicle for countering white media representations that either ignore black pain or individualize it, eclipsing systemic forms of oppression in the process. Within these works, the 'I' often manifests as an elegiac 'we,' and readers are encouraged to become more than passive bystanders. Instead, they are enjoined to participate in the liberation struggle, refusing the enervating forces of state violence, social apathy, and sociocultural amnesia about America's racially unjust past and present."

Similarly, protestors who engage in memorializing through chanting at actions are called to lift up and place themselves in the position of Black people murdered by police—layering their voices and experiences through chants that memorialize victims of white supremacist violence, reflect on leaders and martyrs who have come before, and call forth older traditions of protest and marginalized knowledge systems. As Audre Lorde (2007, 37) wrote, "Poetry is not a luxury . . . [It] is the way we help give name to the nameless so that it can be thought." The flood of voices chanting "Say Their

Names" becomes like libations poured out in African ceremonies that recall ancestors and bring forth their energy (interview with Williams 2022).

Protestors who took to the streets responding to the murder of George Floyd found solidarity in repeating the words Floyd himself pleaded with as Derek Chauvin choked him: "I can't breathe." The imperative mood of this simple, final statement denies speakers and listeners emotional distance and makes Floyd's death something that is brought forth and memorialized again and again as protestors insist that it has not passed, the case is not closed, and justice has yet to be served (Austin et al. 2020, 13–14, 20–21; Brogden and Harper 2021, 40). The chant punctuates the air insistently, and the sound—like many uttered by Black people speaking out against their own oppression—"occurs where it should not" (LaBelle 2019, 33; Scott 2020, 57).

In our interview, Mahnker Dahnweih expressed her belief that chanting is the most powerful form of protest performance:

> For me, the chants are extending a sacred part of my lineage or of my history or my struggle to all these different people, because our chants are all very intentional and they come from somewhere . . . It's this collective way of memorializing and keeping people living in the words that we say. My favorite chant is the power and transformation chant.
>
> [Sallie: How does that go?]
>
> It's the one that goes,
> Power
> Transformation
> I want it
> I need it
> I got to, got to, got to have it.
>
> . . . It's a sacred thing to share. It's a thing around trust, right? If you're here, we're letting you into this tradition and into this world. (interview with Dahnweih 2021)

Through the introduction and co-creation of play elements such as chants, organizers like Mahnker and Jessica open possibilities for transformation and change. In the ritual of protest carried out through these modes of play, protestors, spectators, and the society they share engage in an "exercise of power that constructs for the participants a sense of self, both individually and collectively" (Drewal 1992, 22). For Mahnker, organizing in summer 2020 was difficult but indeed transformative. As we recalled events together during our interview almost a year later, Mahnker's memory was drawn in particular to the massive march on May 30—the 3,000-person caravan that wound its way around the capitol and made its big, hopeful descent down East Washington Avenue:

> Honestly, I feel like that day kind of broke something open in me. As an organizer, there's things you dream about but that you don't think you'll ever see—and I never thought I'd see something like that in Madison. Both in terms of the personal transformations and the organizers that planned that and just working through really traumatic experiences—and in the people, I felt this sense of, like, "we've been here before, and we've been fighting so long, but we're gonna do this again." That just made me, like—it renewed my hope and trust in the process . . . I don't think I've ever really claimed Madison. And I was, like, "I'm proud of Madison." (interview with Dahnweih 2021)

REFERENCES

Unprinted Sources

Interviews recorded during research fieldwork, author's collection: Dahnweih, Mahnker, interview with author via Zoom, February 9, 2021. Williams, Jessica, interview with author via Zoom, May 27, 2022.

Unprinted lecture by Ojeda Penn, March 1986: "Jazz: American Classical Music as a Philosophic and Symbolic Entity." Faculty lecture series, Fifteenth Anniversary of African and African-American Studies Program, Emory University, Atlanta.

Literature

Allen, Phil, Jr. 2022. *The Prophetic Lens: The Camera and Black Moral Agency from MLK to Darnella Fraizer*. Minneapolis: Augsburg Fortress.

Austin, Tiffany, Sequoia Maner, Emily Ruth Rutter, and darlene anita scott. 2020. *Revisiting the Elegy in the Black Lives Matter Era*. New York: Routledge.

Barkley Brown, Elsa. 1989. "African American Women's Quilting." *Signs* 14 (4): 921–29.

Barkley Brown, Elsa. 1991. "Polyrhythms and Improvization: Lessons for Women's History." *History Workshop* 31: 85–90.
Bogad, Lawrence M. 2016. *Tactical Performance: The Theory and Practice of Serious Play*. New York: Routledge.
Brogden, Jim, and Douglas Harper. 2021. "R WE LOUD ENOUGH: Re-inscribing Monuments in the Public Sphere by the Black Lives Matter Movement." *Art and the Public Space* 10 (1): 37–53.
Drewal, Margaret Thompson. 1992. *Yoruba Ritual: Performers, Play, Agency*. Bloomington: Indiana University Press.
Freedom, Inc. 2017. About Freedom, Inc. Accessed July 19, 2022. https://freedom-inc.org/index.php?page=about-us.
Garth Vader. 2001. "Pig Pop." K. Ktus Tribe Records, France.
Hatuka, Tali. 2018. *The Design of Protest: Choreographing Political Demonstrations in Public Space*. Austin: University of Texas Press.
Kress, Gunther. 2010. *Multimodality: A Social Semiotic Approach to Contemporary Communication*. London: Routledge.
LaBelle, Brandon. 2019. *Acoustic Territories: Sound Culture and Everyday Life*. New York: Bloomsbury Academic.
Lorde, Audre. 2007. *Sister Outsider: Essays and Speeches*. Berkeley, CA: Crossing Press.
Rameau, Max, M Adams, and Rob Robinson. 2014. *Forward from Ferguson*. [No place]: Nia Press.
Redman, Henry. 2020. "Wisconsin Law Enforcement Is Everywhere: How Many Agencies Operate Where You Live?" *Wisconsin Examiner*, November 20. Accessed July 19, 2022. https://wisconsinexaminer.com/2020/11/20/wisconsin-law-enforcement-map/.
Scott, Cheraine Donalea. 2020. "Policing Black Sound: Performing UK Grime and Rap Music under Routinised Surveillance." *Soundings* 75: 55–65.
Sithole, Elkin T. 1972. "Black Folk Music." In *Rappin' and Stylin' Out: Communication in Urban Black America*, edited by Thomas Kochman, 65–82. Chicago: University of Illinois Press.
Starhawk. 1985. "Introduction." In *Jambalaya: The Natural Woman's Book of Personal Charms and Practical Rituals*, by Luisah Teish, xxi–xxv. New York: Harper and Row.
Steiner, Sallie Anna. 2019. "Stitched Together: Craft and Community at a Refugee Sewing Group." PhD dissertation, University of Wisconsin, Madison, 71–99.
Teish, Luisah. 1985. *Jambalaya: The Natural Woman's Book of Personal Charms and Practical Rituals*. New York: Harper and Row.
Thompson, Robert Farris. 1984. *Flash of the Spirit: African and Afro-American Art and Philosophy*. New York: Random House.

Tronto, Joan C. 1996. "Care as a Political Concept." In *Revisioning the Political: Feminist Reconstructions of Traditional Concepts in Western Political Theory*, edited by Nancy J. Hirschmann and Christine Di Stefano, 139–56. Boulder: Westview.

Umangay, Umar Keoni. 2016. "(Re)Playing Decolonization through Pele, Aloha'Oe, and Indigenous Knowledge." In *Play: A Theory of Learning and Change*, edited by Tara Brabazon, 73–81. New York: Springer.

Williams, Annette Powell. 1972. "Dynamics of a Black Audience." In *Rappin' and Stylin' Out: Communication in Urban Black America*, edited by Thomas Kochman, 101–6. Chicago: University of Illinois Press.

11

A Frame within a Frame within a Frame within . . .

Concluding Essay

AUDUN KJUS, SIMON POOLE, IDA TOLGENSBAKK,
JAKOB LÖFGREN, AND CLÍONA O'CARROLL

The first chapter of this book emphasized the aspect of play and ritual theory that both kinds of events are framed and therefore stand out. Further, it suggested that one could attempt to make a distinction between the two regarding the ontological status of the framed interaction. It was suggested that transactions in play settings are typically imagined as unreal, while transactions in ritual settings are typically imagined as super-real. Now the time has come to take a closer look at these assumptions, in light of the nine preceding empirical case studies.

THE ONTOLOGICAL STATUS OF THE FRAMED REALM

If we start by searching for the super-real, death and funerary practices would be a promising place to begin. When a deceased member of the community is given a formal departure, the community will typically declare itself in contact with a higher or cosmic or eternal reality, which is often addressed as the receiver of the dead person. Within the vast variation in human funeral customs, the sacred aura seems to be a shared trait. Simply depositing a community member in a hole in the ground, without proper veneration, would be a failing according to any cultural standard.

Hanna Jansson has given examples of ceremonies that are secular, thus not referring to any institutionally sanctioned story world or myth. This make them even better examples of how the framed realms in these proceedings are treated as super-real. In the memorial and ash scattering for Anders (chapter 4, this volume), the attitude was profoundly serious. The ashes were honored with flowers, photographs, and lit candles. Anders's spirit was celebrated with his favorite food and drink, with the words that were spoken, and with the music that was played. Later, when small children replayed the event as a funeral for the butterfly Anders, the gravity of the words and acts was echoed in a performance that was likely perceived as unreal by both participants and spectators. The distinction between the two realms—both acted out with great sincerity—was made clear by the way the adults gently made sure that the butterfly Anders was sent off from a different place than the person Anders. If the pretend ceremony had been held at the exact same place, that would somehow have desecrated it.

To find an example from the other end of the scale, with the realm of the framed interaction clearly marked and referred to as unreal, we could revisit the celebration of Hogswatch in Wincanton, as described by Jakob Löfgren (chapter 8, this volume). The event's story world is taken from a book that is shelved in the literary super-genre of *fiction* and in the first-level genre named *fantasy*; thus, it is institutionally recognized and formally labeled as unreal. The encompassing joking atmosphere also underpins the idea that the framed secondary world is not to be taken in earnest.

If play and ritual are viewed as super-genres that can be used to classify public events, they correspond nicely with the narrative super-genres of *fable* and *myth*. While the persons and places of myth are prefigured as more than real, like Adam and Eve in the Garden of Eden, the fable is prefigured as less than real, like the figures and landscapes of Discworld. But on closer inspection, the distinction's neat clarity starts to crumble—which makes sense, as both words, the Greek *myth* and the Latin *fable*, were originally simply referring to *a story*, regardless of its ontological status.

Before we discuss the mixed and ambivalent forms, there is one more super-genre that needs to be considered. In the case studies in this book, some of the framed events appear to be prefigured as neither more nor less than real. Take, for instance, the anti-racist political protests described by Sallie Anna Pisera (chapter 10, this volume), where the participants were called on to imagine and create a world in which "we protect us" against the violence of racism and capitalism. In these public protests, which spread internationally to the extent that they became a global phenomenon, the key symbol was the eyewitness video that documented George Floyd's killing. The clarity, brutality, and reality of this mediated act were extended through a web of references and used as an allegory that people in different circumstances were able to relate to issues happening in their own communities. The insistence on the reality of this moment was used to create settings in which the protesters could speak and act against oppression and for human rights.

Next to the narrative super-genres of *myth* and *fable*, the super-genre of *history* has been trusted with the realms that are framed as real. It is easy to find other examples of communication settings where the content is framed as real. Take, for instance, the news broadcast (Fiske 1987, 281–308) or the courtroom trial (Kjus 2011, 1–11). Brian Sutton-Smith (1997, 195) warned against making a simple distinction between real life and imagined play. He pointed out that people also imagine the world during mundane and everyday experiences and interactions, and he held that when we enter into play, some of these experiences, feelings, and concepts are detached and relocated so they can be re-experienced, reconsidered, and developed. In addition, it would be a mistake to perceive the distinction between mundane everyday interaction and the intensified interaction of play and ritual (cf. Shapiro 2020, 212) as a distinction between framed and unframed events. Erving Goffman (1986 [1974], 21) showed convincingly how mundane activities, such as sharing a meal, riding the bus, or receiving a stranger at the door, are prefigured by situational understandings that he labels primary frameworks. Interestingly, Goffman (2005 [1967], 57) assumes that the basis for these everyday interaction rituals is the sacred status of the human person, which is protected and venerated—or dragged through the dirt—in various forms of face work. Goffman's concept of primary frameworks resonates well with Mikhail Bakhtin's (1986 [1929/1979]) ideas about speech genres. Bakhtin assumed that all speech is prefigured by inherited understandings of the kinds of utterances that are viable in a given situation, with corresponding notions about what these different speech genres may signify and accomplish.

Since mundane and everyday interaction may also convincingly be described as framed, the heightened interaction of play and ritual should rather be described as happening within a secondary framework (referring to the terminology of Goffman 1986 [1974]) or an intensified framework (leaning on Shapiro 2020). What we have, then, is on the one hand *mundane framed interaction* and on the other hand *intensified framed interaction*; the realm of intensified interaction can be framed as real, super-real, or unreal or as any combination of the three. For this anthology we have invited case studies that contain different mixtures, but it would seem that composite ontology is the rule rather than the exception.

To look at some examples, take, for instance, the football match, as described by Katarzyna Herd (chapter 6, this volume). When the modern institution of sports was established, the games were to some extent disenchanted—removing them from their festival and holiday settings, supplying them with explicit and rational rules, and providing secular reasons for them, related to education, public health, the national economy, or even national security. In sum, the realms of sports were given the shine of belonging to the provinces that are real—even more so in the case of the dominant forms discussed in company cafeterias and reported in newspapers. Recently, long-distance running has emerged as a sport many amateurs perform as if it were their full-time occupation. The activity contributes to their experience of being proper and serious people and is often deemed worthy of being included in one's curriculum vitae (Lindelöf and Woube, chapter 5, this volume).

The sport's aura of reality is one of the factors that may confuse police officers when they are posted to maintain public security at football matches (Herd, chapter 6, this volume). It may take some time before they realize that if they want to do a good job, they must adapt to the dynamics of the game the football supporters play in the stands. The football match abounds with play elements: "There are rhymes that start and end matches; there are songs about specific players or that are aimed at the police or different clubs. You can jump, scream, or wave with scarves" (Herd, chapter 6, this volume). And "you can hate another city for ninety minutes or shout that the police officer is a hooligan without the consequences you would expect in everyday situations" (Herd, chapter 6, this volume). At the same time, these acts are carried out with a gravity that makes the realm of the match difficult to categorize. Its ontological status seems to be constantly floating among the real, the unreal, and the super-real.

Lizette Gradén's study of the Scandinavian American heritage play with the fleeting substance and concept of lutfisk provides a different example with a similar ontological mixture. The place that is referred to is the old country. The strongly coded and always available marker of lutfisk creates a mental passage that allows members of the migrant communities to move freely in and out of the old country (Gradén, chapter 9, this volume). For the Scandinavians who did not migrate, this kind of mental switchbox is hardly needed. To the migrant communities, the Scandinavian homelands belong very much to the realms that are considered real, but referring to them through the playful medium of lutfisk alters the ontological status of these places and creates an ambivalence that helps keep the community's relationship with the old country open and productive. As Gradén (chapter 9, this volume) points out, the old country is not only perceived as real but is given a sacred aura as the place of cultural origin. A serving of lutfisk adds to this heritage salad with a healthy aspect of unreality.

THE WORK OF FRAMING

Ideas about social framing have been very productive within studies of play and ritual. Arnold van Gennep (1960 [1909]) led the way by introducing the metaphor of the doorframe and classifying transition rites as pre-liminal, liminal, and post-liminal. Johan Huizinga (1950 [1938]) followed by describing play activities as both physically and mentally hedged in, ruled by their own internal laws and dynamics. Gregory Bateson (2000 [1972]) paid special attention to the signs that are used to manage transitions from mundane to playful communication. But the social frame, though a useful metaphor, can also be used in ways that are reductive and confusingly simplifying. What do we in fact refer to if we state that an interaction is framed? We want to use the preceding empirical case studies to identify some aspects of the work of framing.

Key Work

It is convenient to start by looking at the use of indexes like those identified by Bateson. In animal behavior studies, several kinds of play signals have been identified, even across species—such as the play face, the play gait, and the play voice. Robert Fagen (1995) noted that such signals not only are introduced at the beginning of play sessions but may also be repeated to uphold the playful interaction. For simplicity, we will refer to the indexes that point toward and invite a specific mode of interaction as *keys*, well aware that we use the word differently than Goffman did.

If we return to the use of lutfisk as a key, we observe that, on the one hand, it is used to establish frames within larger settings, in which people are already engaged. In the town parade or the communal Christmas dinner, the presentation of the lutfisk symbol introduces another particular level of interaction. On the other hand, the lutfisk joking relationship is also frequently activated outside the larger events. The game of inventing new lutfisk jokes is allowed to surface, preferably at unexpected places, within mundane life. Several of the keys mentioned in the case studies work in similar ways. Pisera (chapter 10, this volume) grabs her protest sign, which may have been standing ready in the hall, when she goes out to join the large anti-racist demonstration. This key contributes to frame her as a protester, and her protest is a separate piece within the larger event of the protest march. The visual keys of the modern marriage proposal (kneel down; offer ring) work somewhat differently, as they initiate an interaction between the two parties and turn any bystanders into an audience (Kjus, chapter 3, this volume).

Boundary Work

Most of the events described in this volume are not entered through implicit and meta-communicative keying. They are rather entered through more formal and material boundary work. Karin S. Lindelöf and Annie Woube (chapter 5, this volume) describe how participants in the Spartan Ultra World Championship, after having paid a rather large participation fee, all find themselves at the same hotel. The race itself is taking place on a marked and delimited track, but only after an extensive opening ceremony, including an Olympic-style parade and the appearance of a lightly dressed "Spartan" warrior with a plumed helmet and a deep, masculine voice. Together, the physical walls and fences and the symbolic opening ceremonies bind and prepare the dimensions of space and time for a specific kind of action. The hen party's cabin, the football stadium, and the village of Wincanton, on different scales, serve the purpose of keeping the participants together and shielding them from intruding factors. The opening ceremony serves the extra purpose of coordinating the participants physically while they mirror each other's gazes, moves, and emotions, tuning them to the events that follow. As Löfgren (chapter 8, this volume) points out, if the ceremonies are playful, they communicate the ethos that "we are here to play." Thus, the opening ceremony marks and protects the preferred succeeding interaction.

Catering

Maintaining an intensified secondary frame for a longer period of time demands dedicated catering. Some of the events described in this volume are gigantic in scale. It goes without saying that managing an event like WorldCon, with 70,000 participants, or a top-level football match takes a great deal of planning and organizing, of everything from food and drink to stage equipment and security measures. In the case studies, we learn how even small and medium events, like the hen party or the drive-through lutfisk dinner, require substantial planning and organizing. This work must be done if the participants are to remain comfortably within the frame throughout the passage of the event. Sheila M. Young (chapter 2, this volume) writes that a typical modern Scottish hen party lasts an entire weekend. For those forty-some hours, the organizers must plan not only for the basic practicalities such as food and rest but also for relevant games and activities that keep the momentum going and punctuate the proceedings.

The labors of framing can, to a large extent, be described as catering. Even if the police officers interviewed by Herd (chapter 6, this volume) have to engage in the framed interaction at the football stadium, they are doing this as part of the catering system. The police are at work to ensure that supporters have a safe, uninterrupted game. An interesting example is given by Pisera (chapter 10, this volume), who interviewed organizers of anti-racist protests. She describes how the marches are catered from within through the use of chanted choruses like "drink water" or "turn the group." The organizers see this as one of their largest tasks: to turn participants into leaders who are able to cater for the group when it is in action.

One of the ash-scattering events described by Jansson (chapter 4, this volume) shows what can happen if the catering fails. The frame of a funerary ceremony was not convincingly established, and it did not manage to override the frame of the ordinary Sunday boat trip. As a result, the widow found that her departed husband did not receive the respectful departure she felt he deserved. Jansson concludes that a successful ritual must have the capacity to move the participants, to the extent that they abstain from critical distance and allow themselves to be carried away. The physical conditions for this kind of allowance must be created and sustained. There is both an outside and an inside to the work of upholding a frame through the duration of the intended interaction. The logistic and organizational work may invite and insulate the desired interaction. The insulation even works as an amplification, since disturbing signals are blocked out while desired signals are accumulated. Still, it is the participants who have to provide the desired content. And the most desired content appears to be coordinated emotion.

The performative marriage proposal will be an embarrassment if the emotional engagement of the two parties is not heightened to nearly the same level (Kjus, chapter 3, this volume). The largest attraction of the extreme sports races is probably the way participants suffer and endure together. Pisera (chapter 10, this volume) points out that the coordination of thoughts and feelings starts with the coordination of bodies. Even if outer frameworks need to be in place for such coordination to happen, it is apparently the unforeseen and "naturally" evolving coordination that is most pleasurable for participants, like the moment "when the crowd sat silently on the highway together in quiet relaxation—hundreds of people gathered, enjoying the breeze from the lake amid what was normally a busy automobile thoroughfare." Löfgren (chapter 8, this volume) shows how such unforeseen moments of emotional coordination may be created within the events of fandom, when fans communicate by referring to the mother texts in surprising and inventive ways—for instance, by stealing the beer of a fellow Pratchett fan and leaving a receipt. In the funerary practices described by Jansson (chapter 4, this volume), nothing stands out as more emotional than the improvised spontaneous football match in the pouring rain. Ruth Dorothea Eggel (chapter 7, this volume) describes this kind of interaction as the *magic moment* when one *gets lucky*. Creating such moments seems to be the role of play within the larger ceremonial complexes, and the fact that such moments may occur is likely to be one of the major attractions for those who attend the ceremonies.

Situational Understanding

The importance of situational understanding to the perception of play-ritual genres can be compared to Bakhtin's (1986 [1929/1979], 60) observation that verbal genres are products of, but also constitutive of, the socially recognized situations for making utterances. Keys, boundaries, and catering are aspects of framing, but an important ingredient seems to be missing. What does the catering cater for? What do the boundaries contain? What do the keys point at? The keys invite some sort of labeled and recognized cultural praxis; in other words, they point to a tradition. The aspiring practitioner's ideas about this tradition may be derived from different sources, but any well-founded and realistic idea comes from having participated in the tradition before, such as Pisera (chapter 10, this volume) putting a bottle of milk in her purse when leaving for the political demonstration.

Within ethnographic genre analysis, it has been observed that although there is not necessarily an explicit taxonomy, verbal genres can be identified from their situationally conditioned performance (Ben-Amos 1969, 296). For a person who has not previously participated, ideas about the event will be derived from mediated resources. Some events are relatively rare, like marriage proposals and funeral ceremonies. A suitor's ideas about the proper marriage proposal may have come from word of mouth, TV series, YouTube videos, or, most likely, a combination of these and other representations. When the knowledge only stems from secondary sources, managing a framed interaction represents a challenge. This was discovered by some of the suitors and some of the bereaved in the preceding case studies.

A third resource is to rely on previous experience that one deems to be similar and hopes can bring insights to the new situation. Löfgren (chapter 8, this volume) points out that both the arrangers of and participants in fandom ceremonies rely on their general knowledge about ceremonies when constructing ceremonial events that are not described in the mother texts. Young (chapter 2, this volume) finds that the hen party draws much of its form and content from the children's birthday party.

The only way to become a proficient participant is to place yourself in the field of action and try to get synchronized and become a part of the game by copying and replying to the acts of the other players, much as children do when they engage in play. According to Sutton-Smith (1997), interaction studies reveal that the normal way schoolchildren get involved in play is to place themselves in the area where the action is and copy what the other children do. You need to fake it until you make it. Becoming proficient will demand time, effort, and multiple engagements. This is rather obvious when it comes to people with high-level performance skills. Observing a person who can coordinate a crowd of people, hold their attention, and drive their emotions is awe-inspiring. This kind of leadership is always carried out in a particular genre and setting. Thus, it requires not only general skills but also particular insights and understanding.

It is easier to ignore the fact that a normal participant or member of the audience must invest time and effort in a genre to reach an appropriate level of affection and give relevant responses. This starts with a basic understanding of form and content: what is the structure of a football match? When and why do people cheer? But it goes beyond this, to an understanding of what is apt and what is excellent. Just knowing that something is a joke is a far cry from knowing if it, in this time and place, is boring or improper or if it is perfect in content and timing.

Returning to Bateson's (2000 [1972]) example of the two biting dogs, it takes skill, experience, and situational understanding to know if a particular bite is playful or aggressive, and the dogs do not necessarily agree. The point we wish to make here is that play-ritual events are historical, and, as with other historical events, each of them is unique and contains several equally valid perspectives. This returns us to the stance of chapter 1: such events need to be studied empirically, with attention to the specific and unique. The interesting question is not simply whether a certain key existed, but how it was used, by whom, and to what effects.

INTENSIFIED ENGAGEMENT

Having adopted Matan Shapiro's (2020) view of play and ritual as modes of intensified engagement, it would be interesting to also consider what is intensified and how the intensifying is carried out. First, a theoretical recapitulation: Huizinga (1950 [1938]) assumed that the building of tension is based on how the acts of framing limit the scope of the interaction. Sutton-Smith (1997) described play as an engagement in which some vital aspects of life are relocated and tested in the isolation of a (secondary) framework. Margaret Thompson Drewal (1992) remarked on how an intense performance draws participants to the framed engagement, which makes the strong performance self-reinforcing, as the increased attention heightens the effect and intensity of the performance.

Fun and laughter play a large part in the strategies that synchronize and intensify interactions. Humans are one of the few species that laugh—we are the *homo ridens*. In the various chapters of this book, we hear laughter throughout, although it is not always specified that this is what the actors are doing. When Eggel (chapter 7, this volume) describes gamers turning tedious tasks into "quests," racing through the halls with techno-music blasting, we envision them laughing or at least chuckling or giggling at having succeeded in making the boring fun. The lutfisk parade is considered successful when it is spoken of as "one of the funniest ever." Even Jansson's (chapter 4, this volume) grieving families describe how laughter and tears of joy are intermingled with tears of sorrow. Laughter is a highly communicative act: it can mock and deride as well as knit people together. Laughing with each other is a powerful instrument for community building, and allowing the participants to show that they "get the joke" is a crucial aspect of the playful rituals of Löfgren's (chapter 8, this volume) fan culture events. Being an insider in a group means understanding what is and what is not funny. When are you supposed to laugh and when is laughter strictly forbidden? Jokes and laughter are among the most effective ways of bonding, creating cultural insides and outsides while raising the spirit.

In addition to these more technical dimensions, it is also possible to point to common topical intensifiers. One of them is to play on sexuality and sex appeal. In the hen parties described by Young (chapter 2, this volume), some of the activities display content that is far more sexually explicit that the participants would be comfortable with in normal settings. The bride-to-be, for instance, was asked to perform simulated sex with a male stripper and to reveal the most adventurous place the couple had had sex; also, the entire group was asked to make sculptures of the groom's penis out of modeling clay. Death is another intensifier. The presence of death instantly drives emotions and coordinates behavior. In the early mornings of national days, there tend to be ceremonies at the memorials for "those who made the greatest sacrifice." Addressing the dead sets the standards for a dignified and united celebration. Violence is a third intensifier. Herd (chapter 6, this volume) describes how football supporters play out exaggerated, furious reactions and have formalized ways to express hatred toward the other team. They even challenge the police. Sometimes they break the law, but behaving in a manner that brings them to the very limits of the law appears to be closer to the ideal.

Displaying and putting into play phenomena such as sex, violence, death, and laughter may function as general intensifiers that can be mixed into any performance to spice it up. Still, and following the assumptions of Sutton-Smith (1997), it would make sense to examine how the intensified elements relate to the structures and themes of the larger communicative events. As mentioned, Löfgren (chapter 8, this volume) finds that the fandom ceremonies he studied serve to signal and protect an area in which participating fans can celebrate their playful ethos. In Young's (chapter 2, this volume) interpretation, the hen parties are about strengthening trust within the female friendship group; all the play on male sexuality, including the playful display of sexual organs, communicates that the strengthened bond between the married spouses will not be able to break the feminine circle of friendship. Among the football supporters studied by Herd (chapter 6, this volume), the synchronized shouting, threatening behavior, lawbreaking pyrotechnics, and theatrically exaggerated antagonism express a kind of idealized masculine companionship. Big events may have several foci, and what is judged as most significant will probably vary among participants; even still, one may find that in the overall picture, there is something particular and relevant that is intensified.

THE OLD AND THE NEW

The dichotomy between improvisation and prescribed performance—indeed, between playfulness and solemnity—has inspired debate in various contexts. At the core of these discussions lies the question of how innovation appears in traditional forms of expressions. It is clear that there will always be tension between creativity and tradition, when looking at any given form of expressive culture. This tension can be explored from both sides, from those seeking to maintain classic traditions with little room for variation, and from those who seek innovation, combining traditional shapes with new modulations and imports.

The relationship between creativity and tradition is a recurrent theme in the continuum of play and ritual. Within the field of folkloristics, this relationship has been studied to explore how traditional patterns are transformed in modern contexts, both within communities and through individual agency. This tension manifests itself through formalized activities such as festivals, dances, music performances, and rituals that take place over generations but still evolve with time.

Tradition-based creative expression typically derives from the tension and ambiguity inherent in the meaning-making processes of shared cultural practices. It is often seen during festive occasions, celebrations, or significant moments in the lives of individuals or communities; furthermore, it is often a moment in which performers share stories while simultaneously imbuing them with personal interpretations and expressions.

Although these events may appear spontaneous on the surface, they have an underlying structure that relies heavily on previous iterations for guidance as well as on collective approval for changes to be accepted into the general flow of performance. Therefore, within these performative folk reenactments, funerary or proposal rites, and other performances, we can observe how seemingly unchanging enactment practices actually incorporate some level of flexible adaption according to contemporary needs. A good example is that of football supporters' response to Swedish authorities banning the use of masks at football matches and their creative adaptation to use a lawful loophole to continue to express a traditional tension between them and the authorities (Herd, chapter 6, this volume). In this way, we come full circle, since newly created works based on popular imagery often give rise to further adaptations fueled by performative interaction between audiences and participants. This creative interplay not only serves to represent old narratives in a new form but also provides individuals with opportunities for improvisation.

Not everyone will consider some of the examples from the previous chapters to be folklore. One could argue that an item such as football fans playing with security personnel, which Herd (chapter 6, this volume) writes of, or the practices of extreme runners, which Lindelöf and Woube (chapter 5, this volume) discuss, could not possibly be termed ritual because they lack tradition. They are creative items responding to contemporary cultural phenomena, not defined by timeworn material handed down through generations. Compare this position to John Dewey's (1938) biological interpretation of habit, where experience is seen as something that, when enacted, also modifies the subject. From Dewey's point of view, "Every experience both takes up something from those which have gone before and modifies in some way the quality of those which come after" (35). Against those who would curate folklore as ancient items of tradition (we purposely point no fingers), there is a strong argument that resists items being perfectly represented and accurately identical in every detail (Bronner 1992). Instead, it suggests that the tradition of folk culture resides in the way its acts and items are experienced, that items of folklore are continually enacted and re-created—each time somewhat different (Bronner 2011). Herd's (chapter 6, this volume) footballer activity and Lindelöf and Woube's (chapter 5, this volume) extreme runners' activity fit this perception; they are not only examples of folklore but good examples of the process of creative tradition in action—experiences performed to create new socio-political positions that test, innovate, or reiterate traditional or mythic structures.

Innovation and tradition are the mechanics of change. Creativity in folklore is an immutable force of transmutation, and play and ritual are vehicles of transmission that create the language and action by which individuals psychologically verify, communicate, and socially validate their understandings. In a tradition such as a ritual, the initiate can play within the ritual to carve out a perspective—think here of Thomas S. Eliot's (1982) "Tradition and the individual talent," the inherent capacity of creativity in Simon J. Bronner's (1992) understanding of tradition, or Zygmunt Bauman's (2001) tension between community and the individual. This carving out, this education and inculcation, constitute a perpetual process, the ends of a continuum simultaneously eroding and reconstituting.

THE USES OF PLAY ELEMENTS

We would like to end this book by taking one more look at the relation between the formal versus the playful regulation of events. This relation is interesting regardless of where in the play-ritual continuum an event is located. In hindsight, we realize that this volume has primarily been about the uses of play elements within different play-ritual complexes. This, then, is also where the conclusion should land.

First, we must state the obvious: the forms and effects of play activities are highly variable. We will restrict ourselves to those that have been made visible in the case studies. One of the very visible effects is *attraction*. Play is used to attract attention and establish contact; thus, it is the entrance gate to many social relations. These are both romantic relations, like the thrush singing in the bush, and peer-group relations, like the child searching for an alliance on the playground. The relations established within play provide the participants with social identity, that can be further developed.

When approaching a play-ritual complex that is manifestly framed with physical and symbolic boundaries, play elements can serve to draw potential participants into the magic circle. In Gradén's case study (chapter 9, this volume), lutfisk works this way. The visual displays and the laughter they trigger draw people to the lutfisk float. Through this attraction, they are also drawn to the parade itself and to Svensk Hyllningsfest in Lindsborg, Kansas.

An even more profound effect is that of *modulation*. A large and composite intensified interaction will have several aspects that can be modulated through play. Pisera (chapter 10, this volume) showed how the physical movements of the protest group can be directed through chants and how their needs for information and nourishment can be catered for. Through all the case studies, we see how affects are synchronized and modulated. The successful marriage proposal equally heightens the pulse and attention of both parties. The football match in the rain after the scattering of Anders's ashes modulates the effect generated through the planned and formal ceremony, transforming it through a more active and spontaneous interaction that still resonates perfectly with Anders's spirit as the participants remember it (chapter 4, this volume). Successful play may even transform the understanding and definitions of the social world. After a good game, the relations are different than they were before.

While material and symbolic boundary work secures a place and a time where various kinds of modulation can happen, different modulations are aimed for in different play-ritual genres. The framed interaction is a place where "something" that already exists is intensified and tested. It can be a place where "something" is confirmed or repaired. It may lead to a new pact, where new laws are established, or it can be a protected laboratory for safe exploration.

The events that are most readily classified as ritual are those that establish some sort of social fact. The ash-scattering ceremony (chapter 4, this volume) relocates the remains of the dead community member both physically and cognitively. During the marriage proposal, two people formally agree to get married. Both acts have legal implications. Here, the introduction of play elements can be seen to enhance and develop the effects of the ritual.

In events closer to the play end of the scale, boundaries are used to secure the integrity and liberty of play. In these cases, the formal and material limits protect against play acts spilling over the fence and becoming subject to the interpretational frames of mundane interaction. Eggel (chapter 9, this volume) describes how the participants at gaming conventions use these venues' boundaries and catering to cultivate the indeterminacy of wild games. Her case study shows a level of raw play that is protected by ceremony but could not be confused with it. The interactions have the distinct status of unreality, and they are desired, strived for, and embraced for their own sake.

Fun, jokes, and laughter are important aspects of playful behavior and are some of the reasons people continue to play even after their childhood is long gone. In his description of the Renaissance conception of laughter, Bakhtin (1984 [1946/1965], 66) underlines that "certain essential aspects of the world are accessible only to laughter." In play and in ritual, laughter opens up the unspoken, the intuitive and uncontrollable realities of human life. The case studies have shown different examples of how adults continue to mix fun into everyday life, with its responsible and serious aspects. The women in Young's hen parties (chapter 2, this volume) have created a space for themselves and the bride-to-be to let loose, a culturally sanctioned event where shrieking with laughter at a penis joke is permissible. The contrast between this and the hardships engaged in by the persons participating in an extreme sports event, discussed by Lindelöf and Woube's (chapter 5, this volume), seems huge. However, the underlying logic of creating spaces for explorative and non-productive events, which stand out from the routines of ordinary life, may still be the same. When Pisera's (chapter 10, this volume) anti-racist protestors insist on having fun and experiencing pleasure, it is explicitly framed as a deliberate act of rebellion against a society that threatens to paralyze people with fear and violence.

Even if play can be integrated into other practices, and to good effect, it is doubtful that it can actually be commodified without losing some of its desired qualities. Play consists of back-and-forth movements with open endings. This open-endedness is required for creating movements that are experienced as engaging and liberating. The movements, even the smallest of them, are often highly appreciated. If external benefits are pursued primarily, back-and-forth movements are inhibited and ends are closed. In the first chapter of this book, doing research was compared to playing a game. We would like to end, in the spirit of Huizinga, by encouraging the cultivation of play even within the realms of research. Playing may lead to many advantages, but to bring about good results, the game must be entered on its own terms. The introduction of an instrumental attitude, in which one tries to maximize the benefits, runs the risk of making the game less engaging, less developing, less liberating, and less capable of transforming a situation with unforeseen results. This is one of the many paradoxes of the play-ritual continuum.

REFERENCES

Bakhtin, Mikhail. 1984 [1946/1965]. *Rabelais and His World*. Bloomington: Indiana University Press.

Bakhtin, Mikhail. 1986 [1929/1979]. "The Problem of Speech Genres." In *Speech Genres and Other Late Essays*, edited by Caryl Emerson and Michael Holdquist, 60–102. Austin: University Press of Texas.

Bateson, Gregory. 2000 [1972]. *Steps to an Ecology of Mind*. Chicago: University of Chicago Press.

Bauman, Zygmunt. 2001. *Community: Seeking Safety in an Insecure World*. Cambridge: Polity.

Ben-Amos, Dan. 1969. "Analytical Categories and Ethnic Genres." *Genre* 2 (3): 275–301.

Bronner, Simon J. 1992. *Creativity and Tradition in Folklore: New Directions*. Logan: Utah State University Press.

Bronner, Simon J. 2011. *Explaining Traditions: Folk Behaviour in Modern Culture*. Lexington: University Press of Kentucky.

Dewey, John. 1938. *Experience and Education*. New York: Macmillan.

Drewal, Margaret Thompson. 1992. *Yoruba Ritual: Performers, Play, Agency*. Bloomington: Indiana University Press.

Eliot, Thomas S. 1982. "Tradition and the Individual Talent." *Perspecta* 19: 36–42.

Fagen, Robert. 1981. *Animal Play Behaviour*. New York: Oxford University Press.

Fagen, Robert. 1995. "Animal Play, Games of Angels, Biology, and Brian." In *The Future of Play Theory: A Multidisciplinary Inquiry into the Contributions of Brian Sutton-Smith*, edited by Anthony D. Pellegrini, 23–44. New York: State University of New York Press.

Fiske, John. 1987. *Television Culture*. London: Routledge.
van Gennep, Arnold. 1960 [1909]. *The Rites of Passage*. Chicago: University of Chicago Press.
Goffman, Erving. 1986 [1974]. *Frame Analysis: An Essay on the Organization of Experience*. Boston: Northeastern University Press.
Goffman, Erving. 2005 [1967]. *Interaction Ritual: Essays in Face-to-Face Behaviour*. New Brunswick: Aldine Transaction.
Huizinga, Johan. 1950 [1938]. *Homo Ludens: A Study of the Play-Element in Culture*. New York: Roy Publishers.
Kjus, Audun. 2011. *Stories at Trial*. Liverpool: Deborah Charles Publications.
Shapiro, Matan. 2020. "Dynamics of Movement: Intensity, Ritualized Play, and the Cosmology of Kinship Relations in Northeast Brazil." *Anthropological Theory* 20 (2): 193–220.
Sutton-Smith, Brian. 1997. *The Ambiguity of Play*. Cambridge, MA: Harvard University Press.

Index

Adams, M., 186
adapting (play theory), 22, 40, 65, 69, 74, 153, 158, 176, 208
aebleskiver (dish, Danish), 179
affective play, 144, 149, 152, 154, 160
African American, 187, 192
African diaspora, 186
Afro-centric, 186
agon (competition, a form of play), 61
AIK (Swedish football team), 110, 111, 113–115, 121
Allan, John R., 34
Allen, Phil, Jr., 185
Alzheimer's, 144
ambivalence, 8, 10, 20, 21, 65, 97, 178, 180, 206, 209
American Agricultural Movement, 172
American Police State, 189, 199
American Swedish Institute (Minneapolis), 163, 175, 180
Andersson, Torbjörn, 108, 109
Andreasson, Jesper, 95, 101
animal behavior, 6, 209
animal play, 17
Ankh-Morpork's Guild of Thieves, 144, 146, 155

anthropomorphic, 148, 156
anti-capitalist, 184, 187, 188
anti–Donald Trump, 197
anti-feminist, 18
anti-racist, 184, 185, 188, 191, 207, 210, 211, 220
anti-structure (ritual theory), 21
anxiety-producing, 36, 172
apotropaic, 35
Åre, Sweden, 88–94, 104
ash disposal, 74, 76, 78, 82–84
ash scattering, 27, 72, 74, 75, 79, 206, 211, 219
attraction (play theory), 38, 62, 160, 219
Austen, Jane, 59
Austin, Tiffany, 188, 200, 201
Avedon, Elliot, 40
awe-inspiring (play theory), 214

Bacchi Temple (song), 148
bachelorette party, 39
back-and-forth movement (play theory), 17, 21, 166, 220, 221
Bakhtin, Mikhail, 28, 172, 207, 213, 220
balaclava (mask), 113
ballgame, 9

Bareither, Christoph, 127
Barkley Brown, Elsa, 186–188
Bateson, Gregory, 5, 22, 23, 25, 63, 65, 73, 74, 77, 79, 83, 94, 100, 125, 126, 129, 168, 209, 214
Bath, England, 144
Bauman, Richard, 28, 68
Bauman, Zygmunt, 218
Bear Pub (Wincanton, England), 145
Behn, Ari, 52, 62, 64
Bell, Catherine, 35, 152–154, 160
Bellman, Carl Michael, 148
Ben-Amos, Dan, 213
Bennet, Elizabeth, 59
Bennett, Margaret, 34, 37, 38, 125, 126
Bennett, Stith, 130, 132–134, 139
Bergen, Norway, 55, 62, 67
Bethany Church (Lindsborg, KS), 173
Bett, Henry, 9
Bjørnson, Bjørnstjerne, 56–59
Black (racial reference), 184, 185–188, 190–192, 194–196, 198, 200, 201
Black activism, 185, 192, 194, 196, 200, 201
Black cultural expression, 186, 187, 192
Black Lives Matter movement, 185, 188, 200
Blackburn, Simon, 46
Blehr, Barbro, 73, 75, 168
board game, 5, 145
Boden, Margaret, 130
Boden, Sharon, 35, 36
Boellstorff, Tom, 126, 127
Bogad, Lawrence M., 184, 189
Bouissac, Paul, 41
boundaries (play and ritual theory), 13, 14, 24, 110, 112, 117, 119, 120, 121, 130, 151, 152, 168, 192, 210, 212, 213, 219, 220
boundary work (frame theory), 210, 219
Brain, Kevin, 38
bride-to-be, 38, 46, 56, 64, 215, 220
Briggs, Charles L., 28
British Isles, 8
Brogden, Jim, 184, 203
Bromberger, Christian, 115
Bromley, Catherine, 39
Bronner, Simon J., 36, 168, 218
Brown (racial reference), 185
Brøgger, Waldemar, 53
Burning Man festival, 132
Burstyn, Varda, 94
Busse, Kristina, 149
Butler, Andrew M., 144

Caillois, Roger, 6, 15, 44, 60, 61
call-and-response style, 187, 191, 192
callout, 192
Capitol Square (Madison, WI), 189, 191, 197, 199
card game, 5
carnival, 28, 47
carnivalesque, 27, 28
casual leisure, 40, 42
catering (frame theory), 211, 213, 220
Catholic (religious context), 7, 28
celebration, 22, 54, 65, 143–145, 147–149, 156, 168, 179, 206, 215, 217
Central Europe, 127
ceremony, 6, 7, 9, 21, 27, 74–76, 77, 82, 137, 143–145, 147, 148–161, 201, 206, 210–213, 216
Cervantes, Miguel de, 58
chance, 126, 128, 134–136, 140
Charsley, Simon, 37, 38
Chauvin, Derek, 185, 201
cheating, 20, 121
child lore, 19, 20, 36, 78, 83, 95, 117, 119, 219
childhood games, 4, 6, 8, 9, 27, 34, 40–42
children, 4–6, 8, 9, 13, 16, 19, 20, 27, 34, 40–42, 48, 53, 67, 76–79, 83, 92, 95, 100, 148, 169, 188, 191, 195, 206, 213, 214
children's party, 35, 36, 213
children's folklore, 27
Christmas, 65, 66, 144, 148, 166
Christmas Eve, 13, 64
Christmas food, 164, 168, 175, 178, 210
Chwe, Michael Suk-Young, 144, 153–156, 159, 160
City of Madison (WI), 184–192, 194–196, 200, 202
civil rights movement, 174, 186
Clark, Jennifer, 75
Clarke, Alison, 35, 36
Cock-a-Hoop (game), 40, 41
cocktail making, 39
Codex Manesse, 58
Coffey, Amanda, 125
Cold War, the, 172
Collett, Camilla, 56
Comaroff, Jean, 179
Comaroff, John L., 179
coming of age, 45
commercialization, 35, 36, 165, 175
common sense, 109, 114, 118, 119, 153, 154, 158

Index

communitas (ritual theory), 21, 98, 167, 186
competition, 22, 61, 115, 127, 130, 144, 174
composite ontology, 208
computer game, 27, 95, 125, 127, 136
confirmation (ritual), 13, 46
Constitution Day (Norway, May 17), 20, 168
consumption-orientated ritual, 35, 48
contingency, 134, 139
coordinated bodily movement, 196
coordinated emotion, 212
copy (play theory), 19, 21, 25, 213, 214
cosplay, 138, 145
Covid-19 pandemic, 78, 164, 166, 175, 177, 185
creativity, 25, 73, 97, 130, 150, 170, 179, 180, 187, 216–218
creole, 28, 187
Csikszentmihalyi, Mihaly, 125, 126, 130, 132–134, 139
Cuban Missile Crisis, 172
cultural logic, 88–90, 94, 96, 97, 101, 102–104
cultural phenomenon, 14, 89, 94, 102, 217
cultural praxis, 213

Dahnweih, Mahnker, 186, 190–194, 200–202
Dane County Jail (Madison, WI), 197
Dane County, Wisconsin, 191
Danielsson, Erik, 95
death, 10, 24, 59, 67, 73–76, 79, 81, 83, 84, 185, 187, 188, 195, 201, 206, 215, 216
decolonization, 196
Dewey, John, 217
Dicks, Bella, 125
digital ethnography, 128
digital game, 125–127, 130
Dippel, Anne, 127, 130
Discworld series (Pratchett), 108, 144, 151, 155, 157, 206
disenchantment (cultural theory), 208
disorientation (play and ritual theory), 62
Djurgårdens IF (Swedish football team), 110, 116, 117
Dorst, John D., 28
double framing (frame theory), 63
Drewal, Margaret Thompson, 21, 22, 37, 43, 46, 62, 65, 66, 69, 119, 168, 173, 179, 180, 187, 202, 215
drive-through style, 164, 167, 175, 177, 178, 180, 211

Dundes, Alan, 149
Durkheim, Émile, 6
Dyer, George A., 37
dynamic genre analysis (cultural theory), 28

Earl of Bothwell, the, 57
East Washington Avenue (Madison, WI), 197, 202
Easter, 148, 156
ecclesiastical heritage, 178
Egan-Wyer, Carys, 95
Eggel, Ruth Dorothea, 127, 212, 215, 220
Ehrenreich, Barbara, 99
Elim Lutheran Church (Minneapolis), 174
Eliot, Thomas S., 218
emotion (play and ritual theory), 19, 21, 24, 25, 48, 59, 60, 77, 78, 81–84, 108–110, 115, 130, 149, 150, 211, 212, 213–215
endurance events, 88, 98
engagement ring, 52, 55, 63–66, 68, 210
Engman, Jonas, 77, 168
e-sports, 127
ethnography, 6, 8, 37, 88, 109, 110, 125, 127, 128, 130, 132, 135, 136, 144, 213
evaluation (narrative theory), 66, 67, 133
event (play and ritual theory), 14, 15, 17, 18, 24–26, 28, 35, 37, 43, 48, 83, 139, 168, 193, 211, 213, 218, 220
everyday logic, 118, 119
evolutionism (cultural theory), 8, 10
exaggerated antagonism (play theory), 20, 216
excitement (play theory), 15, 16
existential topic (play and ritual theory), 24, 97, 100, 134, 165, 179
extreme sports races, 27, 64, 88, 89, 91, 92, 97, 100, 102, 104, 212, 217, 218, 220
eye-catching (play theory), 62, 154

fable (super-genre), 206, 207
face work (frame theory), 207, 210
face-to-face interactions (frame theory), 125
Fagen, Robert, 6, 17, 20, 24, 66, 210
Faith Lutheran Church (Forest Lake, MN), 174
fan culture, 144, 215
fan event, 151, 152
fan expressions, 149, 150
fan folklore, 149, 150
fan performance, 152

fan-affective, 149–151
fandom, 149–156, 158, 160
fandom ceremony, 154
fandom community, 150
fandom folklore, 149, 150
fantasy (cognition), 23, 35
fantasy (literary genre), 144, 145, 156, 206
fast food, 36, 167, 175
feeling (play and ritual theory), 19, 24, 44, 73, 99, 134, 150, 158, 207, 212
Fein, Greta G., 19
feminism, 196
fertility ritual, 9
festival, 9, 99, 125–127, 132, 137, 139, 147, 156, 167–180, 208, 217
festival effect (play and ritual theory), 22
festival studies, 26, 27
fiction (literary super-genre), 10, 11, 160, 206
fieldwork, 88, 91, 102, 110, 166, 170
Finn, Adharanand, 94, 97
first-level category (cultural theory), 206
Fiske, John, 207
Fizek, Sonia, 126, 130
flashbulb memory (cognition), 68
flexible adaption (cultural theory), 217
float maker, 171, 172, 179
Floyd, George, 184–189, 191, 193, 194, 196, 200, 201, 207
folkdräkt (traditional dress, Swedish), 166
folklore, 27, 67, 147, 149, 156, 159, 160, 186, 199, 217, 218
folklorist, 6, 7, 9, 10, 18, 20, 28, 149, 165
folkloristics, 8, 216
foodway, 105, 174
football, 15, 19, 27, 75, 77, 81, 82, 107–122, 208, 210–212, 214, 217, 219
football fans, 208, 215–217
Forest Lake, Minnesota, 174
formalize (cultural theory), 12, 18, 84, 131, 145, 153, 216, 217
fossil fuel, 172
Foucault, Michel, 108–110, 112, 119, 121
Fox, Steven J., 3
frame (cultural theory), 37, 60, 63–66, 68, 69, 79
framed realm (play and ritual theory), 205, 206
framing (cultural theory), 53, 63, 64, 128, 132, 171, 209, 211, 213, 214
Franzmann, Majella, 75

Freedom, Inc. (Madison, WI), 190
Friends of Lutfisk (a network), 105
friendship, 45–47, 216
Frimannslund, Rigmor, 57
Frissen, Valerie, 150, 152, 160
fun, 5, 11, 35, 36, 41–43, 48, 55, 66, 80, 95, 108, 117, 130, 135, 143, 151, 159, 160, 177, 180, 196, 215, 220
funeral, 74–78, 81, 82, 205, 206, 213
funerary ritual, 73, 75, 77, 81, 82, 84

game, 3–5, 14–17, 22, 27, 32, 39–48, 65, 67, 69, 73, 77, 78, 82, 90, 92, 95, 98–100, 103, 108–113, 115–122, 126–136, 139–141, 145, 149, 151, 168, 198, 208, 210, 211, 213, 219–221
game developer, 127
game playing, 125, 131
gamification, 130
gaming, 125–129, 132, 220
gaming event, 125–129, 131, 132, 134–141
Garden of Eden (in the Bible), 206
Garza, Alicia, 188
gasohol, 171, 172
Geertz, Clifford, 37, 100, 154, 156
gender-based, 195
general intensifier (play and ritual theory), 216
van Gennep, Arnold, 6, 21, 34, 35, 59, 94, 97, 107, 209
genre analysis, 28, 213
Gerholm, Tomas, 73, 83
Giddens, Anthony, 91
gift-giving (ritual theory), 46
Gillis, John R., 37
Gilmore, Janet C., 174, 181
give-and-take (play theory), 192
Glaser, Barney G., 43, 44
Global North (world region), 94
globalization, 39
Go Bananas (website), 40
Goffman, Erving, 7, 23, 207, 208, 210
Gomme, Alice Bertha, 8, 9, 40
good old days (story world), 65
Gospels (New Testament of the Bible), 164
Gradén, Lizette, 168, 172, 209, 219
grand opening ceremony, 137
Green, Anders, 109
grief, 73, 76, 77, 81, 82, 83, 84
Grimes, Ronald L., 73, 74, 84
groom-to-be, 45, 57

Grossberg, Lawrence, 149, 150, 152
Guild of Thieves (Discworld), 144, 146, 147, 155
gumbo ya ya (everyone talks at once), 187
Gustafsson, Lotten, 14, 65, 73, 96

habit, 217
Hadfield, Phillip, 38
hákarl (Icelandic fermented shark), 179
Hall, Steven, 39
Hamayon, Roberte, 126, 127, 131, 132, 135–140
Handelman, Don, 14, 22, 23, 25, 26, 35, 37, 47, 63, 64, 94, 126, 131, 136, 138, 168
Haraway, Donna Jeanne, 134
Harper, Douglas, 184, 201
Harrison, Rodney, 165
Hatuka, Tali, 189, 192, 194
Haugen, Bjørn Sverre Hol, 65
Heessels, Meike, 75
hegemony (cultural theory), 196
Hellekson, Karen, 149
Heller, Meghan, 132, 134
Hellspong, Mats, 168
Helsingborg, Sweden, 111
Helsinki, Finland, 143–145, 147, 148, 158
Helsinki Exhibition Centre (Finland), 158
hen party, 33–48
Hen Party Superstore (website), 36, 40, 42
Henricks, Thomas, 151, 159
Herd, Katarzyna, 108, 109, 111, 114, 115, 168, 208, 211, 215–217
heritage making, 164–166, 174
heteronormative, 100
heterotopia (cultural theory), 108–110, 119, 121
Hills, Matt, 144, 149–152, 154, 160
Hine, Christine, 127
historical perspective (cultural theory), 11, 99
history (super-genre), 6, 17, 21, 26, 93, 96, 109, 187, 188, 194, 201, 207
Hjorth, Larissa, 128
Hmong (people), 191
Hobbs, Dick, 38
Hockey, Jenny, 74, 75, 77
Hogfather, The (book), 144
Hogswatch (festival, Discworld), 108, 144, 145, 147, 149–152, 155, 157, 158, 206
homo ludens (the playing man), 10, 109, 110
homo ridens (the laughing man), 215

Honneth, Axel, 91
honor, 5, 99, 143, 147, 148, 178
hooliganism, 109, 115
Hoopla (game), 40
Horst, Heather A., 128
Hugo Awards, 145, 157
Huizinga, Johan, 5, 6, 10–15, 36, 44, 93–96, 98, 99, 110–113, 115, 117, 121, 127, 131, 168, 209, 214, 221
human sacrifice, 9
humor, 43, 57, 76, 77, 78, 80, 81, 84, 109, 114, 144, 153, 160, 165
hyper-masculine, 89, 93
Hz. Hizir (Turkish saint), 22
Høeg, Ida Marie, 74

Ibsen, Henrik, 57
idealize (cultural theory), 28, 58, 115, 216
identity (cultural theory), 13, 14, 17, 24, 35, 44, 108, 115, 122, 138, 150, 152, 160, 169, 174, 184, 189, 194, 219
ilinx (vertigo, a form of play), 60
imagination, 24, 25, 29, 169
imperialism, 10
improvisation (play theory), 72, 73, 84, 136, 216, 217
indeterminacy (play theory), 126, 134–136, 139–141, 220
Industrial Workers of the World (organisation), 199
in-game, 130
innovation, 172, 216, 218
institutionalize (cultural theory), 26, 100, 126, 127, 130, 132, 134, 135, 216
intensified framework (play and ritual theory), 208
intensified interaction (play and ritual theory), 207, 208, 219
interactionism (cultural theory), 7
internet, 39, 166
intersectionality (cultural theory), 185
intertextuality (cultural theory), 109, 149–160
Ironman (extreme race), 88
Isthmus (Madison, WI), 189
Ivan, Bomba, 172

Jackson, Carolyn, 39
Jacobsen, Michael Hviid, 74
Jansson, Hanna, 72–76, 84, 206, 211, 212, 215
Jenkins, Henry, 149, 150, 160

Johansson, Janet, 100, 101
Johansson, Thomas, 95
John Nolen Drive (Madison, WI), 189, 196
Johnston, Sarah Iles, 68
joke book, 178
Jones, Tobias, 115
Jönköping, Sweden, 129
Jönsson, Lars-Eric, 77

Karstadt, Bruce, 175, 177, 181
Keinan, Anat, 95
Kekri (East Finnish harvest festival), 147, 148
Kellaher, Leonie, 74, 75, 77
Kenny, Matt, 195
key (frame theory), 210, 214
key work (frame theory), 209
Khan-Cullors, Patrisse, 188
Khrushchev, Nikita, 172
kickoff, 145
kid zone (McDonald's), 36
Kielland, Alexander, 57
Kirshenblatt-Gimblett, Barbara, 165
Kivertz, Ran, 95
Kjus, Audun, 65, 100, 126, 135, 137–139, 207, 210, 212
Klein, Barbro, 7, 73, 76, 83, 167, 179
Knightley, Keira, 59
knowledge keeping, 199
knowledge sharing, 152, 199
Knox, Michelle, 77, 81, 82
Kreinath, Jens, 22
Kress, Gunther, 186
Kvist, Miranda, 97
köttbullar (Swedish dish), 179

ladette culture (UK), 39
Lake Monona (Madison, WI), 189
Lamerichs, Nicolle, 149, 150
Lammes, Sybille, 150, 152, 160
LAN party, 127
Lange, Michiel, 150, 152, 160
late modernity, 91, 92
laughingstock, 114
laughter, 33, 77, 81, 84, 114, 118–120, 160, 166, 169, 172, 173, 178, 180, 215, 216, 219, 220
law enforcement, 189
lawbreaking, 216
Leary, James P., 181
lefse (dish, Norwegian), 176, 179

Legalize It (song), 163
leisure time, 98, 103
lek (freer forms of play, Norwegian), 5
Lévi-Strauss, Claude, 138, 139
licensed behavior, 42
lifestyle, 45, 91, 97, 102
lighthearted, 11, 36, 95
liminal (ritual theory), 21, 34, 36, 42, 45, 96, 97, 119, 126, 136, 137, 209
liminoid (cultural theory), 97, 98, 136
limits (play and ritual theory), 11, 19, 98, 127, 130, 220
Lindelöf, Karin S., 208, 210, 217, 218, 220
Lindsborg, Kansas, 169, 172, 173, 179, 219
Livingstone, Sheila, 37, 38
London Bridge is Falling Down (song), 9
Lord of the Rings, The (book), 144
Lord, Karen, 147, 148
Lorde, Audre, 200
love labyrinth (courtship game), 52, 62, 64
Lowell Lewis, John, 35
Lowrey, Tina M., 35
luck (play theory), 135–137, 140, 212
ludic, 33, 36, 48, 114, 126–128, 130–132, 134
Lund, Dale A., 77, 81
lutfisk (dish, Swedish), 27, 162, 164–181, 209–211, 215, 219
Lutfisk Day (Sweden), 165
Lutfiskens museum (Museum of Lutfisk, Mollönsund, Sweden), 165
Lutheran (Protestant denomination), 13, 15, 174
Löfgren, Jakob, 109, 149, 152, 206, 211–213, 216

Madison, Wisconsin, 184–189, 190–192, 194–196, 200, 202
make-believe, 65, 73
Malaby, Thomas M., 125–127, 131, 132, 134, 135, 137, 139
male-dominated, 38
Malinowski, Bronislaw, 60
Malmö FF (Swedish football team), 110, 116
Malmö, Sweden, 116, 118
Maner, Sequoia, 200
Marquis, Al, 99
marriage, 9, 13, 34, 35, 37, 45, 46, 52–54, 56, 61, 64, 66, 67, 163
marriage proposal, 27, 59, 62, 63, 65–69, 210, 212, 213, 219, 220

Index

Martin, Neill, 34
Martin, Trayvon, 118
Mary Stuart of Scotland (theatre play), 57
Massive Multiplayer Online Game, 130
Mathijssen, Brenda, 75
Mauss, Marcel, 46
May Day, 168
McDonald's (fast-food restaurant), 36, 175
McLean, Albert F., 159
McNeill, Lynne S., 149
meaning making (cultural theory), 173, 217
Measham, Fiona, 38
Mechling, Jay, 27, 168, 169, 179
Melanesia, 16
memorial (funerary practice), 75, 76, 82, 84, 206
meta-communication (cultural theory), 17, 22–25, 129
meta-communicative signal (cultural theory), 17, 23, 63, 179, 180
micro-manage, 34
micro-sociology (cultural theory), 7
Middle Ages, 164
Middle East (world region), 171, 172
Midsummer's Eve, 72, 81
mid-twentieth century, 164, 165
Midwest (US region), 173, 174
migration heritage, 165, 174, 178
mimetic (imitative, play theory), 25
mimicry (imitating, a form of play), 61, 97
Minneapolis, Minnesota, 163, 174, 185
mnemotechnics (cognition), 67
mock ceremony, 152
modulation (play theory), 219
Mollösund, Sweden, 165
Monger, George P., 37, 38
Montemurro, Beth, 39
Monty Python (British comedy troupe), 144, 166
Moore, Sally Falk, 7, 76, 81, 83, 94, 125, 167
Morgan, Philippa, 47
mother-in-law, 42, 47
motif (narrative theory), 17
mourning, 78
Mr and Mrs (game), 40, 41
Muir, Edward, 7, 28
multiple framing (play and ritual theory), 63, 64
museum, 163, 165, 174, 176–178
Myerhoff, Barbara G., 7, 44, 73, 76, 81, 83, 84, 94, 125, 167

myth (super-genre), 10, 68, 206, 207
Märtha-lilies, 52, 64

National Guard (USA), 199
neoliberal, 95
New Year's Eve, 60
Newall, Venetia, 80
nightly visits (courtship custom), 56, 60, 61
Nikielska-Sekula, Karolina, 174
Nilsson, Fredrik, 77
niqab (Muslim face veil for women), 113–115
nonsense (cultural theory), 109, 110, 113–115, 118–122, 152
normativity (cultural theory), 100, 101, 130, 138
Norrick, Neal R., 77
Norwegian Constitution Day (May 17), 168

Oakley, Chris, 107, 109, 116
obstacle course racing, 88
offline, 125, 128
Olmeca (Latino rapper), 195
Olofsson, Birgitta, 16, 97
Olofsson, Patrik, 119
Olympic Games, 94, 154
Olympic-style, 210
online, 80, 125, 127, 128, 130, 166
onstage, 57, 148, 158
ontological status (frame theory), 193, 205, 206, 209
open-ended interaction (play theory), 125–127, 130–132, 134, 136, 221
Opie, Iona, 40
Opie, Peter, 40
Organization of Petroleum Exporting Countries (OPEC), 172
Ormston, Rachel, 39
Oscars (Academy Awards), 145
Oslo, Norway, 52, 55, 62, 63
Otnes, Cele, 35, 46
outhouse, 56
overwhelming (play theory), 59, 63, 69

padding (game), 18
pandemic-safe, 166
paradox (play and ritual theory), 5, 21, 25, 59, 65, 100, 141
Party Pieces catalog, 36

passers-by (play and ritual theory), 189
pastime, 18, 95
peer group (cultural theory), 34, 219
Penn, Ojeda, 186
performance (cultural theory), 27, 36, 65, 68, 69, 91, 110, 112, 120, 122, 151, 152, 154, 168, 172, 180, 187, 189, 193, 196, 199, 201, 213, 215–217
personal protective equipment, 178
Peterson, Tomas, 95, 103
Pin the Tail on the Donkey (game), 33, 40
Pin the Willy on the Man (game), 33, 40, 41
Pink, Sarah, 127, 128
Pisera, Sallie Anna, 207, 210–213, 219, 220
place- and time-bound activity (play and ritual theory), 15, 18, 19, 40, 44, 103, 117, 152, 218
play element, 18, 21, 22, 37, 53, 62, 65, 66, 69, 73, 76, 139, 142, 168, 173, 185, 187, 201, 208, 218–220
play face, 210
play form, 29, 61, 100, 107, 130, 131
play frame, 17, 23–25, 64, 65, 69, 126, 131–133, 139, 140, 168, 171
playfulness, 4, 16, 22, 65, 81, 82, 92, 102, 119, 125, 128, 152, 154, 159, 161, 173, 216
play gait, 210
play-ritual continuum, 3, 5, 26–28, 65, 218, 221
play-ritual event, 28, 214
play session, 20, 210
play setting, 20, 22, 24, 205
play signal, 24, 209
play skill, 22
play voice, 210
play world, 65
play zone, 16, 25, 96, 98, 102, 104
Pleck, Elizabeth, 46
polarization (cultural theory), 46
police, 19, 107–122, 183, 185–188, 191, 195, 197–200, 208, 211, 216
polyphonic (musical theory, cultural theory), 169, 186
polyrhythmic (musical theory, cultural theory), 186, 187
polysemy (cultural theory), 18, 65
Poots, Fleur, 75
pop-up theater, 36
Postill, John, 127, 128
post-liminal (ritual theory), 21, 209

Powers, Anne Marie, 39, 47
practicing (play theory), 95, 131, 192
Pratchett, Terry, 108, 143, 144, 155, 157, 212
Pratchett fan, 149, 150, 212
Pratchett universe (play world), 150, 151, 157
prefigure (cultural theory), 206, 207
pre-historical (cultural theory), 6
pre-industrial (cultural theory), 99
pre-liminal (ritual theory), 209
Prendergast, David, 74, 75, 77
prenuptial, 34
present day (historical period), 7, 53, 59
pretend ceremony, 206
pretense, 73, 78, 80
pre-wedding ritual, 34, 38, 39
primary framework (frame theory), 207
Princess Märtha Louise (Norway), 52
proposal story, 52, 53, 55, 64, 67
Protestant (religious context), 7, 28, 29, 95
psychoanalysis, 149
public attention (play and ritual theory), 62
public health, 175, 208
pyrotechnics, 109, 111–115, 216

quest, 126, 128–130, 133, 135
quest declaration, 128–130
queuing, 174

Radmann, Aage, 108–109
Rameau, Max, 186
randomization (play theory), 136, 140
rapper, 195
reality (ontological status), 18, 25, 28, 64, 65, 83, 96, 100, 109, 205, 207, 208
real-life, 24, 80, 99, 117, 118, 133, 139, 140, 169, 207
realm (frame theory), 139, 140, 168, 205–209, 221
rearrange, 96
reclaim, 155, 184
recognize, 17, 20, 24, 28, 34, 45, 47, 63, 65, 81, 91, 110, 137, 146, 150, 153, 180, 188, 206, 213
recombine, 96
reconsider, 24, 207
recreational sports, 103
Redman, Henry, 189
reenact, 77, 217
re-energize, 38

reestablish, 99, 139
reevaluate, 59
re-experience, 24, 207
Reformation, the, 7, 28, 164
reframe, 80
reggae, 163
reinvent, 76, 84
relocate, 24, 207
Renaissance, the, 220
renegotiate, 139
Renfrew, Colin, 3, 4, 12
re-packaging, 165
repetition, 17, 22, 24, 94, 96, 109, 110, 122, 125, 126, 137, 153, 201
replay, 206
repurpose, 200
reshuffle, 21
response-able, 134
re-staging, 83
restructured, 136
resurface, 3, 168
retelling, 75
reveler, 72
re-voicing, 25
ring dancing, 166
risqué, 38
rite of passage, 34, 35, 37, 44, 48, 59, 98
ritualesque, 18, 27, 28
ritualized, 35, 36, 90, 94, 96, 102, 104, 115, 117, 118, 121, 122, 163, 164, 166, 167, 168, 171, 172, 175, 179
Robertson Smith, William, 6, 8
Robin Hood festivals (England), 9
Robinson, Rob, 186
Robinson, Tony, 195, 200
Robinson, Victoria, 89
Rojek, Chris, 42
role taking, 73
role-play, 15, 18, 22, 27, 61, 138
Role-Playing Games, 130
Roman-style, 199
Ronström, Owe, 7, 12, 14, 17, 18
Rosa, Hartmut, 91, 95
Rudolfsdottir, Annadis, 47
rule-breaking, 33, 190
rules (of games), 5, 11, 14, 17, 18, 20, 24, 27, 65, 88–91, 94, 96, 98, 101–103, 107–111, 113, 114, 117–122, 125, 127, 130–132, 136, 139, 143, 146, 151, 154, 158–160, 171, 208, 209
Rutter, Emily Ruth, 200

Saarikoski, Helena, 152, 160
Saint Lucy's Day (December 13), 64
Santino, Jack, 18, 27, 35
Scandinavian America, 163, 164, 168, 174, 179, 180, 209
Schechner, Richard, 36
sci-fi (narrative genre), 144, 145, 156
Scott, Cheraine Donalea, 201
Scott, Darlene Anita, 200
secondary framework (frame theory), 153, 206, 208, 211, 214
secular (cultural theory), 73, 75, 76, 96, 125, 139, 167, 168, 178–181, 206, 208
secularized ritual, 180, 181
security (play theory), 16, 97, 99, 103
semi-coercive, 44
semiotic (cultural theory), 23, 153
semi-structured, 128
seriousness, 6, 8, 10, 11, 13, 19, 36, 61, 65, 68, 80, 93–95, 100, 103, 108, 109, 111, 115–121, 126, 129, 130, 133, 136, 138, 172, 173, 178, 180, 184, 196, 198, 200, 206, 208, 220
Shapiro, Matan, 26, 37, 43, 46, 207, 208, 214
Sheridan, Molly, 99
shop-bought, 42
shoulder to shoulder, 198
sign waving, 186
signal (cultural theory), 16, 17, 23–25, 63, 96, 129, 168, 180, 209, 210, 212, 216
Simolin, Oona, 148
Sithole, Elkin T., 186
situational understanding (cultural theory), 64, 207, 213, 214
Skeggs, Bev, 42
skepticism, 103
skill (play theory), 10, 14, 15, 22, 23, 98, 132, 140, 214
Smith, Jonathan, Z, 119
Snakes and Ladders (game), 40
social constructivism (cultural theory), 149
social fact (ritual theory), 219
social media, 99, 100, 166, 180, 197
social status (cultural theory), 20, 24, 46, 64, 92
Southeast Asian, 190
southern Turkey, 22
Soyinka, Bambo, 125
spam (junk email), 166
Spam (brand, pressed ham), 166
Spartan (company), 88, 92–94, 96, 98–100

Spartan Ultra World Championship, 88–95, 102–104, 210
speculative fiction (literary genre), 144, 145, 151, 156, 157, 161
speech genre (cultural theory), 7, 128, 207
Spence, Lewis, 9, 10
Spiel (entire field of play, German), 5
spoilsport, 44, 83, 121
Spotify (company), 76
standoff, 186
Starhawk, 188
State Street (Madison, WI), 193, 197, 198
status-enhancing (cultural theory), 91
Stebbins, Robert A., 39, 40, 42, 94
Steiner, Sallie Anna, 186
Stewart, Susan, 109, 110, 114, 117–120, 149–152
Stigum, Hilmar, 56, 60, 61
Stockholm, Sweden, 110, 111, 113, 116, 165
Storaker, Johan Theodor, 67
story world (narrative theory), 157, 158, 206
storytelling, 187, 192
Strauss, Anselm L., 43, 44
Stromberg, Peter G., 151
subculture (cultural theory), 103, 152
subverted (cultural theory), 40, 41, 184, 194
Sugarman, Sally, 20
summer holidays, 54
Sundt, Eilert, 13, 56, 60
super-genre, 206, 207
superhuman, 100, 104
super-reality (ontological status), 25, 65, 100
surprise (play theory), 44, 59, 62, 65, 68, 179, 184
surprise marriage proposal, 59, 62, 65, 68
survival (cultural theory), 8
Sutton-Smith, Brian, 6, 12, 23, 24, 27, 29, 40, 43, 95, 97, 100, 125, 137, 207, 214, 216
Svensk Hyllningsfest (celebration in Lindsborg, KA), 169, 170, 219
Swedish America, 163, 164, 166, 169–172, 175, 177, 178, 180
swift transformation of scene (play theory), 62, 68, 69
symbol (cultural theory), 7, 18, 21, 22, 23, 45, 59, 61, 68, 73, 76, 81–83, 112, 115, 130, 153, 154, 159, 165, 168, 171–173, 178–180, 189, 199, 207, 210, 219
sympathetic magic (ritual theory), 9
synchronize (play and ritual theory), 213, 215, 216, 219

Tambiah, Stanley J., 110, 112
Taylor, Breonna, 200
Taylor, T. L., 128
tear gas, 186, 197–199
techno-music, 129, 215
Teish, Yeye Luisah, 187, 188
tension (play theory), 3, 8, 12, 15, 16, 29, 65, 82, 97, 100, 139, 214, 216, 217, 218
theater, 5, 36, 57
Thompson, Robert Farris, 184
Thurfjell, David, 76
Thurnell-Read, Thomas, 39
time and place (play and ritual theory), 110, 152, 214
Tinkler, Penny, 39
Tolgensbakk, Ida, 119
Tometi, Opal, 188
Tomte Smörgåsbord (parade float), 169
Tosh, Peter, 163
Tourdion (song), 148
tradition, 6, 7, 8, 14, 22, 27, 28, 35, 40, 55, 56, 59, 63, 65, 74, 77, 79, 81, 90, 147, 148, 152, 153, 159, 160, 164–166, 172, 175–179, 184, 185, 187, 192, 200, 201, 213, 216–218
transatlantic, 166, 168, 179
trials (ritual theory), 44
triple framing (frame theory), 64
Trobriand Islands, 16
Tronto, Joan C., 192
de Troyes, Cretién, 58
Trump, Donald, 197, 185
Turner, Edith, 167, 173, 180
Turner, Victor, 21, 36, 94, 96, 97, 98, 99, 136
TV series, 213
Tye, Diane, 39, 47
Tylor, Edward Burnett, 6–9

ultra-running, 95, 97
Umangay, Umar Keoni, 196
uncertainty (play and ritual theory), 3, 16, 60, 65, 68, 134, 198
Uncle Ben's (brand), 179
unexpected change (play theory), 62, 69, 134, 135, 139, 140
unpredictable outcome (play theory), 3, 134, 135, 139
unreal, 19, 24, 25, 74, 79, 139, 205, 206, 208, 209
unreality (ontological status), 25, 65, 100, 220

Unseen University (Discworld), 108
unstructured (play and ritual theory), 136
Upper Midwest (US region), 174
upside down (play and ritual theory), 159
US government, 194

vaudeville, 159
Vedung, Evert, 119
Venbrux, Eric, 75
vertigo (a form of play), 60, 68
Vetinari, Havelock, 155
video game, 126
virtual (ontological status), 24, 25, 100, 126, 140
Visted, Kristofer, 56, 60, 61
volitional, 44

Walter, Tony, 74, 84
Wanseele, Janet Ferrari, 74
war game, 92
Wellington, Chrissie, 99
West, the (world region), 74, 91, 95, 139
West Africa (world region), 21, 187
Westwood, Sallie, 38
white (racial reference), 100, 188, 189, 198–200
white supremacist, 169, 200

Whittaker, Gareth, 40, 44
Williams, Annette Powel, 192
Williams, Jessica, 194, 195, 196, 201
Willies and Ladders (game), 41
Wilson, Donna M., 77, 81, 82
Wilson, Thomas, 39, 47
Wincanton (England), 144, 145, 155, 157, 159, 160
Winlow, Simon, 39
Wisconsin Avenue (Madison), 199
Wolff, Simon Olaus, 61
working-class, 34, 38, 188
WorldCon, 143–145, 147, 148, 152, 156–159
world making, 196
World War II, 10
worldview (cultural theory), 186, 195
Woube, Annie, 208, 210, 217, 218, 220

Ygeman, Anders, 114
Yoruba (people), 21, 62, 187
Young, Sheila M., 34, 36, 37, 39, 40, 42, 45, 46, 48, 211, 213, 215
YouTube (company), 80, 213

Zamboanga, Byron, 47
Zimmerman, George, 188
Zoom (company), 175

Contributors

Ruth Dorothea Eggel. PhD candidate in cultural anthropology. Postdoctoral researcher at the Cologne Game Lab, TH Köln—University of Applied Sciences.

Lizette Gradén. PhD in ethnology and folklore. Associate professor and researcher in the Department of Arts and Cultural Sciences, Lund University.

Katarzyna Herd. PhD in ethnology. Senior lecturer and researcher in the Department of Arts and Cultural Sciences, Lund University.

Hanna Jansson. PhD in ethnology. Lecturer in the Department of Ethnology, History of Religions and Gender Studies, Stockholm University.

Audun Kjus. PhD in cultural history. Senior curator at Norsk Folkemuseum (Norwegian Museum of Cultural History).

Karin S. Lindelöf. PhD in ethnology. Associate professor of Gender Studies, Uppsala University.

Jakob Löfgren. PhD in folklore. Associate senior lecturer / assistant professor in the Department of Cultural Anthropology and Ethnology, Uppsala University.

Clíona O'Carroll. PhD in folklore and ethnology. Senior lecturer in Roinn an Bhéaloidis / Department of Folklore and Ethnology, University College, Cork; research director of the Cork Folklore Project.

Sallie Anna Pisera. PhD in folklore. Museum Lead at Sunnfjord Museum, Førde, Norway.

Simon Poole. EdDoc. Senior leader of Cultural Education and Research at Storyhouse; associate professor of Cultural Education, University of Chester.

Ida Tolgensbakk. PhD in cultural history. Senior curator at Norsk Folkemuseum (Norwegian Museum of Cultural History).

Annie Woube. PhD in ethnology. Associate professor in the Department of Cultural Anthropology and Ethnology, Uppsala University.

Sheila M. Young. PhD in ethnology and folklore. Honorary research fellow at the Elphinstone Institute, University of Aberdeen.

www.ingramcontent.com/pod-product-compliance
Lightning Source LLC
Chambersburg PA
CBHW031147020426
42333CB00013B/541